One of the Guys

Women as Aggressors and Torturers

Edited by Tara McKelvey

SEAL PRESS

One of the Guys
Women as Aggressors and Torturers

Copyright © 2007 by Tara McKelvey

Published by
Seal Press
An Imprint of Avalon Publishing Group, Incorporated
1400 65th Street, Suite 250
Emeryville, CA 94608

AVALON
publishing group incorporated

ISBN-13: 978-1-58005-196-5
ISBN-10: 1-58005-196-0

Library of Congress Cataloging-in-Publication Data

One of the guys : women as aggressors and torturers / edited by Tara McKelvey.
p. cm.
Includes bibliographical references.
ISBN-13: 978-1-58005-196-5 (alk. paper)
ISBN-10: 1-58005-196-0 (alk. paper)
1. Violence in women. 2. Women soldiers. 3. Women and war. 4. Torture. 5. Iraq War, 2003—Participation, Female. 6. Iraq War, 2003—Prisoners and prisons, American. 7. War on Terrorism, 2001—Participation, Female. 8. Military interrogation—United States. 9. Prisoners of war—Abuse of. 10. United States—Armed Forces—Women. I. McKelvey, Tara.

HQ1233.O53 2007
956.7044'31—dc22

2006030699

Cover design by Patrick David Barber
Interior design by Tabitha Lahr
Printed in the United States of America by Worzalla
Distributed by Publishers Group West

Contents

Foreword: Feminism's Assumptions Upended

Barbara Ehrenreich

Even those people we might have thought were impervious to shame, like the secretary of defense, admit that the photos of abuse in Iraq's Abu Ghraib prison turned their stomachs.

The photos did something else to me, as a feminist: They broke my heart. I had no illusions about the U.S. mission in Iraq—whatever exactly it is—but it turns out that I did have some illusions about women.

Of the seven U.S. soldiers now charged with sickening forms of abuse in Abu Ghraib, three are women: Specialist Megan Ambuhl, Private First Class Lynndie England, and Specialist Sabrina Harman.

It was Harman we saw smiling an impish little smile and giving the thumbs-up sign from behind a pile of hooded, naked Iraqi men—as if to say, "Hi Mom, here I am in Abu Ghraib!" It was England we saw with a naked Iraqi man on a leash. If you were doing PR for Al Qaeda, you couldn't have staged a better picture to galvanize misogynist Islamic fundamentalists around the world.

1

Here, in these photos from Abu Ghraib, you have everything the Islamic fundamentalists believe characterizes Western culture, all nicely arranged in one hideous image—imperial arrogance, sexual depravity . . . and gender equality.

Maybe I shouldn't have been so shocked. We know that good people can do terrible things under the right circumstances. This is what psychologist Stanley Milgram found in his famous experiments in the 1960s. In all likelihood, Ambuhl, England, and Harman are not congenitally evil people. They are working-class women who wanted an education and knew that the military could be a stepping-stone in that direction. Once they had joined, they wanted to fit in.

And I also shouldn't be surprised because I never believed that women were innately gentler and less aggressive than men. Like most feminists, I have supported full opportunity for women within the military—1) because I knew women could fight, and 2) because the military is one of the few options around for low-income, young people.

Although I opposed the 1991 Gulf War, I was proud of our servicewomen and delighted that their presence irked their Saudi hosts. Secretly, I hoped that the presence of women would over time change the military, making it more respectful of other people and cultures, more capable of genuine peacekeeping. That's what I thought, but I don't think that anymore.

A certain kind of feminism, or perhaps I should say a certain kind of feminist naiveté, died in Abu Ghraib. It was a feminism that saw men as the perpetual perpetrators, women as the perpetual victims, and male sexual violence against women as the root of all injustice. Rape has repeatedly been used as an instrument of war, and to some feminists, it was beginning to look as if war was an extension of rape. There seemed to be at least some evidence that male sexual sadism was connected to our species' tragic propensity for violence. That was before we had seen female sexual sadism in action.

But it's not just the theory of this naive feminism that was wrong. So was its strategy and vision for change. That strategy and vision rested on the assumption, implicit or stated outright, that women were morally superior to men. We had a lot of debates over whether it was biology or conditioning that gave women the moral edge—or simply the experience of being a woman in a sexist culture. But the assumption of superiority, or at least a lesser inclination toward cruelty and violence, was more or less beyond debate. After all, women do most of the caring work in our culture, and in polls are consistently less inclined toward war than men.

I'm not the only one wrestling with that assumption today. Mary Jo Melone, a columnist for the *St. Petersburg Times*, wrote on May 7, 2004: "I can't get that picture of England [pointing at a hooded Iraqi man's genitals] out of my head because this is not how women are expected to behave. Feminism taught me 30 years ago that not only had women gotten a raw deal from men, we were morally superior to them."

If that assumption had been accurate, then all we would have had to do to make the world a better place—kinder, less violent, more just—would have been to assimilate into what had been, for so many centuries, the world of men. We would fight so that women could become the generals, CEOs, senators, professors, and opinion-makers—and that was really the only fight we had to undertake. Because once they gained power and authority, once they had achieved a critical mass within the institutions of society, women would naturally work for change. That's what we thought, even if we thought it unconsciously—and it's just not true. Women can do the unthinkable.

You can't even argue, in the case of Abu Ghraib, that the problem was that there just weren't enough women in the military hierarchy to stop the abuses. The prison was directed by a woman, Brigadier General Janis Karpinski; the top U.S. intelligence officer in Iraq, who also was responsible for reviewing the status of detainees before their release, was Major General Barbara Fast; and the U.S. official ultimately responsible for managing the occupation of Iraq was Condoleezza Rice. Like Donald H. Rumsfeld, she ignored repeated reports of abuse and torture until the undeniable photographic evidence emerged.

What we have learned from Abu Ghraib, once and for all, is that a uterus is not a substitute for a conscience. This doesn't mean gender equality isn't worth fighting for for its own sake. It is. If we believe in democracy, then we believe in a woman's right to do and achieve whatever men can do and achieve, even the bad things. It's just that gender equality cannot, all alone, bring about a just and peaceful world.

In fact, we have to realize, in all humility, that the kind of feminism based on an assumption of female moral superiority is not only naive; it also is a lazy and self-indulgent form of feminism. Self-indulgent because it assumes that a victory for a woman—a promotion, a college degree, the right to serve alongside men in the military—is by its very nature a victory for all of humanity. And lazy because it assumes that we have only one struggle—the struggle for gender equality—when in fact we have many more.

The struggles for peace and social justice and against imperialist and racist arrogance cannot, I am truly sorry to say, be folded into the struggle for gender equality.

What we need is a tough new kind of feminism with no illusions. Women do not change institutions simply by assimilating into them, only by consciously deciding to fight for change. We need a feminism that teaches a woman to say no—not just to the date rapist or overly insistent boyfriend but, when necessary, to the military or corporate hierarchy within which she finds herself.

In short, we need a kind of feminism that aims not just to assimilate into the institutions that men have created over the centuries, but to infiltrate and subvert them.

To cite an old, and far from naive, feminist saying: "If you think equality is the goal, your standards are too low." It is not enough to be equal to men, when the men are acting like beasts. It is not enough to assimilate. We need to create a world worth assimilating into.

—⟋W⟶

Barbara Ehrenreich is a writer, activist, and novelist whose work appears in publications ranging from *Mother Jones* to *Time*. She is the author of many books, including *Bait and Switch: The (Futile) Pursuit of the American Dream* (Metropolitan Books, 2005) and *Nickel and Dimed: On (Not) Getting By in America* (Owl Books, 2002).

This essay was originally published in the *Los Angeles Times* in June 2004.

Introduction

Tara McKelvey

It was a busload of thugs: Nine suspected assassins and thirty-five accused murderers, rapists, and kidnappers. One of them, an Iraqi major, had been accused of both rape *and* murder. Six feet tall and sporting a tribal tattoo, he was on crutches and had a bandaged arm. That was in May 2003, and Master Sergeant Lisa M. Girman, a thirty-four-year-old reservist from Pennsylvania, was in charge of transporting the Iraqi major and the other suspects from Tallil Air Base to Camp Bucca.[1] That night, something went wrong.

Three Americans were charged with assaulting the Iraqi major, an incident that eventually led to an army hearing and Girman's other-than-honorable discharge from the military.[2] The incident raised questions about innate female aggressiveness, women in the military, and their ability to command and control men—both among enemy soldiers and in their own barracks. It also shed light on widespread assumptions about the maternal, loving traits in women, as well as deeply held fears and anxieties concerning

7

their capacity for doing evil. Finally, it showed the deep revulsion felt toward women who step out of a nurturing role and behave in a violent manner.

In many ways, the incident involving Girman and the Iraqi major on that May evening at Camp Bucca underscores the issues addressed in *One of the Guys*, an anthology about women, power, and violence. The complex nature of the subject, involving gender, the military, and aggression, lends itself to an interdisciplinary approach. As a result, this anthology's contributors come from a variety of backgrounds and represent different strands of feminism, providing a well-rounded look at the subject of women and aggression. Some are academics (Yale, Duke, New York University School of Law). Others are journalists, attorneys who represent detainees, a physician studying the question of American torture, a human-rights activist. Contributors include activist and writer Angela Y. Davis, playwright Eve Ensler, author of *The Vagina Monologues*, and Janis Karpinski, the former commanding officer of Abu Ghraib (she also inspired the book's title).

What exactly transpired at Camp Bucca may never be fully known to anyone except M.Sgt. Girman, the Iraqi major, and a handful of American soldiers who were there. But here is an account of the incident, based on sworn testimony, transcripts from a November 2003 army hearing, and interviews conducted after the legal proceedings, and a look at how it reveals societal attitudes toward women and aggression.[3]

The job of transporting the Iraqi major and the other enemy prisoners of war, as they're known, from the air base to Camp Bucca seemed unusually dangerous. But Girman had trained for this kind of mission and didn't anticipate any serious problems. She seemed up to the task. Her friends and colleagues said she was a "John Wayne" type whom they turned to for tough missions.[3] She joined the army in 1986—the year she graduated from high school. Later she became a reservist. She'd worked as a prison guard in a state correctional institution in Dallas. And before deploying to Iraq, she'd served as a state trooper in Wilkes-Barre, Pennsylvania.[4]

By May 12, 2003, the night of the incident, she'd been through weeks of combat duty. Yet not everybody seemed convinced of her professionalism and her competence as an officer. Another officer said he became concerned about her ability to complete the mission after talking with her briefly. By his reckoning, she seemed overly invested in the task. On a personal level.

May 2003 was a relatively tranquil period in the Iraq War. A month earlier, many Iraqis and Americans rejoiced when the statue of Saddam Hussein was toppled. American journalists filed hundreds of articles celebrating the brave troops who had liberated Iraqis from a despotic leader. Some coverage focused on new phenomena of American warfare—women fighting alongside men and, eventually, the high rate of female casualties. That spring, the story of Private Jessica Lynch dominated the news. It was reported that she had been captured by enemy soldiers, assaulted, and then rescued by American troops.

One thing was clear: Stories such as that of Private Lynch— for all their dramatic twists and turns—were becoming increasingly common. In the Iraq War, women had become part of the military at a level and intensity unprecedented for the American military. In this war, they were getting kidnapped, tortured, and killed—just like male soldiers. They were attacking insurgents, Saddam Hussein loyalists, and others who threatened U.S. troops in Iraq. Many female soldiers were being heralded for their valor and prided themselves on their ability to dish it out and take it—just like a man. "She was hard-charging," said Andrew Barancho, an army sergeant first class who knew Girman in Iraq.[5]

That May afternoon, Girman met with the other officer at Tallil Air Base to talk about the trip to Camp Bucca. (His name is redacted in Girman's army hearing transcript, obtained by the American Civil Liberties Union through its lawsuit against the U.S. Department of Defense.) He expressed concern about her remarks as they were reviewing procedures for transporting detainees. At one point, Girman said, offhandedly, "They've been shown too much respect up until this point."

When the other officer said he wasn't sure what she meant, she responded, "Well, I don't want to make you uncomfortable. I don't want to make you upset, but do you guys get to do any interviews with the EPWs [enemy prisoners of war]?"

Feeling uneasy about her question, he told her prisoner interviews were done only by military intelligence agents at Camp Bucca, the place where they were transporting the Iraqi major and the others.

"I mean personal interviews," she said.

"No, we don't conduct any operations like that," he said.

"What if there is a problem on the bus?" she said.

"We'd stop the bus and take care of it," he said.[6]

He spoke with his soldiers later and told them the security of the prisoners was the number-one priority of the mission. He was worried about the detainees and didn't want them to be harmed on his watch. He told his soldiers to be careful on the road. A half hour after the convoy of prisoners and soldiers left Tallil Air Base, one of the buses broke down. A mechanic fixed a hydraulic pump, and they drove on. Despite the minor mishap—and the male officer's misgivings—the trip proceeded as planned.

Later that evening, they arrived at Camp Bucca and began taking prisoners off the bus. The Iraqi major began hobbling along on his crutches when the male officer heard someone call out, "Is this the guy?"

"Yeah, this is the guy," said someone else. "Get the females over here."

At that point, or shortly thereafter, the officer recalls, Girman and two other soldiers approached the Iraqi major. She started yelling at him to hurry up as they walked along behind the concertina wire. The atmosphere seemed tense. When he slowed down, she shouted at him. When that didn't work, said one witness at the army hearing, "she would kick his trail foot to the side so as to trip him up." Finally, the Iraqi major fell on the ground. His hands were secured in front of him. The soldiers lifted him up in the air and then dropped him on the ground. One of the soldiers grabbed his left arm and wrenched it behind his back.

"He was screaming," said the officer. "I'm going to tell you right now, if you've never heard that kind of scream before—you won't forget it. . . . It was at the top of his lungs. It was as loud as he could scream. He was hollering something in Arabic. He was scared. He was scared for his life."

The soldiers held the Iraqi major's ankles as he was lying on his stomach on the ground and spread his legs. Girman stood between his legs and then delivered "several blows to the groin of this major," said a witness. "I would say she was kicking about as hard as she could kick."

The Iraqi major rolled to his side, screaming in pain. She walked around and kicked him again. Then, the witness said, she "either kicked him in the head or put her foot on his head, telling him to shut the fuck up."[7]

In April 2004, nearly a year later, the battalion commander, Lieutenant Colonel Jerry L. Phillabaum, wrote a memo about the incident. He said Girman had been seeking revenge against the Iraqi major because she believed he was a rapist and deserved to be punished. In fact, Girman thought the Iraqi major had been involved in the kidnapping and assault of Private Lynch. "Vigilante justice," he called it. Insisting he hadn't known about the assault and certainly had not condoned the abuse, Phillabaum accused Girman of assaulting the prisoner, saying she'd acted out her own aggression.

"When M.Sgt. Lisa Girman returned to Camp Bucca shortly before midnight, she took vigilante justice against EPWs that she believed had raped Pfc. Jessica Lynch," he wrote in a later memo.[8]

The narrative seemed to hold together. A female officer, known to be pushy and aggressive, flips out over the rape of an American heroine, Pfc. Lynch. The female officer loses control and plans an attack on an Iraqi major. In the end, she's helped out by her soldiers. They hold him down. She kicks him in the groin. "Poetic justice," as one of the witnesses at her army hearing said. On January 7, 2004, Girman was discharged from the army.

But maybe the story was too good—or too horrible—to be true. Girman says she never assaulted the Iraqi major, or anyone, while she was serving in

Iraq. She didn't even know who the Iraqi major was or what he'd been accused of. She certainly had no idea that he had anything to do with the kidnapping of Lynch. And he may not have. It's true she'd helped subdue the Iraqi major while they were at Camp Bucca. But he'd been recalcitrant—and dangerous. Unfortunately, inexperienced soldiers who'd seen Girman deal with the Iraqi major behind the concertina wire misinterpreted what they saw. They seemed to think she'd been "a little rough," she says. They said she had mistreated the Iraqi major. They described it as a savage attack.

They seemed to have an ulterior motive for accusing her of a crime. She was known among some soldiers as a troublemaker who wouldn't accept the way things were being run at the military base. She'd complained about the lack of clear military procedures at the base, she says. Her superior officers, she says, saw the incident with the Iraqi major as a way to "shut me up and eventually get rid of me." Phillabaum may have had his own reasons for blaming an incident of detainee abuse on her. At the time he was testifying, military officers were interviewing him about several incidents of detainee-related misconduct—namely, at Abu Ghraib—involving soldiers under his command. He knew he was in trouble. He had received reprimands for detainee abuses his soldiers had committed. And in one military investigative report, he was described as "extremely ineffective."[9]

Phillabaum seemed happy to support the accusations against Girman. According to her version of the events, she was a convenient scapegoat. She vowed to fight the military court's findings.[10] On August 19, 2005, the army announced Girman had been cleared of wrongdoing.

Regardless of what happened that night at Camp Bucca, several themes have emerged in the controversy. Some of them are positive: Women have made great strides in the military. They're seen as powerful and commanding within the ranks, and they're often on equal footing with men in the war. But there's a downside: Women are seen as a destabilizing force—either because they're not capable of controlling their passions (says Phillabaum) or because they're outspoken about their views and cause problems for other, less conscientious soldiers (says Girman).

The murky issues of gender and violence and power raised by Girman's case also are central to the Abu Ghraib scandal. Both male and female soldiers at Abu Ghraib seemed to condone the abusive treatment of prisoners. As Janis Karpinski, former commanding officer of Abu Ghraib and one of the contributors to this anthology, told me, they wanted to be "one of the guys." If that meant hurting Iraqis, so be it.

It's hard to say what is most shocking about the Abu Ghraib photos—the picture of Private First Class Lynndie England holding a prisoner on a leash; the one of her pointing at the genitalia of a naked Iraqi man, a cigarette dangling from her lips; or the photo of Specialist Sabrina Harman kneeling next to the frozen corpse of a prisoner, Manadel al-Jamadi, who died during an interrogation in a shower. The pictures, which first appeared on *60 Minutes II* on April 28, 2004, and in the *New Yorker* a few days later, made Americans feel ashamed. American troops had betrayed our country's most cherished values and undermined our ideals of freedom, democracy, and human rights. The photos also forced Americans to examine allegations of abuse of power and torture by women.

In the aftermath of Abu Ghraib, there was a great deal of speculation about the soldiers who were charged with abuse, including, most dramatically, the three women—England, twenty-three; Harman, twenty-eight; and Specialist Megan Ambuhl, thirty-one. Writers, newspaper columnists, and political leaders struggled with the notion of a "few bad apples," as the soldiers were called, and with the larger dimensions of the Abu Ghraib scandal. Everything's been blamed—from societal failures (poverty in West Virginia, where England grew up) to administration hubris (the president wanted to expand his powers during wartime, leading to legal memos that allowed for the harsh treatment of detainees) to the psychopathic behavior of former prison guards (e.g., Specialist Charles Graner).

Conservative analysts wondered about the role of reality television, pornography, and, of course, feminism—all of which, they claimed, led to a cultural atmosphere in which such horrific abuses occurred. It's true that England and Harman flaunted their power as women. They used twisted, sexual gestures to humiliate the prisoners—and then posed coolly for the camera. But it wasn't clear whether these young women were aware of the repercussions of their acts—or even how they affected the Iraqi prisoners. Maybe the women were manipulated or coerced by Graner and other men at the prison. Or perhaps they got caught up in a brutal culture at Abu Ghraib that seemed to allow, even encourage, soldiers to treat Iraqi prisoners as if they were animals. There was a bigger question, though, that went beyond the confines of the prison walls. Why were we so deeply troubled at the sight of women humiliating and hurting prisoners in the photos?

"Maybe I shouldn't have been so shocked," writes Barbara Ehrenreich, author of *Nickel and Dimed*, in the foreword in this anthology. She—like many Americans—had a visceral reaction when she saw the Abu Ghraib photos. It was proof that women, too, are capable of utter depravity. Ehrenreich's initial surprise reveals a set of deeply held beliefs about women and their supposed moral superiority—even, or perhaps especially, among writers and activists such as Ehrenreich who have worked for decades toward the goal of full economic and political opportunity for women. The objective was, of course, that women someday would be in a position where they could do everything men could.

Many young women believe they're already there. Contributors to the anthology *We Don't Need Another Wave: Dispatches from the Next Generation of Feminists*, edited by Melody Berger, explain that young women feel, rightly or wrongly, they're living in a postfeminist United States. Women *are* equal to men. So nobody should be surprised to find that women are also violent and sadistic. Indeed, American women seem to have more power than ever. Secretary of State Condoleezza Rice travels regularly to the Middle East. Nancy Pelosi, House minority leader, is the first woman to head up a political party in Congress. Oprah Winfrey runs a media empire.

But, somehow, things are still different for women. Even as women strive for equality, they find that men seem to hold them to a higher moral standard. Women do, too. Ehrenreich says this is not only naive. It's lazy and self-indulgent.

In *One of the Guys*, Ehrenreich and other contributors look at complex issues, including the way women are held to a more rigorous ethical standard than men; the social factors that contributed to the Abu Ghraib scandal; and questions concerning the expectations of full opportunity and equality for women. If we do want equality and opportunity, what are the implications for women? If we don't, what have we been fighting for?

Playwright Eve Ensler talks about the role of women who interrogate (and abuse) men—the subject of her new play. World-renowned author and activist Angela Y. Davis and other writers examine what Abu Ghraib means to feminists. Ada Calhoun, an editor at the online sex and culture magazine *Nerve*, writes about Specialist Jennifer Scala and her decision to carry Inga Muscio's *Cunt: A Declaration of Independence* into the court-martial of an Abu Ghraib prison guard. (A widely circulated picture of Scala, clutching the paperback, was taken by a photographer for the *Baltimore Sun*.)

In her essay "Split Screens," Karen J. Greenberg, coeditor of *The Torture Papers*, examines the cultural issues raised in a play, *Guardians*, about Lynndie England and a gay, pro-war British journalist who's into S&M. Steven H. Miles, author of *Oath Betrayed*, writes about nurses and female medical practitioners who have been involved in the abuse of prisoners in Iraq, Guantánamo Bay, and other places. Several writers explore the cultural divide between the United States and the Middle East. In "Photography/ Pornography/Torture," Laura Frost, a professor of English at Yale University, looks at the influence of S&M imagery on the Abu Ghraib photos and explains how little they have in common.

In her essay "The 'Sex Interrogators' of Guantánamo," attorney Kristine A. Huskey, who represents several detainees being held at Guantánamo Bay, describes detainees' reactions to being interrogated by American women. LaNitra Walker, a Duke University doctoral student and contributor to the *American Prospect*, compares imagery from lynchings in the American South with the photos from Abu Ghraib, focusing on the role of women in both sets of pictures.

Janis Karpinski, the former commanding general at Abu Ghraib, writes about Lynndie England in an essay entitled "Lynndie England in Love." Karpinski met England the day the young soldier arrived at the prison.

The contributors have a wide range of opinions about the events at Abu Ghraib—and about women and aggression—but they share a curiosity about the subject and an intellectual rigor in their approach. There's a positive message, too. As we learn from this anthology, not every woman who's forthright and strong-willed and ambitious ends up acting like "one of the guys." That's good news.

I Still Don't Get How You Could Put a Leash on a Human Being

Eve Ensler

Eve Ensler's play The Vagina Monologues *has been translated into over forty-five languages and performed all over the world. She is also the head of V-Day, a global movement to stop violence against women and girls. Her most recent work,* The Treatment, *is about a female military psychologist and a traumatized male soldier.* The Treatment *opened in New York in the fall of 2006. She spoke with anthology editor Tara McKelvey about women, violence, and Abu Ghraib from her Manhattan apartment.*

TM: What made you decide to write a play about this subject?

EE: Well, I'm deeply concerned about torture. I think about it all the time. I just can't believe we're living in a country where the government has been sanctioning torture. I've thought a lot about Abu Ghraib and the women who were involved.

Look, everyone defines feminism differently. For me, feminism means reconstructing the world so that the mechanisms of dominance and violence are not the controlling factors. Rather than creating hierarchies based on abuse and submission, we would be creating partnerships based on equality and empowerment. In this world, women wouldn't hunger to be in the military at all. We wouldn't even have a military.

Let me say this: I don't think women are intrinsically better than men. And, yes, I do think there are women who are capable of committing evil acts.

TM: What about Lynndie England?

EE: Well, I imagine she's a working-class woman who's had very few choices in her life. My bet is that at some point she was sexually abused or hurt in a fundamental way. She's been robbed of her self-esteem and went into the military to get some of it back. There, she had a position of some sort of power and prestige. But did it really fix her? No, not at all. It gave her a kind of facade and a cover. I think Lynndie England felt she had to prove herself.

Still, it's just hard to believe. It's hard to imagine that women's hearts have been so hurt and numbed, that women's ability to empathize has been so tragically damaged that we are capable of torture. But it's true. Women are capable of torture.

You also have to consider how soldiers are trained, how racism is intrinsic in the indoctrination. One can understand how someone comes to see Iraqis, for example, as less than human. It's part of the brainwashing.

But even so, I still don't get how you could put a leash on a human being. As much as I try to climb into the psyche of Lynndie England, I still don't see how putting a leash on someone and dragging them around and humiliating them could ever be right in your brain. The only way I can understand it is if

I realize Lynndie England must have felt had she to prove herself. She had to out-macho the most macho in order to prove she was "one of the guys."

I also think that Lynndie England and other women like her perpetrate abuse on others as an outlet for abuse they once may have experienced—you know, an outlet for the rage that results from being violated.

TM: Torture as therapy?

EE: No, I'm not saying it's a good thing. But I am saying that would explain why they behaved the way they behaved. Their positions at Abu Ghraib gave them circumstances where they could act out on some man what has been done to them. These women are making the prisoner feel belittled. They're making him feel like a dog. It's very sexual. That leads me to believe there's some piece that's connected with abuse in their own sexual history.

The situation with Lynndie England asks us to question whether women will be different when they have positions of power. Is it possible for women to have power within that patriarchal system and act any differently than men?

Look, I am not one of those women who will say all we need to do is get women in office. Yes, I think we need to get certain *types* of women in office, but having a vagina is not a prerequisite for being a good leader. We have seen many women in power who have even exaggerated patterns of male dominance.

I want to see women in power who have been through some kind of transformation. These may be women who have been violated, and rather than continuing to perpetuate abuse, they grieve that violation and then devote their lives to making sure it doesn't happen to other people. They don't have to take an AK-47 and go to war. They don't have to torture someone. We call these women *vagina warriors*. The strength of vagina warriors is undeniable. It's real leadership that is completely devoted toward ending violence. It's a total transformation of whatever horrible thing was done to them.

TM: Why didn't Lynndie England go through that transformation?

EE: Where in the world is there help for her to do that? She would need a network of support and encouragement. She would need time for the process of healing.

TM: Do you remember how you felt when you saw the pictures of Lynndie England?

EE: I felt really, really sad for her. And I felt deeply ashamed and outraged about what we had done to people we were supposedly saving. Part of what I'm exploring in my new play is the question of how much of the violation perpetrated by an American soldier is because he's really trying to play by the rules and how much is because he's terrified by his captain who's very much like Lynndie England's boyfriend. This Charles Graner type is always terrifying and reducing men. At one point, the captain humiliates the soldier by saying, "You're soft." It's hard for men to wrest themselves away and say, "I'm not going to be abusive like that. I'm going to stand alone. I'm going to risk being exiled by the tribe."

The only way you could participate in Abu Ghraib is to go crazy. You'd have to agree to another set of moral standards. The only way to do that is to agree to madness. Once you've agreed to madness, you have to go the distance. If we could figure out what stops some people from crossing over that line into abusive behavior, it would be like discovering the cure for cancer. It would be a door unlocking.

TM: Do you think the women who were at Abu Ghraib have taken responsibility for their actions?

EE: We haven't seen that so far. But, really, how many people ever take responsibility for what they've done?

TM: Maybe you're asking them to go crazy. To be conscious of the act—it's unbearable.

EE: Look at the high suicide rate among soldiers. But the point is, they were following orders. You have to think about the people who were higher up the chain of command. None of them have been held accountable. They mutilated those soldiers' souls and I don't know if they'll ever get free.

Sexual Coercion, Prisons, and Female Responses

Angela Y. Davis

The following speech was given at the First Congregational Church of Oakland on December 2, 2005.

I want to talk a little about the importance of recognizing the difference between abstract formal democracy and the kind of democracy that will bring real change, real freedom, real equality, real justice, and truth into people's lives. [Earlier] I was talking about the large numbers of people who are now being put to death, and it seems that what has happened over the last period is that there has been this increasing rationalization of the death penalty and an increasing routinization.

In 1970—I can hardly believe that was thirty-five years ago—I actually faced the death penalty. I was charged with three capital crimes—murder, kidnapping, and conspiracy. I am remembering how difficult it was to fathom how I could actually be put to death three times, which is what the attorney general demanded during the arraignment. He wanted capital punishment three times. But during that period, the death penalty was applied in what appeared to us to be an openly racist fashion.

Now capital punishment was temporarily abolished in California in 1972; and I think that's one of the reasons why it was possible for us to be victorious in my case, because I immediately got out on bail when the crimes for which I had been charged ceased to be capital crimes. In 1973, as we all know, the death penalty was temporarily suspended as a result of the *Furman v. Georgia* case. But three years later the Supreme Court issued a ruling in another case, *Gregg v. Georgia,* indicating that death sentences could be considered constitutional if they were meted out to what the Supreme Court called guided discretion.

Today, we have guidelines for the death penalty. It's all very rational. And these guidelines interface very smoothly with what we might call the abstract individualism of neoliberalism. Create equality by extending the death penalty to white people. Let it not be a punishment that is informed by racism. Everybody should have equal opportunity for death. And if you look at what's happened over the last period, it's true that there are more white people on death row. As a matter of fact, the last couple of executions I mentioned were of white men. But this notion that formal equality can lead us to a better world is deeply flawed. If a white person is sentenced to death for killing a black person this is supposed to be a sign of progress. And of course there was a great deal of celebration a number of years ago when the white supremacist in Jasper, Texas, was sentenced to death for killing James Byrd.

But let me turn to another example. And what I want to do is read some passages from this book around that theme.

In the conversations I had with Eduardo Mendieta, he asked me about the photographs of torture and sexual coercion at Abu Ghraib. And we were talking about the equal opportunity to torture, the representations of women soldiers, which caused some people to react as if this was supposed to be impossible. Women weren't supposed to be capable of inflicting sexual violence on prisoners. And so this was my response:

> *The representations of women soldiers were quite dramatic and most people found them utterly shocking. But we might also say that they provided the most powerful evidence of what the most interesting feminist analyses have tried to explain: that there is a difference between the body gendered as female and the set of discourses and ideologies that inform the sex/gender system.[1]*

And so I said,

> *These images were a kind of visualization of this conjunction. We are not accustomed to visually apprehending the difference between female bodies and male supremacist ideologies. Therefore seeing images of a woman engaged in behavior that we associate with male dominance was startling. But it should not have been, especially if we take seriously what we know about the social construction of gender. Especially within institutions that rely on ideologies of male dominance, women can be easily mobilized to commit the same acts of violence expected of men—just as black people, by virtue of being black, are not therefore immune from the charge of promoting racism.[2]*

Then I went on to say,

> *The series of images to which you refer (I was talking about the photographs of the tortures) evokes a memory of a comment made by Colin Powell at the time of the first Gulf War. He said that the military was the most democratic institution in our society. And it created a framework in which people could escape the constraints of*

race and, we can add today, gender as well. The notion of the military as a leveling institution, one that constitutes each member as equal, is very frightening and dangerous, because you must eventually arrive at the conclusion that this equality is about equal opportunity to kill, to torture, to engage in sexual coercion. At the time I found it very bizarre that Powell would point to the most hierarchical institution, with its rigid chain of command, as the epitome of democracy. But today I would say that such a conception of the military precisely reveals the problems and limitations of civil rights strategies and discourses.

This is true not only with respect to race and gender, but with respect to sexuality as well. Why is the effort to challenge sexism and homophobia in the military largely defined by the question of admission to existing hierarchies and not by a powerful critique of the institution itself? Equality might also be considered to be the equal right to refuse and resist.[3]

And then I went on to say,

This is how I might rephrase your original question. [I can't remember what the original question was, though.] How might we consider the visual representation of female bodies collaborating in acts of sexual torture—forcing Arab men to engage in public masturbation, for example—as calling for a feminist analysis that challenges prevailing assumptions that the only possible relationship between women and violence requires women to be the victims?[4]

When one looks at certain practices often unquestionably accepted by women guards in U.S. prisons, one can glimpse the potential for the sexual coercion that was at the core of the torture strategies at Abu Ghraib. I return, therefore, to the question of those established circuits of violence in which both women and men participate, the techniques of racism administered not only by white people but also by black, Latino, Native American, and Asian people as well. Today we might say we have been offered an equal opportunity to perpetrate male dominance and racism.[5]

Or perhaps to be more specific, people in power regardless of gender or race have this equal opportunity to inflict racist and sexist violence on others.

—⌇⌇→

The following excerpts are from Angela Davis's book
Abolition Democracy: Beyond Prison, Torture, and Empire,
in which the author is interviewed by Eduardo Mendieta.

Barbara Ehrenreich has written that a "certain kind of feminist naiveté died at Abu Ghraib. It was a feminism that saw men as the perpetual perpetrators, women as the perpetual victims, and male sexual violence against women as the root of all injustice." What do Guantánamo and Abu Ghraib mean to feminists?

To naive feminists? Here I would have to place emphasis on "naive." Of course this question of what counts as feminism has been hotly debated for who knows how long. Nevertheless I think that most contemporary feminist theorists and activists acknowledge that the category "woman" is a false universal, thanks largely to the scholarship and activism associated with "women of color feminism." It is true that in popular discourse we have a tendency to use essentialist notions about what women do or do not and what men do or do not. Still, the notion that men are naturally inclined to commit sexual violence and that this is the root of all injustice is something that most good feminists gave up a long time ago. I'm not sure why Barbara Ehrenreich would formulate a response to the Abu Ghraib photographs in this way. A more productive approach would be to think more precisely about forms of socialization and institutionalization and about the extent to which these misogynist strategies and modes of violence are available to women as well as men. When one looks at certain practices often unquestionably accepted by women guards in U.S. prisons, one can glimpse the potential for the sexual coercion that was at the core of the torture strategies at Abu Ghraib. I return, therefore, to the question of those established circuits of violence in which both women and men participate, the techniques of racism administered not only by white people but also by black, Latino, Native American, and Asian people as well. Today we might say we have been offered an equal opportunity to perpetrate male dominance and racism.[6]

So you would rather put the emphasis on the institutions of violence, the institutionalization of certain mechanisms of violence, rather than on whether it is perpetuated by males or females.

Exactly. I am referring to a feminist analysis that enables us to think about these different and sometimes disparate objects and processes together. Such a feminist approach would not always be compelled to engage centrally with "women" or even "gender," but when it does attempt to understand gender, it pays special attention to the production of gender in and through such institutions. More generally, I would say that the radical impulse of feminist analysis is precisely to think about disparate categories together, to think across disciplinary borders, to think across categorical divisions. This is precisely what the Abu Ghraib photographs demand.[7]

Why Did Jennifer Scala Bring *Cunt* into the Courtroom?

Ada Calhoun

A photograph published yesterday with an article about the court-martial of a guard at Abu Ghraib prison showed a book cover that contained an obscenity. The obscenity went unnoticed during editing and should not have been published. Publication of the photo violates The Sun's *guidelines.* The Sun *apologizes for the oversight.*
—*Apology published in the* Baltimore Sun, *March 15, 2006.*

U.S. Army Specialist Jennifer Scala was in the courtroom that March day to testify in the trial of fellow Abu Ghraib guard Sergeant Michael J. Smith, who was accused of torturing prisoners using dogs. Speaking to one of Smith's less violent but more perverse practices, Scala admitted his dogs had licked peanut butter off her bare breasts in front of a video camera, on a dare by another soldier. Ultimately, Smith, the tenth soldier convicted of prisoner abuse at Abu Ghraib, was sentenced to six months in jail.

Into the courtroom Scala carried a copy of Inga Muscio's *Cunt: A Declaration of Independence* (2002), which features an introduction by masturbation icon Betty Dodson and a blurb by rock star Joan Jett. It encourages women to think of themselves as "cunts," in what the author describes as the original, empowering sense of the word. She cites dubious etymology: "'Cunt' is related to words from India, China, Ireland, Rome and Egypt. Such words were either titles of respect for women, priestesses and witches or derivatives of the names of various goddesses. . . ." But Muscio is unconcerned with the facts according to "historians," a term she puts in quotes. Acknowledging that *cunt* may in fact be a word with modern, possibly negative, roots, she writes, "venerable history or not, it's ours to do with what we want."

The *Baltimore Sun* image of Scala confused commentators, for good reason. What are we to make of a soldier carrying a book with such an incendiary title? On the blog the *Huffington Post,* sex writer Susie Bright wrote, "So is Jennifer Scala coming to her senses, and ready to stick it to the man? Or does she just like pissing people off whenever the occasion comes up?" Her headline: "I Can't Wrap My Vulva Around This."

In the weeks that followed, the photo was reprinted online by Baltimore's local alternative weekly, *City Paper,* but the question was never convincingly answered: Why did Scala have that book with her in the courtroom?

Despite repeated attempts, I was unable to reach Scala for comment. But *Cunt* author Muscio weighed in on the webzine *Gelf* and reprinted the item on her website, ingalagringa.com. Of the *Baltimore Sun* image, she said, "When I first saw that photo, I laughed my ass off. The smile on [Scala's] face is just SO perfect. She looks like a devious sprite, having a rollicking good time in what most would consider a nerve-wracking situation."

That smile. In the photograph, Scala is seen in profile, walking away from former Abu Ghraib prison warden Major David DiNenna, who also seems to be in high spirits. She has her brown hair pulled back into a tight bun beneath her beret and is grinning. She has on her uniform, cattish black-rimmed glasses, and tiny earrings. In her hand is Muscio's book, title facing out. Why does Scala seem so happy with *Cunt?* Does *Cunt* seem potentially happy with Scala? The answer to that last question is yes.

Cunt's greatest enemy is the "containment of woman's sexuality" by patrifocal societies. By contrast, the gold standard for good is a "cuntlovin' babe." According to *Cunt*, the Judeo-Christian tradition is evil; goddess worship is good. Television is evil; only independent media can be trusted. Male doctors (especially male gynecologists) and Western medicine (i.e., medicine based on science) are bad; charting your reproductive cycle using the cervical mucus method and a moon calendar is good. Muscio describes her three abortions, claiming the two suction aspirations were bad; the one coaxed with massage and herbs was good. (When the result of the third procedure, at eight or nine weeks, "plopped onto the bathroom floor," wrote Muscio, "it was clear but felt like one of them unshiny superballs. It was the neatest thing I ever did see.")

Muscio, a public speaker and author based in Portland, Oregon, suggests all women are soldiers by virtue of the fact that they are always potential victims of rape. She claims women in America need to be on guard at all times, much as soldiers do in hostile territory. "If indeed, my home sometimes seems to be a fortress that deters enemy soldiers—then aren't I kind of like a soldier, and isn't my life kind of like a war?" She encourages women to think of themselves as predators, to fill their pockets with rocks when they go out alone at night and to fiercely battle agents of oppression—that is, men who suppress women's ability to practice "cuntlove," a term that throughout the book is left conveniently vague: "Every girl and lady who is strong and fighting and powerful, who thrives in this world in a way that serves her, is a rockin', cuntlovin' babe doing her part to goad the post-patriarchal age into fruition."

Vigilante justice is Muscio's ideal punishment for rapists. She suggests women gather into groups and burn huge severed-penis effigies on a rapist's front lawn, pack his car full of rotten fish heads, and pelt him with bloody tampons. She offers no "innocent until proven guilty" caveat and admits no gray areas. Instead, there is this almost erotic description of torture:

> *Wouldn't you just hate like the devil to be pilloried, smeared with dogshit, forced to kneel in front of a high-powered microphone on a raised platform and apologize to the ten thousand women who solemnly marched by you? Boy, that would be an unpleasant day that you might not forget right away, huh.*

She calls this practice "Cuntlovin' Public Retaliation," and it is one of the extra-important terms the book renders in bold.

In the afterword to *Cunt,* Muscio recounts being asked what the book is fundamentally about. Ironically, the word she uses is the same as the one President Bush used to describe the Iraq War's goal: "Freedom."

Some who have read *Cunt* characterize it as an example of Third Wave feminism. Rebecca Walker coined the term Third Wave in *Ms.* in 1992 to distinguish it from the suffragettes (First Wave) and the bra burners (Second Wave).

The online magazine *Bookslut* panned *Cunt* eloquently ("Muscio is selling non-answers packaged as answers, New Age pop psychology packaged as sociology"), but concluded that the book epitomized Third Wave feminism, "a movement that preaches all men are potential rapists." Wikipedia describes Muscio as a Third Wave feminist.

By extension, anyone who saw that book in Scala's hand may have drawn the conclusion that she was a Third Wave feminist and that what she did at Abu Ghraib was a feminist act. But I've had a firsthand education in Third Wave feminism, and *Cunt* is no example of Third Wave feminism as I understand it.

In 1992, at the age of sixteen, I discovered a *Bikini Kill* fanzine. This was before gender-inclusive language became a joke. At the time, there was nothing like this zine.

In the early nineties, those few dark years before widespread Internet access, zines were the vehicle by which creative, angst-filled teenagers and twentysomethings talked to each other. Ideas were disseminated via xeroxed paper tucked into CD covers, stapled and mailed, placed strategically in bookstores. In retrospect, it was very colonial-era, very *Poor Richard's Almanack*. But it also worked.

"Revolution Girl Style Now" was what the choppy, half-scrawled, half-typed, cut-and-paste *Bikini Kill* zine promised. It attempted to explain what it meant, on a cosmic level, when guys catcalled you; what date rape was; how to handle not being taken seriously because you were a girl and young and angry.

I immediately photocopied it for all my friends. That fanzine and those that followed it spread like a neofeminist virus through New York and, judging by how suburban malls started stocking T-shirts with "Revolution Girl-Style" slogans, the rest of the country. I carried my zines around proudly, much as Scala brandished her copy of *Cunt*.

What stuck with me was the fanzines' plea for an internal revolution, a kind of self-audit. In 1992 it was revolutionary for a teenage girl to be told by other teenage girls, "Be a dork, tell your friends you love them." Or, "Don't allow the world to make you into a bitter abusive asshole." I believe those zines and bands were symptomatic of, and fuel for, a generation with a fundamentally different take on relationships between men and women.

In an effort to pin down exactly how Third Wave feminists are different, I've looked at books like *Third Wave Agenda, Her Way, Catching a Wave, Manifesta, No Turning Back*, and *The Fire This Time*. Barbara Ehrenreich says the Third Wave is characterized by anger; Gloria Steinem says it's a "generation of translation and backlash."

Third Wave Foundation cofounder Amy Richards says this new generation of feminists seeks to "bring to light otherwise subliminal messages that are concealed within a culture that pretends to be ignorant of them." According to *Third Wave Agenda,* "Third Wave feminists must remain aware of the complex ways that power, oppression and resistance work in a media-saturated global economy."

If Jennifer Scala were truly aware of the complex ways power works, one might expect her to feel anger toward those above her in the chain of command. By Smith's account at least, the military encouraged Scala and her colleagues to abuse prisoners in order to soften them up for interrogation. From the outside, it seems like she's just a pawn in a far larger game. And yet, there she is in the courtroom, smiling.

There's a lot about identity politics in many of the books about the Third Wave, about how the personal is political. Indeed, the midnineties saw many of us whipped up into a froth of liberal righteousness. In 1995, at my first college, I was as anticonsumerist as Inga Muscio. I became a vegetarian, used a Keeper (what Muscio and others recommend instead of tampons), and feared the Pill (which was okay because I was too angry at the gross abuses of the patriarchy to have a lot of sex). I interrupted a class I had on Christian church history to praise the (in retrospect, pretty loony) radical feminist theologian Mary Daly.

But I became less sanctimonious with time, and I feel that the Third Wave's pendulum, too, quickly swung back to a genuinely progressive middle ground, and that out of all that, a generation of inherently decent, fundamentally feminist adults has emerged.

To the untrained eye, the feminism that came out of the nineties' zinefest may seem indistinguishable from that of *Cunt,* but it is very different. Third Wave women, as I know them, are financially independent. They're happy alone, or they're looking to create families with partners rather than providers. They are political activists, conscious consumers, and respectful employers.

They enjoy sex and have an innate sense of their own value and potential. They are self-aware and adventurous, and live supportive lives with men and with each other.

The Third Wave as I've experienced it calls for women to be strong and independent. Were the female guards at Abu Ghraib operating independently? Exercising free will in an empowering fashion? It's a hard case to make.

In the abstract universe of a freshman women's studies class, *Cunt* might be exciting, just like Valerie Solanas's infamous *SCUM Manifesto*. But in the real world, the one in which Muscio has received copious requests for her home-abortion method, it is not at all quaint. It is a bad book, stupid and sociopathic. It preaches hate with the same disregard for logic and humanity exhibited by Jerry Falwell or *The Protocols of the Learned Elders of Zion*. All such fanatics place political ends over human decency.

But the Third Wave is about human decency. It began with young women demanding to be taken seriously. If political correctness at one point became a kind of witch hunt in academic circles, it's become far less draconian with time. The goal of identity politics in its current mainstream iteration is to encourage respect for other cultures. Diversity and inclusivity are second nature to most young people today.

On her website, Muscio explains where her deep anger and rage at men come from: She grew up in "a socially blighted backass racist town," and her mother was raped by two men as a child. These are tragedies, and psychically damaging, but they do not make anything Muscio says noble or valid. She now preaches the same disregard for the rule of law that she grew up with.

Confirming Muscio's extremist position is her latest book, *Autobiography of a Blue-Eyed Devil: My Life and Times in a Racist, Imperialist Society*. This book is really more of a muddled, stream-of-consciousness rant about slavery, Native Americans, and foreign policy. Muscio calls history as it's taught in the schools "lightly veiled white male supremacist racist propaganda." She refers to "the United States of Amerikkka," yammers on about Hugo Chavez, and makes statements like "Fuck Columbus Day." Gone is the blurb from Joan Jett.

On reflection, it makes sense that Jennifer Scala would have had *Cunt* with her in the courtroom that day, and that she would have had a smile on her face. The book encourages women to take pleasure in harm done to men, particularly harm done to men who are part of the "patrifocal problem."

Who might represent the patriarchy to someone in Scala's position?

Muscio singles out Islam several times in *Cunt*, referring at one point to a quote from the Koran as an example of "chicken-shittedness." The prisoners' religiously based sexual taboos certainly wouldn't have implied cunt-love. The Iraqi prisoners recoiled from menstrual blood and nudity, both of which reportedly were employed by guards.

But the U.S. government just as easily could have been the implied object of cunt-lovin' rage. An article in the *New York Times* claimed, "Among all the abuse cases that have reached military courts, the trial of the dog handler, Sgt. Michael J. Smith, had appeared to hold the greatest potential to assign accountability to high-ranking military and perhaps even civilian officials in Washington." But that didn't happen. According to CNN, Smith did not show remorse for his actions. He did say he wished he'd gotten written permission from his superiors first.

Scala's testimony helped convict Smith of an indecent act. It did nothing to bring down the so-called patriarchal system. The feminism I know may have proved more helpful to her. It's built on the premise that men and women should work together to make a better world. It is built on a sense of fairness and justice and decency. What does *Cunt* offer?

Let's just say if I were a woman who had participated in or witnessed the torture of men, I would find it a comfort.

Split Screens

Karen J. Greenberg

One drizzly afternoon, I attended a reading of a new, two-character play at the Culture Project in New York City's East Village. Within moments, my sleepy demeanor was transformed into an alert hunger for more. Home to plays that deal with the moral dilemmas of current politics, the Culture Project has staged such plays as *The Exonerated,* which protested the death penalty, and *Guantánamo,* the story of individual enemy combatants. The play I watched that afternoon was entitled *Guardians,* written by the young, Oxford-educated, American playwright Peter Morris. It premiered in 2005 at the Edinburgh Fringe festival and received a 2005 Fringe First Award. Morris has twice won the Sunday Times Playwriting Award. It's no wonder. *Guardians* presents the most insightful study to date of the intersection between the political and human dimensions of the torture story now gripping the American conscience.

Guardians offers insight into the torture issue from the perspective not of legal experts or administration critics and apologists, but of two individuals swept up in its wake. The play presents two competing monologues: one in the voice of the American Girl (inspired by Lynndie England), reflecting on what's happened to her with a crude, Appalachian-tongued ignorance; the other in the voice of a British reporter, named English Boy. He is a tabloid journalist who longed for a career in pornography but "settled" for the more respectable journalism. To advance his career, he has fabricated pictures of torture.

These two people, personally implicated in U.S. torture policy, for better or worse don't quite get it and aren't able to see much beyond their own lives. Both sense that they are bit players in a larger drama that has revealed the cruel perversions and intentional deceit of a world that exists as much inside the corridors of power as within S&M parlors and the abusive lives of some families in rural America.

By fabricating pictures of British soldiers conducting torture, the English Boy achieves his dream of becoming a columnist. Interwoven in his disdain for the war and his blatant opportunism are his confessions about his life as a gay man who enjoys belting his boyfriend and watching him be physically abused by other gay men. The English Boy is initially attracted to the boyfriend because he has been through army training and reveled in its practices: "You don't think. Don't think about work, paying the rent, anything. You just do what you are told." It dawns on the English Boy, "He's a submissive. It's a match."

The spanking session that begins the English Boy's relationship with the army veteran leads to an epiphany. "Frankly fucking is fucking and . . . and this was *transcendent*. I wanted to live in that moment. Wanted the experience to linger. . . . I wanted something to hold on to. A souvenir." He grasps the powerful potential of fabricating pictures and equates his deceit with that of the United States and Britain in the buildup to the war. "Let's call what I did 'framing the guilty.' I looked at the war, I called it criminal, and I fabricated evidence to stop it. It's the same way the war got started, after all. Framing the guilty's what Britain and America did to Saddam Hussein."

Essentially, both the American Girl and the English Boy are reckoning with their countries' occupation of Iraq—not as a policy matter, but as an expression of human indecency. For each of them, torture is familiar terrain. In the words of the American Girl, "If it sucks more to be a *girl* in the army, well fuck it, you try bein' a girl in West Virginia. That really sucks. . . . Like the drill use ta say in basic training, he'd say: YOU, WEST VIRGINIA. YOU A VIRGIN? And I'd say: SIR YES SIR. And he'd say: GUESS THAT MEANS YOU CAN RUN FASTER THAN YOUR BROTHER THEN . . . . But my point is that yeah, I *can* run faster, faster'n my whole family, thank you very much. That's the plain truth of it, and I run straight into the arms o' the army 'cause that's my way of running *out* of West Virginny."

Throughout, she equates her status as scapegoat with that of the role of women in general. "But that's the thing about being a girl. You can just keep on taking it. . . . They think they're stronger 'cause they hit ya. But they just don't know what it means to be *so* strong you can lie there and take it." We discover, instead, that she is bewildered when she's rebuked for her involvement in something as natural and everyday as physical abuse. There is little moral outrage about torture here, little sense of shame, just plain personal resentment coupled with a sense of institutional abuse that mirrors the abuse she has known since childhood.

The dark import of the play is that there is something logical, something consistent, and something almost predictable about what happened, and yet it's excruciatingly, humanly sad. As the American Girl says, "*I served.* I served my country, now I'm servin' time for a mistake. And someday, all y'all are gonna say: Hey, hold on a minute, she only got into all that shit 'cause of a whole nother bigger mistake. But nobody ever went to prison for *that* one. And that ain't fair. That ain't right."

In addition to a searing understanding of the personal details of the Abu Ghraib incident, Morris's play reflects a deeper problem: the disconnectedness of the American public. The English Boy and the American Girl never speak to one another. Each is living his/her own story: One is rewarded for participating in the illegal excesses of the war; one is punished for representing those excesses. Each interprets war, contending that everything is the same, yet everything is exceptional. Within each narrative, further contradictions underscore how both characters are victims, given their context, and victimizers of others. By contrasting the stories in a theatrical version of split-screen cinema, Morris casts the American public's response to the Abu Ghraib scandal as a sort of split-screen syndrome.

The split-screen syndrome grows out of a basic contradiction that has existed since 9/11: We assert that the post-9/11 world has created a new paradigm; at the same time, we insist that we can go on existing in the world as we did before. That fundamental contradiction gives rise to others: The nation is both vulnerable and powerful, both victim and victimizer, both aggressor and defendant. Confronted with competing realities, the public has chosen to live with cognitive dissonance rather than try to resolve the contradictions. The U.S. president and his advisers insist that the country has been forced to take action against terrorists; in so doing, the leaders must "take off their gloves" and break the old rules. The country is told, however, that the government is behaving absolutely normally, absolutely legally, absolutely according to the Constitution. Everything is the same and everything is exceptional.

To some extent, embracing the old paradigm, with its powerful national image, is an understandable form of symbolic and psychological self-defense. But it contributes to the perception that we alone must shoulder the burden of protecting ourselves from terrorism. With little public scrutiny, the government created the Department of Homeland Security, passed the USA PATRIOT Act, went to war in Afghanistan, and invaded Iraq. The unspoken pact forged between U.S. citizens and its leaders centers partly around safety, but more essentially around "normality," or the illusion of it. As the American Girl says, "C'mon and see what I'm made of, 'cause you ain't gonna split me in half no matter how hard ya come."

—∿→

Like it or not, the United States has adopted a new paradigm designed to enhance national security in the age of terror. The new paradigm relies on certain factors, some of which are debilitating for American democracy, as revealed by the cruelty of the English Boy and the passivity of the American Girl in *Guardians*. In the name of safety, the Bush administration has created a national security strategy in which torture is a logical outcome. Declaring necessary unprecedented presidential powers, the administration has undermined the processes that sustain democracy—transparency, honesty, and an integrated public discourse. Torture, like the war on terror, has been done in secrecy, and the policy has been carried out with an eye toward escaping accountability. When confronted with accusations, the government relies on "speaking power to truth," just as the English Boy does in the name of the deeper principle of personal survival.

This split-screen syndrome—in which normality and abnormality, vulnerability and power, democracy and domination jostle, side by side—has laid ground for a crisis of identity, apparent not only in the government but also among ordinary citizens. It is not possible to live as before and to not live as before. It is difficult to embody the oppressor and the oppressed. The result is a notable paralysis manifest in the public's passivity, shifting its focus from government policy and accountability to a collective fear of potential dangers.

Perhaps the most frightening aspect of *Guardians* is the message it sends about the future. The quest for justice is futile. "And those guys are like God," the American Girl tells us, referring to the president and his advisers who sent the country to war, "'cause you can blame 'em for all the shit that happens—you *should* blame 'em, 'cause it's their fault—but you can't catch 'em and haul *their* ass into a court-martial like you're doin' with me. Know why? 'Cause you don't got pictures a them. They're invisible. 'Cause they're the ones *behind* the camera."

U.S. citizens have been living in a state of limbo, akin to the "legal limbo" that lawyers in the Department of Justice's Office of Legal Counsel predicted on first receiving the infamous memos on the treatment of detainees. Where do we go from Abu Ghraib? *Guardians* suggests that this is a complicated question that calls into question basic notions of American identity. The follow-up to Abu Ghraib, therefore, is not just about punishing individuals and redressing wrongs; it is about restoring a sense of security based on open-eyed realism, not head-in-the-sand denial, and an understanding of ourselves not just as victims of terror, but as victims of a policy, never clearly explained, that now has gone awry.

—⟳→

If Morris's split-screen diagnosis is correct, there remains the question of whether attempts to redress the excesses of power are ultimately futile. One possible way to set the record straight would be to demand transparency and accountability by establishing a congressional investigation or a congressionally appointed independent commission. As Arthur Schlesinger Jr. once said, "The investigative power may indeed be the sharpest legislative weapon against executive aggrandizement," even sharper than Congress's ability to legislate. Such an investigation could be charged with examining the road to Guantánamo and Abu Ghraib, including efforts to divert and cloud public understanding of what happened. It could revalidate the importance of legal processes that rely on evidence, testimony, and cross-examination. The investigation also might look at the broader issues of interrogation as a skill and help us gain some historical perspective on executive powers.

The testimony and facts amassed by such a commission would help illuminate the real motives behind detainee abuse and the government policy of coercive, extralegal interrogation methods. In *Guardians,* the American

Girl is submissive to Charlie's increasingly perverse sexual demands, which include punching her and forcing her into a ménage à trois. She sees his demands about the prisoners as just one more form of rape. She sees him standing over her "with a broke-off mop handle in his fist. And this time, I can read it, the look in his eyes says . . . *You got problems with what I'm telling you to do? You take those problems and you take 'em out, take 'em all out on this brown person's ass. . . .*" The play echoes testimony from Lynndie England's trial about how she wanted to please individuals in positions of authority and had difficulty comprehending complex language. Morris's England may be obedient, but it's a survival strategy—if you "take a lickin'" you "keep on tickin'."

The sadomasochistic elements in both *Guardians* monologues share certain characteristics. They are overwhelming and as such transformative. As the English Boy says, "I pulled my leg back to kick him, and realized that . . . that I was actually drooling. So wholly possessed I couldn't even keep my mouth shut. The last thing I remember, really, is me, slack-jawed, slavering, slipping away into . . . some other world. Like a spastic, a pedophile, some subhuman creature charging forward, fully in the grip of its own mindless concupiscence. An American." The American Girl describes her fooling around with Charlie as "one of those things that just sweeps over you like, like a combine harvester munchin' over the amber waves of grain. You get plucked, and shucked, and spun every which way till you don't even know what you're doin' anymore, or it's *you* that's doin' it. I sure didn't." In confusion lies exculpability.

As the play reveals, we cannot conclude that every abuse is motivated by a clear-headed and rational desire to obtain information that could not be obtained in other ways. It suggests that American torture policy was motivated, at least to some extent, by a cruelty that Americans must eventually explain to themselves and to one another. In addition to the frustration and even fury at our lack of progress in the war on terror in general and in suppressing the

Iraqi insurgency in particular, there remains the impulse to abuse. As James Gilligan, professor of psychiatry at the University of Pennsylvania, writes in his illuminating study *Violence*, "The whole story includes, inescapably, the lives of the victimizers. . . ."

This, then, seems to be the ultimate question raised by Morris: Who, really, are the victimizers? To Morris, they are regular Americans, from the president down to Lynndie England. But a deeper understanding could be gained through an independent inquiry. Testimony, after all, ends silence and could shed light on the inchoate impulses displayed at Abu Ghraib. It would help clarify the American character in this new age and integrate the split screen into a cohesive picture. Until we do this, Abu Ghraib leaves not just a gap in the historical record, but a point of denial and disconnect in American consciousness. Until then, the American public will have to glean what it can from the words of this young playwright, trying to fathom how the victim turns victimizer, only to return to the status of victim.

"'Cause look. Everybody in the world seen me doing what I did wrong. Which—here's the funny part—it only proves that really, I'm nobody. 'Cause the powerful people? The folks I was takin' orders from? They're invisible.

"But try it now. Do what I did, follow that chain a command. All the way up to the Preznit. 'Cause ya know, I almost feel bad for the Preznit a little. I think he's a fuckin' disgrace, but I feel a little bad. 'Cause ya look at him and ya know he's like me. He's in over his head, no fuckin' clue, but there he is—still smiling for the cameras."

The Women of Abu Ghraib

Francine D'Amico

The Iraqi prison scandal starkly reveals the assumptions beneath the U.S. military's gender camouflage—that is, the multiple overt and subtle ways gender is deployed in the military context to include or to marginalize, to honor or to stigmatize.

In examining public, media, and official responses to the documentation of the recent abuses, I find two gender dimensions. First is the gender dimension in the abuse itself, which includes the purposive sexual humiliation of prisoners and what now appears to be the deliberate use of female guards to exacerbate that humiliation through a reversal of gender roles. Second is the gender dimension of the larger group dynamic in which women, despite all their contributions to military service, are still seen as "outsiders" in what many perceive as a definitively masculine institution.

It is no coincidence that the two soldiers' names most recognizable to the general public in the second Gulf War are those of Private First Class Jessica Lynch and Private First Class Lynndie England. One is cast in the gender-traditional role of victim, the other in the gender-incongruous role of victimizer. Their two stories demonstrate how ill-fitting our "either/or" gender expectations are, especially in the context of the Iraq War.

The thread running through their stories is the same: Both wanted to fit in, to be part of the larger group. As Lynch said to her rescuers, "I'm a soldier, too." Yet the inclusion they sought was elusive: They remain highly visible because they are women in a gender-nontraditional institution.

Most military men and women treat each other as colleagues, with professional respect. But there remains a small but disruptive minority who creates and sustains a hostile climate of both gender harassment ("women can't hack it") and sexual harassment (including sexual assault and rape), sadly illustrated by scandals at Aberdeen Proving Ground in 1997, at the U.S. Air Force Academy in 2003, and recently in the Iraqi theater itself. This gender dimension plays out in military group dynamics.

Social scientists have documented that people in groups behave in ways they never would as individuals. This group dynamic is most compelling for those whom core members of the group define as "outsiders," people who must work hard to fit in, to be accepted. As someone who has studied military gender dynamics for twenty years, I mention this not to excuse some U.S. soldiers—both men and women—who commit these crimes, but to try to understand them. Gender cuts both ways. Women who refuse to participate are not "players"—not one of the guys. And men who refuse have their masculinity mocked and risk ostracism.

Confusion over Treatment

This powerful and gendered group dynamic operates in a larger permissive context in which political leadership refuses to call detainees "prisoners of war," causing confusion about the treatment accorded prisoners under both international and domestic law. In this legal limbo, such practices as housing common criminals with prisoners of war and identifying "high value" prisoners as suspected 9/11 terrorists rather than as insurgents in the Iraqi resistance make military police uncertain of whether prisoners are entitled to the full protection of the Geneva conventions.

Like the detainees, the "prison abuses" should be called what they are—war crimes or atrocities—and should be punished as such. Sex has often been used as a weapon of war; and sexualized forms of torture have been deliberately applied to subjects under interrogation to erode their sense of humanity as well as their gender identity. For example, in the secessionist wars in Yugoslavia, husbands were made to witness their wives being raped so they would be shamed for having failed in their gender role as protectors, a tactic now being documented at the International Criminal Tribunal for the former Yugoslavia.

Consider the immediate context of the following group dynamic: Military police (MPs) at Abu Ghraib and other Iraqi prisons are mainly reservists, far from home, family, community. They work in overcrowded and understaffed facilities, and most, according to the report by investigating officer Major General Antonio Taguba, have not had adequate training to handle prisoner interrogation.

There is confusion in the chain of command, with military police officers telling guards one thing and military intelligence staff telling them another. The prison compounds are under attack much of the time, yet the MPs cannot fight back because their job is to guard the prisoners. They feel frustrated and helpless.

Sexual Tension Among the Ranks

Additionally, the atmosphere is sexually charged: Most are young people, far from home and spouses/partners, yet they are forbidden to fraternize. Sexual banter is as common there as it is among young people on college campuses, but acting on sexual attraction risks censure. Sexual deprivation compounded by fear is channeled into inappropriate behavior.

The Taguba report is revealing; Taguba criticizes Brigadier General Janis Karpinski, military police commander for Iraq's prison system, for both a failure of leadership because the abuses happened on her watch and for being "emotional" during questioning, the latter mentioned twice in the report. The gendered implications of this description are obvious: Women are emotional, men are rational, as though they are different species (men are from Mars, women are from Venus).

Appropriately, Karpinski was relieved of her command and censured, an action that will prevent further promotion and effectively force her retirement, since in the military hierarchy one must move "up or out."

Taking Orders from Women

Yet I have to wonder if other women officers have experienced what Taguba's report documents as consistent refusal by Karpinski's subordinates to comply with her orders: Is this simply a failure of leadership or concurrently a gender-related failure of compliance bordering on insubordination? As one soldier put it at a court-martial in another incident not long ago, "I don't take orders from women."

Karpinski's reaction to initial reports by detainees of abuse was one of disbelief. This was not simply feminine naiveté; most other military and political officials also refused to believe the allegations until there was irrefutable evidence. Karpinski is guilty of having too much faith in the people under her command. This is not a gendered trait; Taguba's report also cites a dozen other officers (all men) for failing to recognize the severity of the situation and intervene.

Karpinski clearly tried to make changes in the prison staff to rectify the situation: She twice disciplined Lieutenant Colonel Jerry Phillabaum, MP battalion commander at Abu Ghraib, for ineffective command, first with a general officer memorandum of reprimand in November 2003 for lack of leadership and then with a suspension in January 2004 for dereliction of duty.

Through June 30, 2006, U.S. military fatalities in Iraq and Afghanistan total 2,831; of these, fifty-eight are women, despite service rules that ostensibly prohibit military women from serving in "direct combat" jobs. I point this out not to minimize men's sacrifices but to recognize that military women are also in harm's way. If we must remember the name of a woman soldier from Abu Ghraib, let it be that of Private First Class Rachel K. Bosveld. A nineteen-year-old from Wisconsin, she was with the 527th Military Police Company.

Bosveld died in 2003 from injuries she sustained during a mortar attack on Abu Ghraib. She was buried in Berlin, Wisconsin, on November 7, 2003, which would have been her twentieth birthday. She had previously been awarded a Purple Heart for surviving a September 12 grenade attack on the Humvee she was driving; her second Purple Heart was awarded posthumously.

Other members of the Bosveld family also have served our country: Her father, Marvin, and her brother, Craig, are army veterans, and her stepbrother, Aaron Kribs, is a marine stationed at Camp Pendleton. In a recent interview, her father said he always called Rachel a "chosen child" because she was adopted, and her brother described her as an artist and a musician. Her family nickname was Sweetpea. We honor the memory of Pfc. Rachel Bosveld not because she was a woman soldier, but because she was a soldier.

Gender Representative

Most military men and women had no role in these incidents and are, according to recent interviews, as repulsed by what happened as are we civilians. There is a disturbing tendency to interpret England as a "gender representative." She is no more representative of military women than Graner is of military men, so why are her actions used by some with a political agenda to suggest women don't belong in the military? It would be deemed ludicrous to suggest that Graner's actions represent those of military men.

England was a woman in what is still a very male environment: Approximately 15 percent of U.S. military personnel are women, and only about 10 percent of personnel deployed in Iraq and Afghanistan are women.[1] Like other servicewomen, she lived in a fishbowl. Her actions are wrongly extrapolated to all other servicewomen. Her participation in the abuse demonstrates that men have no monopoly on brutality or moral depravity. Nor do women have a monopoly on moral virtue, as the courageous actions of Specialist Joe Darby, who blew the whistle on the atrocities, illustrate. All human beings have an impulse to good and an impulse to evil, and gender does not determine which will triumph.

The Misogynist Implications of Abu Ghraib

Lucinda Marshall

The Abu Ghraib–inspired backlash against feminism was predictably swift. Women being portrayed as front-and-center participants in the sexualized torture that took place at the prison challenged our comfortable assumptions about how women are supposed to behave. Right-wing pundits wasted no time in implicating the role of feminism in causing the atrocities.

Linda Chavez of the deceptively named Center for Equal Opportunity quickly suggested that the presence of women in the military actually encouraged such "misbehavior." Attempting to bolster her claim, she inexplicably cited reports of sexual harassment in the military and the pregnancy rate of female soldiers in the gulf.

George Neumayr, columnist for the *American Spectator*, opined that what happened at Abu Ghraib "is a cultural outgrowth of a feminist culture which encourages female barbarians." He went on to quote Elaine Donnelly of the Center for Military Readiness as suggesting that feminists are good at creating "equal-opportunity abusers."

In hindsight, we can see the deliberate element of stage management involved in the release of the Abu Ghraib photos. We need to ask why, out of the thousands of photos that surfaced (and were made available to Congress), only the few highly sexualized photos were released to the public.

We now know that torture and abuse have been a systemic part of the U.S. campaigns in Iraq and Afghanistan. Between the time the abuses occurred at Abu Ghraib and September 2005, more than four hundred inquiries were made into detainee abuse in Iraq and Afghanistan, and 230 military personnel received punishment.

We also now know that responsibility for these policies goes to the highest levels of command, and that the use of female guards to taunt male prisoners is acknowledged by the military as a known method of interrogation, not something invented by a few female soldiers in the field. Indeed, given that women make up more than 15 percent of those on active military duty (and a much smaller percentage of those in command), the notion that a few low-ranking women were significantly responsible for what happened at Abu Ghraib is ludicrous.

The vilification of Private First Class Lynndie England is perhaps the most deliberate and misplaced attempt to blame women for Abu Ghraib. It's as if England is reprising the role of Hester Prynne in *The Scarlet Letter*. Dog leash in hand, she epitomizes the evil of Abu Ghraib. "The accused knew what she was doing," said Captain Chris Graveline, the lead prosecutor at her trial. "She was laughing and joking. . . . She is enjoying, she is participating, all for her own sick humor." Virtually guaranteed a conviction by a jury of five male officers, the U.S. military saw in her prosecution a ritual cleansing of the stain of torture and abuse that oozed out of Abu Ghraib.

That England had a history of mental incapacity and learning disabilities and was ordered by Charles Graner, her lover and superior officer, to pose was simply not deemed relevant. She was the one caught holding the dog leash. Conveniently omitted was the fact that the infamous picture was reportedly cropped to cut out other soldiers. Also overlooked was the fact that Graner shot the picture and wrote its caption, "This is what I make Lynndie do." Ironically, she was acquitted of a conspiracy charge pertaining to the leash. Grainer also shot numerous other highly sexualized photos both of female soldiers and of female detainees.

Perhaps what horrifies and discomforts us the most is the blatant connection between pornography and the violence of war. As anyone who has been to the movies lately knows, the combination of sex and violence is a popular form of amusement. And in the world of adult film, eroticized violence is often an element of hardcore pornography.

The military arena, where torture and sexual violence are standard fare, provides the opportunity to up the voyeuristic ante with actual, rather than staged, versions of these acts. This makes it disturbingly easy for politicians and the media to label many of the images as *merely* pornography, rather than torture and abuse, as if it were just a matter of politically incorrect entertainment.

Shortly after the Abu Ghraib story first surfaced, Arab-run websites posted photos that purported to show Iraqi women being sexually abused by U.S.-led coalition soldiers. Unlike the pictures of men being abused, these pictures were summarily dismissed as fakes when it was discovered that they had been posted on pornography websites. I have seen these pictures. They show violent sexual acts being committed against women. Whether the photos show acts as they're occurring or being staged is not the point; the pictures clearly show abuse and should be considered as such.

The Bush administration's assertion that Abu Ghraib was an isolated incident, and its attempt to atone for it with England's highly publicized trial, looked farcical in light of the many reports and stories showing an undercurrent of sexual deviance in parts of the military. Consider the success of Internet entrepreneur Chris Wilson, who generously offered military personnel serving in Iraq and Afghanistan free access to his porn site in exchange for pictures of action in the war zone. It is perhaps fitting that the depravity of war should find its fullest expression on a site that peddles pornography. The pictures submitted by soldiers to Wilson's site show all manner of mutilated bodies and evidence of torture being committed by U.S. troops. It is obvious that the soldiers sending in these pictures took great pride in the displays of their handiwork.

These pictures of torture and abuse also make it clear that pornographic venues per se are not a reason to discount the veracity of photographic evidence. One of the pictures that *East Bay Express* reporter Chris Thompson saw on Wilson's site illustrates the point:

> [A] woman whose right leg has been torn off by a land mine, and a medical worker is holding the mangled stump up to the camera. The woman's vagina is visible under the hem of her skirt. The caption for this picture reads: "Nice puss—bad foot."

As Wilson's site clearly shows, soldiers often feel perfectly comfortable taking ownership of the sexualized violence they've committed. It's even something to brag about.

Placed in historical context, sexual depravity in the military has always been present but has rarely been of a consensual nature. Male soldiers have always been considered entitled to the "R&R" provided by prostitutes and sexual slavery; rape and other forms of sexual assault (including that of female soldiers within the ranks and their own family members) have been included in the arsenal of power tools on which militarism and patriarchy depend. The misogynistic assumptions of militarism that lead to the sexual use and abuse of women are not limited to war zones, as we have clearly seen in the reports of sexual abuse at the United States Air Force Academy and at Florida's Patrick Air Force Base, where in 2006 a senior noncommissioned officer was charged with arranging for an enlisted woman to have sex with several people, including someone charged with inspecting the base.

As the horrors of Abu Ghraib started to unfold, Iraqi men were quoted as saying that they had been humiliated both by being made to feel like women and by being tortured by women. Sexualized torture of men by women is scandalous both to Iraqis and Westerners alike, and its use amounts to the deliberate use of misogyny as a weapon of war.

But far more misogynistic is the almost total lack of attention to the ample evidence of sexual assault against Iraqi women at Abu Ghraib. Quite simply, sexual abuse against men is considered torture; sexual abuse against women by men is business as usual.

There is no doubt the abuse against women took place, according to reports by the military, numerous human rights organizations, and NGOs (nongovernmental organizations). Most of the women were detained not because they were suspected of having committed crimes, but in hopes of getting their male relatives to provide information, according to documents released by the U.S. military in January 2006. Such detentions are a violation of international law.

In Iraqi culture, the abuse, intimidation, and sexual assault of a woman is considered to be a reflection on the manhood of her husband and male family members. The abuse affects the family's honor. A woman who is raped or assaulted is seen as bringing shame upon her family, making her doubly victimized by being subjected to not only a crime but denial, ostracism, or even death. The Iraqi legal system offers women no protection from being victimized again by their families. Because of this, Iraqi women are afraid to report rape and other forms of violence, making it impossible to truly document these crimes.

Feminists must ensure that the sensationalizing of the role women played at Abu Ghraib not be allowed to obscure the real causes of the atrocities that took place there or the far more prevalent violence male soldiers have inflicted both on female soldiers and on civilians, including women.

Shock and Awe: Abu Ghraib, Women Soldiers, and Racially Gendered Torture

Ilene Feinman

In the United States, the Bush administration, Congress, public intellectuals, and mainstream media outlets have represented and analyzed the exposure of torture through the photographic and testimonial evidence from Abu Ghraib prison in ways that have obscured the role of gender and race in both perpetrating and representing that torture.

Significant clues to this effect are seen in the overrepresentation of white women soldiers as perpetrators of torture relative to both their actual participation at Abu Ghraib and their numbers in the military, the absence of accounts of the torture of women prisoners, and the public's widespread surprise (feigned and otherwise) that our soldiers are even capable of torture. The insistence on the "few bad apples" theory in the months following the release of the Abu Ghraib photos served to exonerate the rest of us from culpability, and served the administration by keeping the "authority" for carrying out the torture among the lowest-ranked officers in the U.S. military—in itself contradictory, given the hierarchical command structure of the forces.

Perhaps the most profound ramification of the scandal, however, was the way in which it forced our focus on women as torturers. This focus serves to reify the role of white men as torturers. We seem to expect their brutality; men perpetrating torture is far less interesting to the public, as evidenced by the proportionally smaller focus on men's role in the scandal.

There is a complex story of racialization here: that of the military police and clerks at Abu Ghraib, the majority of whom are white (and portrayed as "trailer trash whites"), and of the prisoners, who are Arab Iraqis. Moreover, in the United States, the presentation of homosexuality as deviance, and its violent performance as torture, underscored the heterosexism fueling the raging debates about homosexuality and marriage.

This essay analyzes the racially gendered figure of the woman soldier, the extent of masculinism that shapes the core constructs of military culture, and the complex process of othering that is entailed in military endeavors. It also examines how and why U.S. women soldiers become public signifiers, generating and grounding the debates about the meaning of rules of interrogation, about women POWs, and about women's rights protection. This analysis demonstrates that the function of women as the focus of the torture revelations, disproportional to their actual presence in either the military or the group of soldiers convicted of torture, serves to both anomalize the incidents of torture, and to discredit "unintelligent and incapable women," while ignoring the very rank command structure that authorized the torture in the first instance.

U.S. Troops' Use of Torture

The Abu Ghraib images were explosive renditions of brutality that sparked a number of responses and questions. The ubiquitous response in the United States was the citizenry's (and politicians') public surprise and horror that U.S. soldiers were using torture to interrogate prisoners. While the citizenry's response made sense, the administration's did not. The International Committee of the Red Cross (ICRC), Amnesty International, and Human Rights Watch have all documented torture as a practice by the U.S. military. The ICRC confidentially reported its findings and concerns to the administration regarding the armed forces' use of torture in Afghanistan and Iraq well before the Abu Ghraib scandal broke. ICRC Director of Operations Pierre Kraehenbuehl said, "We were dealing here with a broad pattern, not individual acts. There was a pattern and a system."[1] In addition, the ICRC asserted that 70–90 percent of the prisoners at Abu Ghraib were arrested by mistake through systematic roundups in neighborhoods. Thus, it's more likely than not that the administration—including Donald Rumsfeld, though he acted surprised for the media—and the leadership of the intelligence committees of both houses of Congress knew what was going on long before the Abu Ghraib photos leaked to the media. The argument that no one actually ordered the torture seems improbable, since the low-level courts-martial proceedings and Attorney General Alberto Gonzales's memos regarding the "quaint provisions" of the Geneva conventions, as well as Rumsfeld's signed instructions to the prison guards at Abu Ghraib, have become public.

While there is detailed admonition in Department of Defense training manuals against using torture, there remains a long, documented history of U.S. military training for and involvement in torture. The School of the Americas (now called the Western Institute for Security Cooperation) is a notorious site for such training. This, of course, does not make the United States stand out among other nations. One need only read the ICRC, Amnesty International, and Human Rights Watch reports for a startling glimpse of the international company we keep as users of torture, both political and civilian. As a nation we represent ourselves as protectors of freedom and democracy, yet our practice evinces something else entirely. In choosing to use Abu Ghraib as a prison, we reopened what, under Saddam Hussein, was the most notorious torture prison facility in Iraq. We continue to support national leaders with incontrovertible histories of defiling freedom and democracy via basic human rights violations, including the use of torture. We are signatories to the Geneva conventions against torture and yet we busily create exceptions for ourselves. In short, the public release of the Abu Ghraib photos served to out the United States for something that has too long gone ignored or unrecognized by the majority of Americans.

Who's Really Calling the Shots?

It is important to recognize the compartmentalized, top-down structure of the military command, and thus to consider the Taguba report (March 2004) on the Military Police Brigade, the Fay-Jones report (August 2004) on the Military Intelligence Brigade, and the Schlesinger report (August 2004) on the investigations themselves in terms of the light they shed on military procedure.

General Taguba, who was instructed to investigate the role of the MPs in the emerging scandal, investigated within a very limited framework. Each of the investigations proceeded in a hierarchical fashion down the ranks. Though the Military Intelligence Brigade was investigated in the Fay-Jones report, the blame rested solely on Colonel Thomas Pappas, who was in charge of the 205th Military Intelligence Brigade in Baghdad. Pappas was under the command of Major General Barbara Fast, head of military intelligence in Iraq. Although Fast was the leader from whom the instructions would have been given, she was not held culpable. Then–brigadier general Janis Karpinski, a midlevel leader in charge of the military prisons and MPs, and her soldiers were the main focus of the investigation. Those in Karpinski's charge were allowed into the infamous cellblocks, but she was restricted access, under the guise that interrogation was their sole function.[2] Karpinski and Pappas were both demoted and reprimanded in the aftermath of the scandal. To date, none of the ranking officers above them has been held directly responsible or court-martialed. While the investigations continue at the lower levels, it remains to be seen how deep or high these investigations will go.

The young MPs and clerks were poorly trained for what turned out to be their mission, as their original mandate was to hold prisoners of war for brief periods with no involvement in interrogations. Interrogations were only to be used by military intelligence to "soften up" prisoners.

There are instructive linkages between the U.S. prison system and MP units. Many MPs came out of prison guard and police force careers at home. One of the more notorious Abu Ghraib MPs, Specialist Charles Graner, was a poorly reviewed and regularly reprimanded prison guard in the Pennsylvania state prison system. His violent practical jokes on other guards and propensity for beating up prisoners were widely known and frowned upon, and he had a long record of domestic violence.[3] While stationed in Iraq, he and Private First Class Lynndie England, the most infamous of the female torturers (actually a clerk for the MP), conceived a child together; he has now married former specialist Megan Ambuhl, another of the female soldiers convicted of torturing prisoners at Abu Ghraib.

It's important to recognize the context for this set of revelations about torture and the Bush administration's acceptance of using it, as well as its use in the U.S. prison system (albeit "against the rules"). The architects of the rebuilding of the Iraqi prison systems have long, unsavory connections to the U.S. prison system.

Lane McCotter, who directed the reopening of Abu Ghraib as a U.S. military prison, also had an unsavory record as a U.S. prison official. Formerly the director of the Utah Department of Corrections, he resigned in 1997 under a cloud of scandal when he defended the practice of using restraining chairs on prisoners after an inmate died while being restrained. McCotter went on to become an executive for Corrections, a division of Management & Training Corporation, a Utah-based firm that operates thirteen prisons in the United States, Canada, and Australia. He was sent to Iraq as part of a team of prison officials, judges, prosecutors, and police chiefs picked by Attorney General John Ashcroft to rebuild the country's criminal justice system.

In 2004, in the middle of a firestorm about the severe human rights violations at Abu Ghraib, Guantánamo, and various prisons in Afghanistan and Iraq, U.S. Ambassador to the United Nations John Negroponte was appointed ambassador to Iraq. Negroponte himself had been investigated for human rights violations in Honduras when in the 1980s he supported the contras in their guerrilla war against the democratically elected government of Nicaragua. A year after becoming ambassador, Negroponte became the first person to serve in the newly created post of director of national intelligence.

The torture revelations must be analyzed as a logical outgrowth of the Bush administration's willingness to use torture as part of its interrogation practices, as well as in the context of the particular use of subordinated and possibly subaltern figures as scapegoats for our broader military-political practices. At a minimum, U.S. leaders, as well as the administration's diplomatic appointments, have demonstrated a cavalier attitude toward due process, human rights, and integrity of law. There is also recent evidence that the dog handlers in some of the most infamous photographs were in fact given instructions to use their dogs in illegally violent ways.

Women Can Torture, Too

Women soldiers' participation in the brutal acts of torture stands as the single most shocking revelation to emerge from Abu Ghraib. Perhaps this explains the relentless repetition of the photos, which resulted in distorting public perception about women soldiers as perpetrators of violence and torture. Given the number of women in the military police and in the forces more generally (a consistent 15 percent), their involvement in the Abu Ghraib scandal was exaggerated.

I was contacted early on by the media for my comments on the visage of Lynndie England, Sabrina Harmon, and Megan Ambuhl in the disturbing poses we saw in the press. At that time, I was still thinking about Lori Piestewa, Jessica Lynch, and Shoshana Johnson, all three of whom foreshadowed the ways in which the public would read the women involved in the Abu Ghraib scandal. Piestewa, of the Hopi Nation, died in an attempt to drive her convoy to safety; Johnson, who is African American, returned gunfire. Both soldiers, women of color, were deemed heroines, and yet they were hardly covered in the press. Jessica Lynch, a white woman, became the poster child for the meaning of women in the military, despite her own account of hiding out in the bottom of the Humvee and arguments that her rescue was staged. Before Abu Ghraib, female soldiers in Iraq were portrayed as Jessica Lynches—hapless young women who needed to be rescued by heroic male soldiers. No wonder the public was so startled by the account of women torturers.

A common reaction to women as torturers at Abu Ghraib came in the form of questions: Why (or how) could women do this? How could women torture, degrading themselves and their captives simultaneously? Doesn't this prove that women are just as brutal as men?

My reaction was not one of feeling let down, nor did I feel that this signaled a new stage of women's degradation. I understood that women can be socialized to objectify and brutalize other human beings, just as men can. I knew that women were sitting in roughly 15 percent of the available billets in the military, and thus were likely to appear in those ratios in any given scenario. Especially in the low-ranking, low-power reserve military police units. The women at Abu Ghraib, therefore, seemed neither out of place nor disproportionately involved. To my mind it would have been surprising had there been no women in those images. Unfortunately, the training of soldiers depends on the ability to objectify and thus dehumanize the enemy. Training is equally dependent, for women as well as men, on adhering to a strict hierarchy of command. To disobey orders is to invite court-martial.

Whether we're considering the female POWs or the women soldiers convicted of torture at Abu Ghraib, it's evident that, as a culture, we do not yet understand how to think about women in the military—much less women in combat. There is incredible ambivalence in the U.S. mainstream press about women in positions of power or control, however symbolic; and there's a parallel ambivalence and disappointment among many American feminists about how the women involved in the Abu Ghraib scandal conducted themselves. The ongoing focus on this small group of female MPs and clerks has opened up a public discourse around sex, race, and sex roles.

When I see those images of women soldiers standing over the degraded Iraqi prisoners, I think of women combat pilots who flew their first sorties over the Persian Gulf in the early nineties as part of the U.S. mission to keep Hussein out of Kurdish territory. The first official female combat pilot who was interviewed after her first sortie said she had fun and was ready to do it again.[4] Equally capable as male soldiers to be warriors, she and her sisters were trained systematically alongside male counterparts to perform their technical duties, to drop their "clean bombs,"[5] and see the designated enemy as other/nonhuman in order to facilitate brutalizing them in whatever way orders defined.

Scholars of women in the military have written about the ways women have argued for expanded roles in the military and for equal rights and responsibilities for the sake of their careers, as well as for the same aspirations that men express in terms of patriotism and enthusiasm for the fight.[6] Women's interest in the military is as varied as men's. How women are perceived, treated, and implicated in wrongdoing in the military relative to men is of course another matter.

(Un)Gendered Military?

Given the stark contrast between public focus on female torturers and their actual numbers among those court-martialed, in addition to the relative number of men to women in the military, I would argue that women in the military are used as an enormous symbolic wellspring of unresolved issues around gender equality and military masculinism.

Data on military demographics demonstrate that in 2002 females comprised a total of 17 percent of the forces' population. This breaks down as

17 percent of the army; 17 percent of the navy; 24 percent of the air force; and 5 percent of the marine corps.[7] The numbers of active duty personnel as of September 2004 indicate 35,112 women officers out of 228,124 total (or 16 percent of all officers) and 174,929 enlisted women out of 1,861,074 total (or 15 percent of all enlisted).[8] The fact that women are holding at approximately 15 percent of the forces given their 50–52 percent representation in the general population indicates a continued dearth of interest among women to join the forces in representative numbers.

This small percentage of women in the forces, and the officer ranks overall, is reflected evenly in their apparent numbers relative to the Abu Ghraib prison scandal. Based on the number of times images of women were replayed as "photographic evidence" in the press following the Abu Ghraib scandal, one would assume that women were a majority of the military police inflicting the torturing. This reality is an interesting study in the meanings of women's participation and the use of those women, rather than in how or why women were present at the start.

Were the women soldiers at Abu Ghraib more or less feminine than the general population of women? They are likely representative, within the same range of girly to tough as any other sector. So what is happening when they share the willingness to perform acts of violence against Iraqi men? Did they employ the same tactics or use their sexual identities to violently manipulate Iraqi women detainees? How is military training shaping women's understanding of themselves in relation to male soldiers, female soldiers, and citizens of the countries where they are deployed? How are women functioning symbolically in the broader debate? How are they constructed, particularly in the depicted acts? Given that women's physical presence is far smaller than their symbolic presence in the Abu Ghraib photos, we have to ask, To what use are they being put?

Understanding the Abu Ghraib scandal requires two levels of analysis. The first approach is to consider the debates sparked by the public representations of the scandal. The second is to consider the evidence and patterns that have emerged through the courts-martial and parallel disclosures about the extensive use of torture as a prime interrogatory method. The press has released some images to the public, but release of subsequent photos has been controlled by the Defense Department. Given the method of the photos' release, it is not possible (without security clearance) to count the real numbers of men and women who were actually involved. We are left to make our own determinations based on the released photographs and the convictions and charges in the courts-martial. And though we know that similar abuses are being reported from Guantánamo and prison sites in Afghanistan, these occurrences do not have the same photographic evidence that might otherwise bring them into broad public discourse.

The fact that we don't have evidence about actual number of torturers presents several interesting themes. First, there are far fewer women MPs than would be assumed by the frequency of showcasing women as torturers. Second, the numbers disclosed, in terms of how many men and women tortured prisoners, seem to mirror the ratio of women to men in the military at large; so there does not seem to be a gender anomaly here. Thus, female MPs are, in fact, overrepresented as torturers; in contrast, one might note that which was not visually represented at all—namely that the Taguba report notes the abuse and rape of women detainees at Abu Ghraib. Photos depicting these acts have been withheld by Congress and have not leaked to the media. Images were released that showed simulated rape of men, featured women as torturers, and depicted forced homosexual positions. Images of women being raped and tortured were not. Why?

Racialized Gender and the Gendered Military

We know from various testimonies that female MPs and some clerks, posing as brutal dominatrices and sirens, were used as tools of interrogation at Abu Ghraib and Guantánamo—but to what extent were they complicit and to what extent coerced? How did we get from visages of gender-neutral soldiering to gendered torture?

The women MPs and clerks (all white) in these torture scenarios express their racialized and gendered selves on two different registers. The first is one in which, as white women soldiers, they exercise power over Arab male prisoners of war. In this case, they act on instruction from their superiors in the hierarchical command structure of the armed forces. They have power, in effect, but only inasmuch as their commanders bestow it. In this way, they are positioned as parallel to their male rank counterparts. Their superiors and their superiors' superiors, however, are typically men. (Outranking most of those men, however, was one woman: Major General Barbara Fast, head of military intelligence.) Therefore, when the female MPs are commanded to take power and express power over the prisoners to achieve an aim set by their commanders, they are not in positions of autonomous power. In an environment where fully 85 percent of the forces are men, are women soldiers acting from positions of power at all?

Certainly, they do not have ultimate power as assistants to interrogators. In fact, they are interpreting and enacting the commands sent to them from above; arguably, they are extending their power within the small confines of their jurisdiction in order to express a sense of power—a sense that is immediately challenged when they face court-martial and their pleas to having acted on order are summarily dismissed.

The focus among American feminists—who have tried to make sense of women's role in the torture—and among people who oppose women in the armed forces has been to ask whether women were exploited and debased by using their sexuality to manipulate prisoners. Were these women soldiers simply pawns, or were they players equipped with their own arsenal? I find this focus to be problematic. When we only ask questions about women, when we are only appalled and confused by women soldiers' acts of brutality, we continue to cast women as victims and men as brutes. When both are stereotyped into these roles, Rush Limbaugh's comment about the photo of prisoners stacked in a pyramid looking like a fraternity rush signaling our boys letting off a little steam turns out to be exactly the point. Male-orchestrated torture is "normal," part of frat culture, part of hazing into the military. By focusing on women's intentions as the only aberration, we are not taking seriously enough the equally troubling male-perpetrated violence. Our analysis of the women and men of Abu Ghraib has resulted in their removal from our expectations of civilized norms. We have marginalized them to the point that we expect the women were coerced into the behavior by the men and the men . . . well, trailer-trash men are brutes, right? We expect them to be violent, so our curiosity ends with them and does not proceed up the chain of command to those who hold the real power.

Carol Mason teaches us that the portrayal and subsequent analyses of these low-level participants lead us to assume that these men and women are hillbillies, liminal figures who, by their uncivilized behavior, underscore how much this torture is an aberration from our civilized soldiering, our feminist women, our society. She argues that this is a classic typecasting—seeing the hillbilly female as a she-man, a gender-bending trope of uncivilized and disorderly femininity.[9]

The second register on which these female MPs express their gendered and racialized selves has to do with a woman's power over her male prisoner and the constructions of racialized gender in the interplay between white woman and Arab male. Utilizing the assumptions of distinctly gendered cultures, the white female U.S. soldier proceeds to violate the physical and religious (or cultural) integrity of the Arab male prisoner. From smearing (fake) menstrual blood on the Arab prisoner to enacting sexually explicit behaviors and sexually harassing him, the white female soldier creates a stunning environment of humiliation and distress. Male interrogators also humiliate and defile prisoners utilizing rape, forced sex act simulation, groveling, and impure contact with shoes, feces, and other prisoners.[10] But there is a unique dynamic to be examined here with the use of female soldiers' symbolic racial power and sexuality to break down prisoners of war. This is a racially gendered theater of subordination.

Women's Agency and Military Command Structure

The Abu Ghraib scandal created an opportunity to think about the ways in which it could be possible for women to participate in barbaric acts of torture contextualized by questions of power in general and women's power in particular within the military. Women are, after all, tools of the masculinist military within which they are trained. The particular function of women (white women soldiers) raises the question of whether they are being used, or using themselves, as sexualized and sexist tools of a racist, masculinist militarism that freely deploys tropes of sexual power as the main tool of oppression against Arab prisoners of war.

Because women's level of involvement in torture policies and training is roughly equivalent to their ratio in the forces, women's "sudden" or "unique" propensity for violence is neither abnormal nor cause for alarm. Nor are they simply victims of male sexism. We need to continue to analyze the military as a hierarchical, deeply obedience-based institution that is still foundationally racist and masculinist and has no trouble absorbing women (of all colors) and men (of color) into that paradigm and utilizing their bodies as sexualized, racialized weapons. Sexualized torture entails women MPs, interpreters, and clerks engaging in activities (perhaps with the exception of smearing fake menstrual blood) that would stereotypically sexually arouse their heteronormative American male soldier comrades (see the panoply of pornographic tropes for evidence of parallels); but in this context, against Arab men, the behavior is designed to shame. Multiple layers of women soldiers' sexualities are deployed here: shaming Arab men with American women's presence and sexuality; exciting and sustaining American men's understanding of their sexuality as power; and dominance. Author Carol Burke writes about

the historic practice of sexually violent marching cadences.[11] Thus tweaked
by women soldiers' integration, the culture of sexually dominant masculinist
militarism is sustained.

Thumbs-Up: Bush and England

Military masculinist performances by President George W. Bush and
Private England tell a similar story of performing tropes of power: "Mission
Accomplished." Bush dons a fighter pilot outfit of the Top Guns—invoking
the powerful symbol of a war hero though he has never fought in a war;
England sticks her thumb up in a "mission accomplished" pose, a cigarette
dangling from her mouth, nonchalant about the power she has just taken
over the group of Arab male prisoners, standing hooded and naked against
the wall. What are these two gendered performances doing as centerpieces of
the imagery of the Iraq War? Multiple images of the women MPs and clerks
at Abu Ghraib depict the thumbs-up sign, demonstrating a camaraderie
with Bush, thumbs-up on the deck of a military ship. There is a signaling of
positions of power that is recognizably masculinist and militarist. Yet both are
curiously staged and evocative. No one can deny that although Bush was never
an active soldier he has waged war, nor that although England and her fellow
female soldiers were not men they tortured their prisoners in traditionally
masculinist ways. These masculine tropes are not accidental, and yet they are
both real and simulated.

In terms of the women's behaviors and the significance of the performance of military masculinity cum violence, I am reminded of the analysis
of popular military films exploring connections between sex roles and
military prowess, from *Top Gun* to *G.I. Jane*.[12] In *Top Gun*, a woman can be
an intellectual specialist in military affairs, but nothing competes with the
warrior's direct experience. In *G.I. Jane*, a woman can be a warrior if she can
become the man, shaving her head and commanding her master sergeant to
"suck [her] dick."

The increase in coeducational racially gendered training in the forces (notwithstanding the severe sexualized violence against women in the military by military men) has provided women with similar strategies of power over and objectification of "the other" (i.e., enemy combatants) as men possess. They are equally conditioned to divorce themselves from the humanity of the other. Military boot camp is far from gender-neutral training, designed in precisely gendered and racialized ways, and inscribed with precise power relations and dynamics. Women are now being trained to respond equally to their male counterparts with a racialized, patriarchally constructed tool kit of behaviors.[13] Soldiers from any of the military branches in any of the billets, regardless of gender and given their duty to fight, are trained to distance themselves from the designated enemy and be inured to killing.

Cultures of Sexuality and Torture

It is worth remarking that according to journalist Seymour Hersh the "study" text of Arab culture in the administration and the Pentagon was Raphael Patai's *The Arab Mind*.[14,15] It is particularly dense with reference to the intensely circumscribed sexuality of men and women in Arab culture and has been widely criticized for its contribution to the practices of orientalism, plaguing U.S. understanding of the cultures of the Arab world, as if it were one entity. Nevertheless, this social and political caricature of Arab cultures has been exploited by U.S. interrogators.

Much of the American public views Arab societies as sexually suppressed and segregated. The fact that U.S. citizens talk about sex, have political and cultural wars about sexuality, and continue to fight for control of women's reproductive bodies does not mean we are open, egalitarian, or even sexually integrated as a culture. This is demonstrated by the ways we revert to the same social debates decade after decade. Take the question, What do career moms want? How radical it would be to ask, What do career dads want? U.S. culture is rife with examples of sexual inequity. That the society remains amazed by the fact that women use the capital they are granted (or have won) in civilian culture to participate in warrior culture is a signal that we somehow understand women to be incompatible with warrior culture. Even pop culture has a handle on this: Women warriors like those featured in *Elektra, Mr. & Mrs. Smith,* and *Kill Bill* utilize their feminine wiles to effect a seduction that gets them what they need.

How then to explain the shock that is professed at women soldiers who use their sexual arsenal to manipulate prisoners of war, even if the order comes from the man (or woman) above? Surely it's the case that sometimes the female soldier is happy to comply for her own reasons; other times she is manipulated. We may never know which is true in any given case. Consider Graner testifying under oath that he forced England, and England testifying she chose to do it herself.

The furor over women soldiers participating in torturing prisoners of war in Abu Ghraib and elsewhere has served several interesting purposes. The focus on women has allowed for posturing that has enabled "normal" Americans to distance themselves from the torture. Consider the following rationales: Real women (including real feminists) would never behave that way; the torturers—male and female—must be stupid and uncivilized to do what they did. Much was made of England's learning disabilities and mental illness. Her defense lawyers used these circumstances to soften her conviction.

The sexualized torture photographs opened up all kinds of reactions and debates, but they also exposed secrets. They provided a moment of voyeurism into domination as sexual fantasy and its concomitant horror—the severely sex-constrained, puritan social mores of the United States (which is quite prevalent for all its liberalized show). They initiated a renewal of the cry from Concerned Women for America and Eagle Forum that women don't belong in the ugly man's world of the military. They cannot handle it. In the case of Abu Ghraib, of course, it seems that the women served instrumental roles in helping effect the violations of the sexual mores of Arab cultures by their witnessing and participant observation, no less than their abominable acts of degradation such as masturbating on or in front of prisoners and smearing fake menstrual blood on the prisoners. In other words, they can handle it just like the men.

Women Tortured Offscreen

In war, historically constant and not at all unique to the United States, racially sexualized violence against women has been routinely used to punctuate the defeat and destruction of an ethnic group. One need only read the tomes on recent wars in Yugoslavia, Afghanistan, Darfur, Iraq, and elsewhere, both with and without United States intervention, to see that this is a regular practice of war.

As the shock waves over torture at U.S.-run prisons spread, the inquiry into evidence that women were also being tortured in the prisons was skipped. While fewer women than men were imprisoned at Abu Ghraib, the harm imposed on those women was deeply significant. A series of articles has exposed the abuse and torture of women detainees, drawing on the investigations of Iraqi women lawyers. On May 20, 2004, the *Guardian*'s Luke Harding reported about a letter smuggled out of the jail by a woman prisoner to the women lawyers attempting to gain access to them in the prison. The note claimed that the U.S. guards were raping women detainees. Amal Kadham Swadi and a group of Iraqi women lawyers are pursuing these cases. The pressure was so great on the U.S. forces that the women originally rounded up were released after the exposure of torture at Abu Ghraib. The Taguba report confirmed the accuracy of the woman detainee's smuggled letter and remarked that "among the 1,800 digital photographs taken by U.S. guards inside Abu Ghraib, there are images of a U.S. military policeman 'having sex' with an Iraqi woman."[16] The report also indexed videotapes and photographs of naked Iraqi women prisoners and other photographs of women forced at gunpoint to reveal their breasts.[17]

Tara McKelvey detailed the findings of a Department of Defense report disclosing the torture of women at Abu Ghraib as follows:

Forty-two women have been held at Abu Ghraib, according to a U.S. Department of Defense statement provided at the request of a U.S. senator and forwarded to me, though none are interned there now. (Many of the women were released in May, shortly after the scandal broke, and the last woman was let go in July.) Overall, 90 women have been held in various detention facilities in Iraq since August 2003, says Barry Johnson, a public-affairs officer for detainee operations for the Multi-National Force, the official name of the U.S.-led forces in Iraq, speaking on a cell phone from Baghdad. Two "high-value" female detainees are now being held, he says. More women may be in captivity, he adds, explaining that "units can capture and keep them up to fourteen days." In addition, approximately 60 children, or "juveniles," are being held.[18]

Although most women prisoners were released after the Abu Ghraib scandal went public, there is evidence that women and children are being captured as ransom to pressure their male relatives (suspected of resistance work) to turn themselves in. According to McKelvey, the women can be held for up to fourteen days.

Much of our shock and awe stems from the fact that men were being sexually devalued and defiled by female MPs; the flip side of this, similar violations by our male soldiers of women prisoners, inspires neither shock nor awe. To the U.S. public, female, white soldier torturers were visible; tortured Arab males were visible; U.S. white men were visible; one or two U.S. men of color soldiers were sometimes visible; and Arab women, tortured, or even being held as prisoners, were made invisible.

Current Revelations and Machinations

At this stage in the process, after several investigations into Abu Ghraib—as well as other sites of torture interrogations from Guantánamo to Bagram and Bucca to the latest revelation of torture interrogations, in old Soviet camps and extraordinary renditions—we in the United States have been exposed to multiple facets of the horrid reputation and behavior of our government abroad, as well as evidence of our collective responsibility for this situation.

Even now, when I would expect the administration to be contrite or at least subtle about the contours of torture interrogations, they continue to fight internally over what the instructions to interrogators should say and whether they should employ language from the Geneva conventions. The Senate bipartisan passage of language on the defense bill to outlaw (in fact reaffirm the international illegality of) torture was strong-armed by Vice President Dick Cheney. The administration declared that the CIA should be exempt from constraint on torture. The language agreed upon for the Department of Defense documents and the *Field Manuals* echoes the Geneva conventions; yet the CIA is excluded from those proscriptions. The amendment to the defense appropriations bill does not exclude the CIA. On December 15, 2005, President Bush agreed to sign the Defense Authorization Act, but he also introduced a Presidential Signing Statement on December 30, 2005, specifically referring to HR 2863—the Department of Defense, Emergency Supplemental Appropriations Act that contained the provisions against torture. In this signing statement, the president reiterated a common theme of his presidency: reserving powers to the controversial notion of the "unitary executive" and effectively citing executive authority to withhold from Congress anything he deems to be in the interest of national security or the efficacy of the exercise of presidential power.

That we torture and are protected from lawsuit by "terrorists" assumes first that torture is an effective means of interrogation, and second that all detainees are terrorists. Moreover, since the signing of the Defense Authorization

Act, there has been a more focused disclosure of torture sites in Iraq and Afghanistan, increased calls to shut down Guantánamo coming from the FBI and elsewhere, and the disclosure of U.S.-sponsored extraordinary rendition to countries renowned for their regimes of torture but that are not in the public spotlight.

For now, it seems that the cases resulting from Abu Ghraib will have to stand in for the pattern of torture as interrogation around the world in our name. Many cases are being investigated and pursued elsewhere but they are beyond the scope of this chapter.

The Courts-Martial

All nine of the army reservists investigated at Abu Ghraib were charged and found guilty. Their sentences ranged from a few months to ten years. Karpinski was demoted to colonel. As I write, investigations of the military intelligence wing are underway, and the first dog handler to be charged has been sentenced to ten months in prison. The military command structure is segmented (military intelligence and military police are investigated separately), and the investigations go down the ranks, not up. It is unlikely that the leadership in the Pentagon and the White House will ever be directly scrutinized for these crimes against humanity.

Karpinski is being held responsible for this abuse, which happened under military intelligence and CIA purview. In her book, *One Woman's Army*, and in subsequent interviews, she claims to have been restricted from the "hardened site" where interrogations happened. Yet her soldiers were there. The sexual politics framing the debates about military women remind us that the arguments for and against women in the military have been grounded on the idea that women, as they are socialized, would bring a "civilizing" force to the military; in Cynthia Enloe's words, "The military is too important a social institution to be allowed to perpetuate sexism for the sake of protecting fragile masculine identities . . . and the military is too important."[19] Broadly speaking, success in this approach would either improve the military or destroy it. Without acknowledging the operationalization of sexual politics at play in the scandal, Karpinski came to be branded as incapable of having appropriate (read *civilizing*) control over the men and women in her command.

Ultimately, she is responsible, yet she is also a pawn in a larger playbook of the generals above her and the more powerful military intelligence command hierarchy. As cases have proceeded against the MPs and clerks, and now against lower-level military intelligence, Karpinski's claims at having been kept out of the interrogation spaces, and evidence of overriding orders from military intelligence and the CIA, have begun to vindicate her.

What's It All About?

In the months following Abu Ghraib, I had to consider why women soldiers would torture, and what it is about the broader culture that persistently reaffirms images of women as above or incapable of such horrors. On the one hand, feminist analyses have taught us much about the ways that gendered behaviors are socialized—that they are continually renegotiated both within and among individuals, that they imply systems of meanings and interruptions in those systems on a continual basis. Why then have we seen mostly expressions of shock that women could be capable of such violence? The prevailing sense of women's roles in the United States, especially relative to soldiering, continues to appear as contradictory: Women can be soldiers, but as women they will be different than men soldiers. We expect them to somehow elide the brutality of soldiering as it is currently practiced.

The numbers cited above establish that the women who were ultimately found to have participated in these torture scenarios are proportional to their general presence in the military. I don't foresee there being a higher "refusal" rate among women in the near future; nor do I foresee a magnetic draw of women to this kind of work. Given that the military is a well-thought-out socialization machine into which individual young men and women enter and out of which soldiers emerge, is it surprising that young trainees (men and women alike) are refashioned into hierarchy-respecting, power-wielding fighting machines? They are, after all, trained to be soldiers. Grisly observation though it may be, the behavior of the female soldiers at Abu Ghraib proves that women are quite capable of performing the noble and ignoble tasks of soldiering with aplomb.

What is it about military culture that persistently reaffirms and utilizes sexually and racially saturated mind games to deal with getting up the gumption to fight, to interrogate, to torture? Is it that the United States is a particularly sexualized culture to the extreme that we go immediately to sex as a tool for every situation? Look at the movie rating system in the United States and you immediately see a pattern in which "routine" violence is presented in PG-13 movies, while explicit sexual activity (beyond affirmations of heteronormativity such as kissing, hugging, holding hands) is confined to R-rated movies. In the United States, not unlike Muslim cultures, people have strong feelings and beliefs about sex, its boundaries, and its permissions. And yet violence is doled out in movies across the spectrum—in cartoons, video games, and popular music. Moreover, as many studies have sadly confirmed, we have a propensity for couching violence in sexualized terms. All of this to say, it is not surprising to see that interrogators have a swift and detailed repertoire of sexualized violent routines to deploy on "suspects."

Abusing Sex as Power

We are still left with women soldiers being the ones instructed to use their bodies (or facsimiles thereof) to degrade the male prisoners of war. In this double degradation, women are being instructed to use their sexualized behaviors to defile and intimidate the male detainees while their U.S. comrades watch, participate verbally, and thus defile both female soldiers and male detainees. We cannot forget the evidentiary accounts of male soldiers raping female prisoners of war and children who were taken up as prisoners.[20]

The broad perception around Abu Ghraib was that the women soldiers were pawns of the men. Why do we not have such an outcry of soldier as pawn when we—*if we*—discuss the male soldiers' rape of women prisoners at Abu Ghraib and elsewhere? Or an outcry of how it is that men are so manipulated by societal expectations of their masculinity as brutality, a profile that from all accounts is absolutely manipulated and nurtured by the Pentagon? We rarely discuss the use of sexualized violence by our male soldiers in war. What does that absence of discussion signal about our acceptance of male soldiers' sexualized violence?

Of course, we want to make sense of and express our outrage at how inhumane our soldiers can be to prisoners of war, how desperately out of step our soldiers' training is with even the basics of the Geneva conventions on the treatment of prisoners of war. We want to at least imagine ourselves, as a culture, to be more civilized than that, more civilized than the images and accounts of what has been done in our name to prisoners of war. Unfortunately, we perpetuate some of the worst abuses by our solitary and obsessive focus on the appalling notion that women would use their sexuality as a tool in carrying out their mission as U.S. soldiers. We are outraged and embarrassed that women would use their sexuality to dominate and thus humiliate male prisoners of war. So we fashion them as victims of men's power, allowing us to gently elide the issue of U.S. military brutality and in effect normalize male soldiers' brutality by leaving it unmarked.

Make no mistake: Female soldiers live in a complex web of power and powerlessness as members of the U.S. military. However, it is no less or more abhorrent that they humiliate and dominate (violating Geneva) male prisoners with their sexual performances than male soldiers raping female prisoners. I suggest we reframe the question. Let's start by asking what it is about the U.S. military that makes it rely in such an uncivilized way on the sexual power of its soldiers. This would open a new discourse about the use of rape (perpetrated by male and female soldiers against male and female prisoners and male soldiers against female soldiers), about the continued oppression of lesbian and gay soldiers, and about our sexually racialized constructions and demeaning of human beings as comrades in arms and prisoners of war. In this way we might come to terms with what a military ought to look like and how it ought to conduct itself if it really were responsible to and representative of a democracy at home.

Gender and Sexual Violence in the Military

Jumana Musa

When I first saw the photos from Abu Ghraib, I was shocked and disgusted. However, what struck me was not the fact that abuses were occurring in U.S.-run facilities—Amnesty International had been reporting such incidents for over two years. The nature of the abuses gave me pause. This was not the type of torture and ill-treatment one sees on *24*—broken fingers, torn-out fingernails. The photos depicted treatment that exploited every gender and sexual taboo in the Arab world—men dominated by women, men posed in homosexual acts, men treated as dogs. Although the Bush administration tried to pin these obviously deliberate and exploitative acts on "a few bad apples" or "some rogue soldiers on the night shift," the conscious design of the tactics indicated a deeper knowledge of the Arab psyche.

The photos from Abu Ghraib were evidence of a larger policy designed to take advantage of the Arab equivalent of "male pride," to gain intelligence, assuming any was to be had.[1] Most of the various positions depicted in the now-infamous photos were intentionally employed to attack not just the

81

men's physical integrity, but their very existence as men. It was reported the men were photographed not just for the amusement of the soldiers involved, but so the photos could be used as leverage to turn the men into informers. This leads one to conclude that photos depicting men being dominated not just by women, but by American women were intended to be the ultimate diminution of male pride.

The use of female interrogators and gender roles in interrogations was not limited to Abu Ghraib. There are reports of prostitutes being used in interrogations at Guantánamo Bay.[2] While it is unreasonable to assume the U.S. government brought in prostitutes, reports indicate that women were used to interrogate detainees in ways that men from sexually conservative societies interpreted as actions only prostitutes would engage in. Some of these allegations have been confirmed by the U.S. government in its periodic report to the UN Committee Against Torture. Among the abuses they've verified thus far were those of a female interrogator in a tight shirt straddling a detainee in a virtual lap dance and a female interrogator wiping red ink, made to look like menstrual blood, on a detainee. These images call into question the techniques designed to attack the male role in society and male pride, and the role assigned to female military interrogators. Would the chain of command ever ask male interrogators to engage in sexual taunts to elicit information from detainees? Could one imagine a commander asking a male interrogator to put on some tight shorts and sit on a detainee's lap?

Both the tactics employed against Muslim detainees and the use of female soldiers in effectuating them raise questions about the nature of the torture and inhuman treatment of detainees. First, could such a sophisticated and targeted design really have been the work of "a few bad apples"? Second, were female soldiers and interrogators asked to assume roles and take actions that their male counterparts would not be expected to engage in? And finally, does the nature of one's culture or religion have any effect on the definition of what constitutes torture or other cruel, inhuman, or degrading treatment or punishment?

I will first turn to the question of the nature of the tactics employed against detainees in Iraq and at Guantánamo. Revelations of other incidents of torture and inhuman treatment that emerged after the Abu Ghraib photos became public indicate that the photos were a result of a larger policy and practice. They were not the spontaneous acts of soldiers on the night shift. They revealed a far more refined understanding of Arab and Muslim culture than most enlisted soldiers would have.

Several news stories make reference to the much-discredited orientalist book *The Arab Mind*, and its use in the upper echelons of government to understand Arab culture in the post–September 11 era. Written in 1973 by Raphael Patai, the book purports to give insight into the Arab psyche. As Seymour Hersh writes in his *New Yorker* article "Torture at Abu Ghraib":

> *The book includes a twenty-five-page chapter on Arabs and sex, depicting sex as a taboo vested with shame and repression. "The segregation of the sexes, the veiling of the women . . . and all other minute rules that govern and restrict contact between men and women, have the effect of making sex a prime mental preoccupation in the Arab world," Patai wrote. Homosexual activity, "or any indication of homosexual leanings, as with all other expressions of sexuality, is never given any publicity. These are private affairs and remain in private."[3]*

The use of this racist book among top policymakers further undermines the notion that these tactics were hatched by a battalion of reservists deployed to Iraq, many working in detention facilities for the first time. The intent to attack the male identity and sexuality is clear. For example, the photo of Lynndie England holding a detainee on a leash depicts a situation in which not only is the man put in the position of a dog, an animal the Koran teaches is dirty, but he also is being subjugated to the nonbeliever woman. Not only does the detainee become the lowest form of being, he is dominated as well. He is stripped not only of his male pride but of his humanity, perfecting the indignity.

Some argue that the photos are a testament to the misogyny and homophobia rampant in the military. I think this oversimplifies the issue. As scholar Jasbir K. Puar puts it:

> The reaction of rage misses the point: this violence is neither an exception to nor a simple extension of the violence of an imperialist occupation. Rather, the focus on the purported homosexual acts obscures other forms of gendered violence and serves a broader racist and sexist, as well as homophobic, agenda.[4]

She goes on to discuss the various reactions to the photos, and poses the question of whether people's reactions to the images of homosexual acts were informed by their own homophobia. Were these acts "un-American" because they depicted acts of torture and other cruel, inhuman, or degrading treatment, or because gay sex is un-American? I believe these acts involved a strong degree of gendered violence, but also a form of violence to the male identity. That this was the course of action taken in response to a call for more intelligence indicates that the use of gender and sexual violence was the response to calls to intensify interrogations.

Since September 11, there has been an increasing focus on domestic and sexual violence within the military, highlighted by a few key events. The first involved four shootings in April 2002. Three men returning to the United States from deployment in Afghanistan and another man already on base all shot and killed their spouses, triggering a review of the way the military addresses domestic violence.[5] In fall 2003, there was a great deal of reporting about an increase in sexual violence in the military, particularly in combat zones.[6] The common thread between the two was a lack of accountability. Many victims reported difficulty in having reports investigated and perpetrators held accountable, as well as in accessing services. These themes—sexual and gender-based violence existing in an environment where perpetrators act with impunity—seem linked to the events at Guantánamo and Abu Ghraib.

Although government spokespeople tried to paint the Abu Ghraib photos as an isolated incident, evidence later suggested that the public release of the photos was the only unusual part of the situation. A firsthand account given to Human Rights Watch from a soldier only identified as "Officer C" of the 82nd Airborne Division indicates that the lesson of Abu Ghraib was not to stop the behavior, but to get rid of the evidence:

> [At FOB Mercury] they said that they had pictures that were similar to what happened at Abu Ghraib, and because they were so similar to what happened at Abu Ghraib, the soldiers destroyed the pictures. They burned them. The exact quote was, "They [the soldiers at Abu Ghraib] were getting in trouble for the same things we were told to do, so we destroyed the pictures."[7]

Ample evidence reveals that sexual and gender-based violence in the military is treated with impunity. And the racism apparent in the treatment of Iraqi detainees is an extension of an already-existing problem.

Many questions have been raised about the position in which female soldiers and interrogators were placed. Interrogation techniques that have come to light reveal a willingness to exploit women's sexuality to achieve a larger objective. While some may argue that using all means necessary regardless of individual cost is the nature of the military, the question remains about whether male soldiers would have been used in this manner. Those who speak of the homophobic nature of the military would argue otherwise; would an organization that does not allow openly gay men in its ranks, really allow men to be used as sexual objects to elicit information from other men? The Abu Ghraib photos depicting detainees posed in homosexual acts indicate that homosexual tactics are used against detainees, yet no male soldier or interrogator has been reported to use sexual tactics with male detainees to elicit information.

Some observers blame feminism for women's role in the Abu Ghraib abuses; the women were trying to prove they could be as tough as men. Others argue that women's willingness to participate in such sexually explicit abuses is part of the desensitization caused by the proliferation of pornography. But neither theory addresses the deliberate design of the techniques. As Gary Myers, attorney for one of the Abu Ghraib defendants, said, "Do you really think a group of kids from rural Virginia decided to do this on their own? Decided that the best way to embarrass Arabs and make them talk was to have them walk around nude?"[8]

Erik Saar, a soldier and former translator for the interrogators at Guantánamo, details in his book, *Inside the Wire,* an interrogation in which a female interrogator wore a tight top and taunted the detainees with her breasts and pretended to wipe menstrual blood on men.[9] This was not the only report of using fake menstrual blood or wearing skimpy clothing.[10]

The decision to use female guards and interrogators for male detainees from communities where men have little unregulated contact with women who aren't their wives or family members does not just exploit gender roles and cultural mores; it also takes advantage of the military women.

Whatever individual women thought they were doing at Abu Ghraib and the Bagram Collection Point, it looks now as if they were being exploited, used, and blamed for degeneracy that was mandated at the top. Procedures, rationales, policies, and incentives for selecting and training women for deployment in our military police and military intelligence units in the Islamic world shaped individual actions. Feminism and pornography do not explain women's role in the sexual humiliation and torture committed in the U.S. military prison system in Iraq, Afghanistan, and possibly elsewhere.[11]

—WW→

The discrepancy is not only apparent in the different duties men and women were asked to assume in interrogation. It is also apparent in the way senior officers were (or were not) held accountable. The most glaring example is the disparity between two generals—Brigadier General Janis Karpinski, who was in charge of Abu Ghraib, and Major General Geoffrey Miller, who oversaw intelligence gathering at Guantánamo. Karpinski bore the brunt of the blame, was reduced in rank, and was relieved of her duty. Miller escaped the entire scandal unscathed.

When commanders in Iraq determined they were not getting the kind of actionable intelligence they needed, Miller was brought in to "Gitmoize" Abu Ghraib.[12] Later investigations found that interrogation tactics "migrated" from Guantánamo to Abu Ghraib, and recommended that Miller be sanctioned.[13] Despite that recommendation, General Bantz Craddock, head of the U.S. Southern Command, declined to reprimand Miller, despite evidence of his direct involvement in designing the interrogation regime that resulted in violations at Guantánamo and Abu Ghraib. Just as women sacrificed themselves in interrogations, they were the first to be sacrificed when it came time to hold people accountable for the policies that resulted in such abuses.

The final question raised by these incidents is whether the definition of cruel, inhuman, or degrading treatment changes depending on the culture and religion of detainees. After the photos became public, it was widely argued that these tactics—the nudity, the sexual behavior, and the use of women in dominant positions—were particularly offensive to Arabs and Muslims. Does that mean that Christian U.S. soldiers would be less affected by being forced to pose in homosexual acts or by being subjugated to Arab female soldiers?

Some argue that Arab and Muslim men are particularly vulnerable to sexual humiliation and subjugation by women. As Seymour Hersh wrote:

Such dehumanization is unacceptable in any culture, but it is especially so in the Arab world. Homosexual acts are against Islamic law and it is humiliating for men to be naked in front of other men, Bernard Haykel, a professor of Middle Eastern studies at New York University, explained. "Being put on top of each other and forced to masturbate, being naked in front of each other—it's all a form of torture," said Haykel.[14]

Indeed, this seemed to be the purpose Hersh referred to Patai's book on the topic.[15] However, this runs counter to a fundamental tenet of the *Field Manuals,* which offer soldiers in the field this guidance on the subject of interrogations: "If your contemplated actions were perpetrated by the enemy against U.S. POWs, you would believe such actions violate international or U.S. law."[16]

I can imagine that any U.S. soldier witnessing a fellow soldier posed in a homosexual act, handcuffed with panties on his head, or with a snarling dog in his face, would find these acts in violation of international law. When confronted with the "urban myth . . . that Arab men had an inordinate fear of dogs," Tony Lagouranis, a former Army interrogator who served in Iraq, put it this way:

I heard that all the time, but not from Arabs. I mean, that just seems silly. It's like everyone has a fear of a growling German Shepherd when you're tied up and helpless. And it's like when people were saying, "Arabs, they really hate being sexually humiliated." I mean, who wants to be sexually humiliated? That's not a cultural thing, that's a human thing. So I attribute a lot of those comments to just pure racism.[17]

The notion that what constitutes cruel, inhuman, or degrading treatment varies from culture to culture, thus making interrogation rules unknowable, would require a complete overhaul every time an enemy from a different religion or culture is encountered. John T. Parry addresses this in his article "Just for Fun: Understanding Torture and Understanding Abu Ghraib," published in the *Journal of National Security Law and Policy:*

> *Instead of directing us to focus on the suffering (including mental suffering derived from humiliation that includes religious or sexual taunting), which reflects a relationship of a perpetrator and victim within a context of state power and as such is a core concern of human rights advocates, crude ideas of cultural relativism (that is, claims that some kinds of people suffer more or less than the norm that "we" represent) distance us from a common denominator of pain. . . . In a word, and particularly in the context of Abu Ghraib, these are Orientalist approaches to torture that obscure the actual effects of coercive practices.[18]*

The gendered and sexual nature of the tactics employed at Guantánamo Bay and Abu Ghraib are not culturally unique in their ability to cause harm, nor are they detached incidents conceived of by a few soldiers working the night shift. As Puar writes in her article "Abu Ghraib: Arguing Against Exceptionalism":

> *Although the presence of women torturers should at least initially give us pause, the simulated sex acts must be thought of in terms of gendered roles rather than through a notion of sexual orientation. Former prisoner Dhia al-Shweiri notes: "We are men. It's okay if they beat me. Beatings don't hurt us; it's just a blow. But no one would want their manhood to be shattered. They wanted us to feel as though we are women, the way women feel, and this is the worst insult, to feel like a woman."[19]*

The calculated policy of sexual and gendered violence directed at detainees in U.S. detention facilities overseas is indicative of a larger culture that exploits women as it devalues them. As Jasbir Puar concludes:

> *The systemic failure of U.S. military operations at the prison is thus due to the entire assemblage of necropolitics, and sexuality reveals itself not as the barometer of exception, a situation out of control, an unimaginable reality, but rather as a systemic, intrinsic, and pivotal module of power relations.*[20]

To try and separate the soldiers' actions at Abu Ghraib, Guantánamo, and elsewhere from the larger culture of gender devaluation and sexual aggression is to discuss the symptoms without naming the illness. Until the discussion about these tactics moves beyond the specific acts to the larger environment in which the acts were committed, the problem will continue to manifest itself in its myriad forms.

Women Soldiers and Interrogational Abuses in the War on Terror

Steven H. Miles

That women have been involved in all aspects of the abusive interrogations during the war on terror was brought to light by the Abu Ghraib photographs. The pictures of Private First Class Lynndie England—standing beside a pyramid of naked prisoners, appearing to drag a naked prisoner across the floor with a leash, pointing to the genitals of a naked man—shocked the world. Nurse Helga Margot Aldape-Moreno saw the "pyramid of naked guys who had sandbags over their heads . . . almost like cheerleaders," and she heard guards yelling at them.[1,2,3] She examined a man who had collapsed from being beaten and left him there without reporting the abuse.[4] The photograph of smiling Specialist Sabrina Harman giving a thumbs-up over the ice-packed corpse of prisoner Mon Adel al-Jamadi is especially disquieting—she looks so pleasant.[5]

As England described the abuse, "We would joke around, everyone would laugh at the things we had them do."[6] Aldape-Moreno did not evacuate the prisoner for medical care or report the beating or the pyramid of naked, crying prisoners. Master Sergeant Lisa Girman and several soldiers were accused of beating and kicking several prisoners at Camp Bucca. At least one detainee was pinned to the ground while soldiers spread his legs and kicked him in the groin.[7,8]

Declassified military documents show that other women played a role in managing or creating the brutal interrogation system:

In 2002, Lieutenant Colonel Diane Beaver, a judge advocate general (JAG) attorney working with the Guantánamo prison, proposed the policy of harsh interrogations. She wrote that the Defense Department was above all interrogational laws and treaties except the U.S. Constitution. She wrote that death threats "[and] exposure to cold weather or water [are] permissible with appropriate medical monitoring. The use of a wet towel to induce the misperception of suffocation would also be permissible if not done with the specific intent to cause prolonged mental harm and absent medical evidence that it would."[9] Secretary of Defense Rumsfeld approved Beaver's proposed outline of interrogation policy in November 2002.[10]

Captain Carolyn Wood was in charge of intelligence staff at the detention center at Bagram Air Base in Afghanistan when the Red Cross protested the brutal treatment of prisoners, including the process of suspending prisoners from chains.[11,12] Under her watch, two prisoners died within a one-week period after being suspended and beaten. Eight months later, in 2003, she assisted in setting up the interrogation center at Abu Ghraib and wrote an interrogation rules poster that was posted on the wall of the Abu Ghraib interrogation wing. In part it read, "Wounded or medically burdened prisoners must be medically cleared prior to interrogation" and "Dietary manip (monitored by med.)."[13]

*Brigadier General (One-Star) Janis Karpinski commanded the 800th
Military Police Brigade and was in charge of the fifteen detention
facilities in southern and central Iraq, including Abu Ghraib.*

*Major General (Two-Star) Barbara Fast was the senior officer in
charge of intelligence in Iraq.[14] She was intimately involved in creating
and managing the interrogation program at Abu Ghraib during the
time when the photographed abuses took place.*

Women physicians, like their male colleagues, concealed or delayed public
knowledge of deaths from torture. Flight Surgeon Anne Rossignol was called
to the interrogation room where resuscitation of a prisoner, Abed Hamed
Mowhoush, was in progress. He had been beaten for much of his sixteen-day
imprisonment and then suffocated after being stuffed headfirst into a sleeping
bag, which was wrapped with wire. Rossignol did not know about the beating
or the sleeping bag. An interrogator told her that Mowhoush had simply
collapsed; she did not ask for more details.[15] Extensive bruising on his arms,
legs, head, neck, pelvis, and the front and back of his torso, and the facial blush
indicative of suffocation, were readily apparent to on-site investigators and the
pathologist. A Pentagon press release cited her opinion that Mowhoush died
of natural causes. For months she remained publicly silent after the autopsy,
which was also concealed from the public, showed otherwise. In other cases,
Dr. Elizabeth Rouse delayed signing death certificates so that those deaths
were not known to the broader world. She misplaced and temporarily lost
the specimens of the murdered Nagen Sadoon Hatab, disrupting the trial
of his accused murderers. I am not aware of any record suggesting that she
challenged the Armed Forces Institute of Pathology's refusal to allow DNA
testing of the located remains, a move that would have allowed the trial to
proceed in an orderly fashion.

Gendered Interrogation Abuse

Gender refers to how a culture views the significance and meaning of being male and female. For example, why are the pictures of the degraded male prisoners at Abu Ghraib readily available when the pictures of degraded women prisoners are classified? Why has the Defense Department released the death certificates, autopsies, and investigations pertaining to male prisoners, but a hand-scrawled note in a memo is the only hint of the death of a woman prisoner?

Commentators and bloggers have a variety of gendered perspectives on the abuses committed by frontline women soldiers. Some focus on the sexual relationships between male and female abusers. Specialist Charles Graner had a sexual relationship with England while they abused prisoners at Abu Ghraib. He married another abusive Abu Ghraib guard, Megan Ambuhl, when he returned home. Others have smirkingly floated rumors that some of the women who abused prisoners were lesbians. There is evidence that women soldiers were goaded to perform sexualized abuse by their male colleagues. England says the staff sergeant Ivan Frederick told her to pose pointing at the penis of the masturbating prisoner in the Abu Ghraib photograph.[16] A male interrogation chief at Guantánamo instructed a woman interrogator to rub perfume on a prisoner's arm with her hand; other women interrogators under male supervision rubbed their fingers through prisoners' hair or over their bodies.[17] In one incident, MPs held a prisoner down so a female interrogator could straddle the prisoner in a manner suggestive of what the army report called a "lap dance."[18] Such directives from male supervisors to female coworkers could constitute a form of sexual harassment in that the approaches were novel, unapproved, and improvised without the subordinate women interrogators being prepared to perform such acts. Alternatively, some of the sexualized interrogational abuses seem to fall within what Muslim chaplain James Yee called Guantánamo's "secret weapon," the use of Islam as a way of life against the prisoners.[19] Interrogation plans were designed to exploit the religious commitments of prisoners against them.[20,21] Male soldiers at Iraq and Guantánamo often used sexualized violence and degradation. This typically included prisoner nudity, nudity in front of women, forcing prisoners to wear women's underwear on their heads, gay baiting, and insults and threats directed toward the female relatives of prisoners. Of her own initiative, one female interrogator reddened her fingers with ink and touched a prisoner on the neck, saying, "By the way, I am menstruating." The United States government also made a sexualized attack on the marital fidelity of Chaplain Yee as a part of its false accusation of treason.

Accountability

Sabrina Harman was convicted of conspiracy to maltreat detainees, maltreating detainees, and dereliction of duty, and was sentenced to six months. Lynndie England was convicted of conspiracy, maltreating detainees, and committing an indecent act; she was sentenced to three years. Megan Ambuhl, who passively witnessed the abuses at Abu Ghraib, plea-bargained a deal to get some charges dropped; she was convicted of dereliction of duty. Her website argues that low-ranking soldiers, like herself, are scapegoats for the policies and failures of senior commanders.[22] Lisa Girman's administrative discharge for overseeing the beating of prisoners was reversed on appeal in 2005. Major General George Fay in his report on the scandal recommended that Nurse Aldape-Moreno, who abandoned the beaten man in the room with the "dog pile" of prisoners, be disciplined for failing to report the abuse.[23] The women who provocatively touched the prisoners at Guantánamo were found not to have engaged in misconduct. The interrogator who used the menstrual blood ruse was verbally reprimanded.[24]

Major General Fay recommended consideration of disciplinary action against Carolyn Wood for failing to implement the necessary checks and balances to detect and prevent detainee abuse and other matters pertaining to abuse.[25]

Janis Karpinski was relieved of command of the 800th Military Police Brigade and demoted to colonel. Although the demotion was carefully constructed to not include culpability for the abuses at Abu Ghraib, she is the highest-ranking soldier to receive such severe punishment. Barbara Fast and other two-star generals who managed the prisons where abuses occurred have not been prosecuted.

Dozens of men were investigated for many serious beatings and murders. With a few exceptions, they escaped sanctions or received only light punishments. Even homicides have gone unpunished. Given the incomplete nature of the public records of military investigations, it is not possible to come to any firm conclusions about the relative rates of punishments handed out to men and women, although it seems that women have been more likely to be identified and sanctioned.

Women and the Profession of Arms

Erin Solaro

In the midst of a highly questionable war, the United States has done something unprecedented and extremely positive. It's time to notice.

Between September 2001 and September 2006, the United States sent more than 151,000 women to war as volunteer professional soldiers (and sailors, marines, and airmen). By December 2006, that number will be closer to 200,000. Approximately 2 percent of the dead and wounded are women, a historic percentage. Women formally serve in all roles and positions other than as direct groundtroops: special operations, infantry or armored troops, and in most field artillery positions. Yet, military necessity has ensured that women are increasingly serving alongside men, in the small infantry and special operations units from which they are barred by law. Terminology is artfully used to disguise women's roles: They are "attached," not assigned.

Women served in the American Civil War not only as civilian nurses and spies subject to summary execution, but also surreptitiously as combat troops, though they were usually expelled if their gender was discovered. American women served during World War II as auxiliaries. Yugoslav and Soviet women served as regular combat troops, with Soviet female snipers earning particular distinction. Women fought in Israel's War of Independence; and though subsequently excluded from combat positions and units, women are trickling back into those positions. And women have always served as resistance fighters, partisans, insurgents, and guerrillas, fighting in defense of their hearths and homes.

But present-day American servicewomen are serving as genuine volunteers, and not as auxiliaries. They are professionals, participating in combat, the central function of the military. As women increased from 1.6 percent of armed forces in 1973 to approximately 15 percent in 2005,[1] the right issued dire predictions of what would happen when women were allowed to take up the profession of arms. They foresaw waves of pregnancies as women tried to get out of arduous duty, orgies 24/7 because most men had no higher priority than sex, and combat failures galore because women couldn't fight and the men wouldn't know whether to protect them from the enemy or rape them themselves. Moreover, the guys wouldn't be able to handle women as peers.

In summer 2004, I went to Iraq to observe the role of American servicewomen. I was embedded with the First Brigade Combat Team of the First Infantry Division at Camp Junction City, near Ramadi, one of the flash-point cities of the Sunni Triangle, and with 2nd Battalion, 4th Marines inside Ramadi itself. In spring 2005, I went to Afghanistan, embedded chiefly with Parwan Provincial Reconstruction Team (PRT) at Bagram Air Base and Ghazni PRT at Forward Operating Base Ghazni.

When I left for Iraq, Private First Class Jessica Lynch had been eclipsed in the media by the "mean girls" of Abu Ghraib. This media feeding frenzy diverted our collective attention from a very important story: the profound change in the status of servicewomen, a change that has its own cultural implications.

Before 9/11, speculation about how women would perform in combat as volunteer professionals was just that, speculation. Positive speculation derived from the actual combat performance of women in other cultures defending their families and homes, while negative speculation ignored their experiences. We now have a database, unique in the history of the world and virtually definitive, about American women as volunteer professional soldiers in expeditionary combat with men. No, they are not engaging in trench warfare or D-day–style beach assaults, but they are increasingly involved in the kind of combat the U.S. military does *now*. Their performance has impressed even most skeptics.

Concerns about women's strength and stamina—aggravated when not caused by the military's different weight and physical fitness standards for women compared with those of men—have been assuaged by the fact that most women have performed *far* better in the field than the standards indicated were possible. Likewise, concerns about how women would handle combat stress have been greatly reduced since women started attaching to all-male combat units. They are expected to share in whatever combat comes along. And their role has expanded far beyond that. I knew of female soldiers who had spent so much time working with 2/4 Marines in Ramadi—when 2/4 had taken the highest casualties in the corps—that the Marines wanted them to live and work with them full-time as regular infantry. I knew of other women serving in Iowa National Guard infantry platoons in Afghanistan. And that was just what I personally saw.

We were told that American women participating with American men in combat would require immense, almost violent social engineering. Yet their involvement has happened easily, almost naturally. Why, then, was there such resistance to opening the military, much less combat, to women? Why did it take so long for America to even begin a rational discussion of the right and responsibility of women to participate in our common defense, long held as an important and inherent part of citizenship?

There are two answers. The easy one is that mainstream contemporary American feminism devalued military service in particular and citizenship in general. Feminists argued that the military was naturally misogynist, homophobic, and heterosexist because it was majority male by demographic and masculine by ethos, while women were naturally peaceful and shared interests transcending national boundaries. But law, including any laws guaranteeing women's equality, is only opinion unless it is backed by the enforcement power of a nation-state. The widespread refusal of feminists to sanction the participation of women in the military as citizens responsible for the common defense was a transparent attempt to have equality of rights without equality of responsibilities.

But there is a more complex answer that has to do with biology as tragedy, not destiny. Before women could become members of the profession of arms—not auxiliaries, of interest only because a war was underway, or de facto conscripts choosing between dying armed and clothed, or unarmed and naked—they had to stop dying in childbirth. For women to enter the military as professionals who are no less subject to combat than men, and as able to choose a combat specialty for themselves as men do, means stepping out of biology, out of the prism of gender through which they are currently viewed.

Like women, men face and negotiate limitations imposed upon their will and their intellect by their bodies. But for women, biology is not about height, weight, muscle mass, aerobic capacity, or even pregnancy. It is about the risk of death in childbirth. Until recently in the developed world, the risks posed by birth usually negated a woman's abilities, both physical and mental. High maternal mortality rates made it economically unwise to invest in an expensive education for a daughter who might die soon after menarche.

My book, *Women in the Line of Fire*,[2] extensively delves into statistics on maternal mortality. I found that approximately 840,429 women died while giving birth to living children between 1900 and 1960. I found that approximately 840,429 women died during childbirth itself between 1900 and 1960. This statistic does not include women who died of complications of pregnancies and childbirths, or women who were "only" injured (often seriously) during reproductive events.[3] I did not even attempt to estimate the number of women who died in the seventeenth through nineteenth centuries, when access to food, sanitation, and obstetric care were even more limited than they were in the 1900s.

In her seminal 1963 book, *The Feminine Mystique,* Betty Friedan exposed the simmering discontent of American women with the narrow scope of their lives. Her work resonated with women *and* men in a way that the early suffragists' struggle to give women political rights did not. In 1848, suffragists held the first women's rights convention at Seneca Falls; it took another seventy-two years to ratify the Nineteenth Amendment giving women the right to vote, to make the laws by which they were governed. By 2005—only forty-two years after *The Feminine Mystique* was published—women's legal and social standing, their educational and employment opportunities, and their relationship with men had changed beyond recognition, almost entirely for the better, and with shockingly little resistance—despite the defeat of the equal rights amendment.

Between 1848 and 1963, women's pregnancy survival rate increased dramatically. In 1920, the year the Nineteenth Amendment was ratified, the average American woman had a 2.44 percent risk of maternal mortality: Nearly one woman in forty-one died in childbirth, a rate comparable to that of the average South Asian woman in 2000. By 1940, the year of America's first peacetime draft, the average American woman's risk of maternal mortality had dropped to .9 percent, below the risk of the average Middle Eastern and North African woman in 2000. By 1945, during World War II, which saw both food rationing and an enormous influx of doctors into the armed services, American maternal mortality had been cut to .54 percent, and all but the most fragile of women could expect to survive their reproductive careers. By 1955, the average woman's lifetime risk of maternal mortality was .18 percent, and 1960 saw a further reduction in risk.

It was no longer economic folly to educate most women for more than domestic duties. It was also clear that housekeeping and child rearing did not and could not consume the full energies and intellects of most women. As men ceased to be the routine agents of the deaths of their wives, and as fathers ceased to give their daughters in marriage to the men who were likely to kill them, the human worth of women relative to men increased and emotional relationships between the sexes changed.

The practical, emotional, and intellectual aftermath of high maternal mortality rates was the fundamental reason why few American women were recognized as citizens except when it came to paying taxes and conferring citizenship upon their children, especially sons. Yet in the early 1960s, a revitalized feminist movement swiftly developed, concurrent with the introduction of safe hormonal contraception. Despite the defeat of the Equal Rights Amendment in 1982, the eighties saw the coming of age of the first generation to be born to parents whose lives and relationships were not formed by the unconscious knowledge that the mother might die in childbed.

Putting American maternal mortality into a military context, consider that between 1900 and 1940, approximately 762,613 American women died in childbirth. The Pentagon's figures for total American war deaths (i.e., both combat and noncombat losses) between the American Revolution and the end of World War I (twenty-four years of war spanning 143 years) totaled 637,272. (Since American participation in World War II began in 1941, those losses are not figured into this calculation.) The Pentagon's figure for Revolutionary War losses is low by about 21,000 to 22,000; and I have included Confederate battle and nonbattle deaths, but not the estimated 26,000 to 31,000 Confederate prisoner-of-war deaths. Even with those adjustments, maternal deaths from 1900 to 1940 alone far exceed the numbers of those who died in American wars until 1940.[4]

The conclusion is inescapable. For most of American history, from the first Virginia landings until deep into the twentieth century, childbirth was more dangerous than military service, even in the infantry. The few years when military service, especially in the infantry, was more dangerous than childbirth are concentrated around the Civil War and World War I. But those concentrations of battle deaths were an aberration. The norm was the steady bloodletting of at least one woman in every hundred for the birth of a child in what should have been her most intellectually and economically productive years. That only began to change in 1940.

To a significant extent, the sociocultural meaning of maternal mortality obliterated women's individuality except at the most surface level of dress, hairstyle, and taste in domestic furnishings. American—and world—history is filled with men who survived combat to lead distinguished public lives. Vulnerability to death in combat was a function of politics, not biology, especially not reproductive biology, let alone caused by the other sex. Death in combat was an aberration, whereas maternal mortality was a natural constant, natural for women to suffer and natural for men to impose. You have to look long and hard to find women who survived not merely the tragedy of human reproductive biology but also the judgments it imposed upon female worth.

Since these maternal deaths occurred year in and year out, they must have stood like the very judgment of the gods against the equal human worth of women. As the Judeo-Christian god says, "I will greatly multiply thy pain and thy travail; in pain thou shalt bring forth children; and thy desire shall be to thy husband, and he shall rule over thee."[5] No wonder many men felt so strongly that it was their duty to protect women while at the same time also believing in women's inferiority. During World War II, the Korean War, and the Vietnam War, it was commonly believed that combat service was a duty American men owed their wives, mothers, and daughters; from this perspective, that looks an awful lot like a sustained cultural attempt to redeem a blood debt with blood.

—ᴡᴡ→

When we discuss women's traditional exclusion from and growing participation in what are known as the direct ground combat arms, we are dealing with two major issues. The first is that of combat, of dying, killing, and suffering. Under no circumstances does the risk to firefighters or law enforcement officers compare to that of soldiers in the direct ground combat arms. Sixty years after its end, World War II still claims a powerful hold on the institutional memory of the U.S. military, especially the army. During that war, the army could and did burn through its basic tactical unit—the infantry battalion, an organization of approximately 900 men—in a matter of days, leaving virtually all the original soldiers dead or wounded, and their replacements dead or wounded shortly afterward.[6] This was not because the army was lavish with the lives of its soldiers; indeed, compared with other major combatants, it was practically parsimonious. It was simply the nature of that war.

The greatest need for troops is always in the infantry at the rifle company level, where living conditions are harshest. In the 1990s, the military was willing to open aerial but not ground combat specialties to women because, despite the *very* high casualty rates combat aircrews suffered during World War II, living conditions even at austere air bases are always better than those in foxholes. As one old soldier shyly told me, it's hard enough to spend the winter in a cold, wet foxhole without your period; he'd lived in a foxhole in Europe during the hard winter of 1944. As commissioned and warrant officers, female aviators were judged far more likely to know what they were getting themselves into than most junior enlisted women.

The second issue concerns geography. Since the Civil War, the United States has had the geographic luxury of being able to play away games. It is one thing for women to take up arms as members of a militia, to defend their nation against imminent invasion. It is another to use women as volunteers, such as highly trained aviators, special operations troops, or combat troops in expeditionary warfare. And many men are deeply unsettled by the idea of drafting women for combat as regular infantry in expeditionary wars.

General William Westmoreland famously held a press conference to announce, "Maybe you could find one woman in ten thousand who could lead in combat, but she would be a freak, and we're not running the military academy for freaks." He also said that "no man with gumption wants a woman to fight his battles."[7] There are plenty of men who would never describe a woman able to lead in combat as a freak, but who do agree that they don't want women to fight their battles for them. And if they wear or have worn a uniform and feel that way, they do not necessarily believe that women are not citizens fully entitled to participate in the life of the republic, or believe that women's only stake in the life of their polity or culture is their personal biological survival. There are men who parse the issue this finely: They respect female participation in other realms of the military and of combat, but they feel that most direct ground combat, especially in expeditionary warfare, especially by draftees, ought to remain a male domain. The carefully limited beliefs of such men reflect a dimly articulated, but genuine, and only recently outmoded, moral balance.

This belief was that women, who as a matter of biology had no choice but to risk and often lose their lives and health in giving life, should not also have to risk life and limb to defend their children, hearths, and homes when men were available to do so. When we think of men as natural killers, and therefore best suited to combat, it is because until 1940, their victims were likely to be not their enemies, but their wives, women they often genuinely loved. One way—perhaps the only way—a man could salvage his self-respect after risking or even costing his partner her life in childbirth was to hazard his life in war, to defend her and their children.

Only sixty-five years have passed since 1940: Men are still living who were born to women who risked their lives to bear them. They are no longer the senior leadership of the U.S. Army, but they are a significant part of its institutional memory. The military is less isolated from the larger civilian society than many civilians think; but it is an institution that has preserved anachronistic sexual attitudes because they encapsulate the need for men to regain self-respect by choosing to risk death after having been the common cause of female deaths in childbed. General Peter J. Schoomaker, the chief of staff of the United States Army, was born in 1946. His life has not been uninfluenced by that demographic fact and the cultural attitudes toward women that it engendered; his parents almost certainly knew of women who didn't make it through a pregnancy, and those deaths would have occurred in a time of steeply declining maternal mortality rates. Graduates of West Point's class of 1980, the first to include women, have just begun to be promoted to general officer rank. They will be among the first general officers whose lives have been shaped by the possibility of equality for women; not merely the possibility of equal opportunity, service in the combat arms aside, but equal human worth.

In May 2006, *Army* magazine, the journal of the Association of the U.S. Army, published a fascinating article by General Frederick J. Kroesen (retired), a combat infantryman and veteran of World War II, Korea, and Vietnam. He was born into a generation when sons were expected to redeem the blood their mothers shed giving them life by defending them in war. Kroesen writes the following:

> *The awarding of a Silver Star to a female soldier for her performance under fire should be a significant factor in the continuing argument about women's role in combat. Her performance earned a well-deserved recognition, but it also calls attention to the fact that other women routinely are earning Combat Action Badges for their solid professional performances under fire. Their actions and reactions ought to remove*

concerns about . . . their reliability under fire and their dedication to and accomplishment of their missions.

My own recommendation is that the Defense Department should issue a ruling requiring the services to identify every [military occupational specialty] that demands physical qualifications that every soldier assigned must demonstrate. . . . Applying consistent requirements will not discriminate between male and female; it will instead eliminate those whose assignments unnecessarily burden or endanger other members of their squads or sections.

Such a rule should eliminate charges of discrimination, prejudice or male chauvinism. . . . Such a rule will not satisfy the arguments and concerns of those of us who believe men are the warriors who protect our civilization, women are the nurturers who guarantee the future and the twain should not be committed to the combat task. . . . But it seems that America has, by commission or omission, ignored or accepted or endorsed the role now being played out in today's wars and any revisions of the role will have to await a future assessment of rights and wrongs.[8]

Despite his ambivalence, General Kroesen keeps faith with female soldiers.

In private correspondence, another retired four-star general, himself an infantry veteran of Korea and Vietnam, called my attention to Kroesen's article. The background of our correspondence was the Korean War and the general's service in a rifle company that sometimes suffered more than one hundred casualties, dead and wounded alike, each day. He wrote me that combat was not just about dying, but also about killing; that he thought it was the role of women to give life, not take it; so he thought that men were better at close-range killing than women; and that he did not want women to fight his battles for him. The general also wrote with a proud pleasure of the courage and expertise of servicewomen; of a woman's civic right and responsibility to enter the military; of the need for the military to revise standards to reflect their actual capabilities; and that he hoped my work would change his opinion that men were better than women at close-range killing.

I cannot do that for him, for the simple reason that we are only beginning to see women participate in the profession of arms, and there is a dearth of research on women engaging in serious, sustained military aggression. Everything we have seen from Iraq indicates that however different women's dominance posturing is from men's, they engage in military aggression about as well as men do. What emotional price they will pay depends not only on neurobiological differences between men and women, but on how easy we make it for women to come to terms with the fact that they have killed. When people break down in combat, it is not because they love violence. It is because killing tinges your soul, so that your dead enemy's soul enters into you, even when you have in no way killed dishonorably, much less engaged in murder.

What I can say to the general, and by extension to men like General Kroesen, is this: There has been a timeless quality to women's lives. Across cultures, women have generally labored inside the household, and when we worked outside, it has usually been at jobs with a domestic analogue. Even when men did the same work—cooking, sewing, and bookkeeping—their wages have been higher and their work has commanded more status. They might well be the sole support of many children and a crippled wife. And, until recently, they most likely were the parents to see their children to adulthood. Men were the heads of the house. They, not their wives, were citizens. In Anglo-Saxon culture, a wife was a *feme covert*, a woman whose status was covered by her husband; she owed him, not the state, responsibilities. Her rights were those he permitted her, while the state guaranteed her few rights against his wishes.

In 1920, American women began to become citizens in their own right. Over the next four generations, as the maternal death rate collapsed, the human status of women relative to men soared. Their growing status as citizens, falling maternal death rates, and increased human worth make the increasing participation of American women as regular soldiers in offensive combat operations abroad a normal and morally necessary part of our political evolution as citizens. This also means end the formal exclusion of women from the ground combat arms and their inclusion in any future draft. Unchosen reproductive risk is slowly being replaced by chosen political and military risk.

But this is also part of women's human evolution. Pregnancy will always be painful, demanding, and dangerous, but women are now able to control their fertility and survive their reproductive careers. Their reproductive biology no longer stands like the judgment of the gods against the human worth of women; it no longer defines and limits and diminishes women. High maternal mortality rates meant that death was present between a woman and her man, shared their bed, was present in sex, and was omnipotent in delivery. Collapsed rates of maternal mortality have changed the very context of sex, and mean that man is no longer so natural-born a killer that he even kills his mate in their bed. Just as the moral risks and physical burdens of the common defense must now be shared by women, the giving of life in sex and pregnancy becomes male as well as female.

America is not seeing the coarsening of its women because the men who have always risked their lives in the defense of the republic and their own families have become weak cowards. Rather, we have lived to see the women of our polity step fully out of the timeless tragedy of reproductive biology and into the normal passage of historical and political time, into the fullness of human worth and moral judgment.

Guarding Women: Abu Ghraib and Military Sexual Culture

Elizabeth L. Hillman

Since September 11, 2001, the United States has cast its war on terrorism as a new type of conflict, a war that can be won only by defying legal constraints and drafting new rules of engagement. The use of torture as a means of extracting information is the most controversial of those new rules. American soldiers' brutal treatment of Iraqi prisoners and other detainees took place after the Departments of Justice and Defense, hoping to land an intelligence coup, reinterpreted existing law to permit more aggressive interrogation methods. For many, the image of American soldiers grinning over hooded, naked prisoners was impossible to fathom except as a consequence of this new type of war on terrorism. The battle against an apparently stateless, irrational enemy seemed to necessitate tactics of questionable legality, tactics that were implemented by soldiers too undisciplined or sadistic to prevent a human rights disaster.

Observers have also struggled to make sense of women's participation in the abuse of prisoners of war. Among the most jarring images to come out of Abu Ghraib were those of a female soldier, Private First Class Lynndie England, photographed while smiling and pointing at the exposed genitals of captives and holding a leash attached to the neck of an Iraqi prisoner. After the exhaustive investigations, public fallout, and internal recriminations subsided, only a few low-ranking enlistees had been court-martialed.[1] A few junior and midlevel officers were reprimanded and only one high-ranking female officer, Brigadier General Janis Karpinski, was subjected to formal censure.[2]

Some critics have blamed the inclusion of women among combat troops for the soldiers' degrading behavior. They suggest that servicewomen be excluded from frontline military duty in order to improve military discipline and minimize service members' opportunities for heterosexual encounters.[3] When England returned from Iraq pregnant with the child of Specialist Charles Graner, one of the ringleaders of the Abu Ghraib abuse, she became a lightning rod for criticism of servicewomen's performance and vulnerability.[4] Others blamed the military for exploiting unwitting servicewomen to shame Iraqi prisoners into compliance with interrogators. The Abu Ghraib debacle gave new life to doubts not only about whether women ought to be performing dangerous military duties, but about whether they should be part of the armed forces at all.

Yet blaming the mistreatment of prisoners at Abu Ghraib and other American-run detention facilities on the exigencies of the war on terrorism, or on the presence of women in the United States military, ignores a key culprit: the military's sexual culture. Whatever new legal terrain the war against terrorism has carved out, the sexualized torture that took place at Abu Ghraib was not new to the armed forces. Sexual humiliation, taunting, and abuse were a part of American military culture long before 2001.[5] Beginning with reports of egregious sexual harassment at the Tailhook convention of naval aviators in 1991, extensive media coverage has documented the military's inability to control sexual exploitation in its ranks.[6]

The service members who stripped, beat, raped, and perhaps even killed Iraqi prisoners were practicing a particularly ugly form of the sexual degradation and domination that have appeared in many military sex scandals. Servicemen in positions of authority have sexually assaulted less powerful targets in many recent incidents. Drill sergeants raped army trainees at Aberdeen Proving Ground in the mid-1990s;[7] three servicemen gang-raped a twelve-year-old Japanese girl in Okinawa in 1995;[8] "mock rapes" were part of a 1990s U.S. Air Force Academy training program intended to help cadets survive a POW encampment. Sexual harassment is routine in military workplaces, and sexualized degradation is an integral part of military rituals like the navy's celebrated "crossing the line" initiation of those crossing the equator for the first time.[9]

The homosexual content of the Abu Ghraib guards' sexual abuse is also consistent with modern American military culture. Taunting accusations of homosexuality are the most common forms of derision encountered in military training. The recent parade of military sex scandals includes several involving violence against suspected homosexuals, including the 1999 murder of Barry Winchell by fellow army enlistees who thought he was gay.[10] Sexual orientation discrimination is as powerful a force in military culture as is gender discrimination. The message that homosexuality is a shameful weakness, and that gays and lesbians are appropriate targets of violence, is reinforced by the "don't ask/don't tell" policy and by the military's informal culture of lesbian-baiting and same-sex harassment.

Recent scholarship has documented many of the troubling consequences of military sexual culture, including its toleration of heterosexual rape,[11] exploitation of sex workers (especially overseas),[12] and violence against gay men. This culture places not only prisoners, but also servicewomen and men suspected of homosexuality at particular risk. The restrictions on women's military service, particularly the ban that prevents women from filling certain "combat" positions and the policy of male-only draft registration, have diminished the status and limited the promotion opportunities of women in uniform.[13] Reports of sexual assaults and harassment of military women by servicemen have prompted congressional investigations and negative media coverage of the armed forces.[14] High rates of domestic violence in military families have also captured public attention, particularly after a series of wife murders committed by soldiers recently returned from wartime duty.[15] Many service members, and many military families and civilians, have experienced sexual humiliation and physical violence at the hands of American soldiers and sailors.

In order to show how the incidents at Abu Ghraib were, in part, a manifestation of a distinctive sexual culture rather than a consequence of women's service or a result of the war on terror, this essay analyzes three courts-martial from twentieth-century military history. These cases are drawn not from the highly publicized sex scandals of the recent past, but from the 1950s and early 1960s, when the roots of the armed forces' attitudes toward gender and sexuality were formed as a newly modernized military justice system integrated legal process into military culture.[16] During this period, before the recruiting demands of the all-volunteer force opened the door for more women in uniform, women did not constitute a sizable percentage of the force. Yet sexual harassment and abuse were features of military life, present not only in military prisons, but in other military workplaces as well. Because courts-martial, then as now, reinscribe the boundaries of acceptable conduct for service members, the records of military criminal prosecutions are a rich source of insight into the norms of military culture. The military crimes described below include a case of prison sexual assault, a case of sexual play that went too far, and a case of fraternization, a military crime whose designation protects the class and rank hierarchy of the armed forces. Preserving the military's hierarchical, hostile culture and separate society also preserves the likelihood that incidents of brutal, sexualized violence will continue—in military detention facilities, in the dorm rooms of U.S. Air Force Academy cadets, in army training barracks. Courts-martial do not simply document aberrant behavior. Quite the contrary. They reveal the cultural norms and institutional structures that have created and perpetuated gender-based, sexualized abuse in military workplaces.

Military Prison Abuse

The May 2004 court-martial of Jeremy Sivits, the first soldier to face trial for his role at Abu Ghraib, was not the first time that courts-martial have dealt with the sexual exploitation, or sexual exploits, of American service members in prisons. Like civilian prisons, military prisons have long been associated with both forcible and consensual homosexual encounters. In many ways, the sexual hierarchies of military stockades echo those of civilian detention facilities. But the armed forces' official condemnation of homosexuality and emphasis on male aggressiveness created a special irony when imprisoned soldiers sought to prove their manhood through sexual aggression toward other men.[17] Forbidden or not, homosexual acts were part of the way male soldier-prisoners communicated with each other and tried to protect themselves from the violence that often took place behind bars, sometimes out of sight of the soldier-guards and sometimes with their tacit consent. During the 1950s, when the armed forces grew into a large, permanent force, service members convicted of crimes were often sent to military prisons before being returned to active duty or discharged from the service. The emphasis on sexual performance and masculinity that shaped soldiers' expectations and behavior was exaggerated in the isolated, all-male environment of stockades and brigs. These were not prisoner-of-war camps, but facilities run by military police and corrections officers, and populated by American service members sentenced to confinement at courts-martial.

Yet the sexualized abuse that was sometimes permitted among military prisoners reflected a culture similar to the one that led to Abu Ghraib. In May 1956, at one of a series of courts-martial involving what the U.S. Court of Military Appeals described as "a bizarre and sordid incident," Private William

G. Miasel was convicted for assault with intent to commit sodomy for his part in a gang rape in the Fort Polk, Louisiana, stockade.[18] Seven men, including Miasel, tied down a prisoner on a bed in what Miasel termed "a joke." Miasel testified that he was afraid of one of the prisoners in the group, a man who had been "bullying" and physically intimidating him. To avoid a fight, Miasel pretended to commit sodomy on the victim, thinking his act would make him appear a "big shot" and would protect him from sharing the fate of the prisoner being assaulted.[19]

Miasel's effort to portray the incident as a joke, part of the usual teasing that occurs among young men in all-male environments, was contradicted by his own statements. Aware of the hierarchy of the stockade and cognizant of the threat of rape, he responded to the situation as a person who took the threat of forcible sodomy seriously, not as a man being teased. Miasel knew that becoming a sexual aggressor was a practical way to adapt and survive in the culture of the stockade. That the assault targeted another man, rather than a woman, signaled strength, not weakness. Despite the military's assumption that homosexuality implied weakness, homosexual acts established informal hierarchies among men in both prisons and isolated military units.

Miasel was eighteen years old in 1956, when he decided to play along with the prison gang-rape crew and pretend to sodomize a fellow prisoner. Young and afraid, he opted to protect himself at the expense of another young man. The situation of both male and female prison guards at Abu Ghraib was not entirely different from that of Miasel. Soldiers guarding prisoners in Iraq faced a physically challenging and frightening situation in an overcrowded, dangerous prison. They used the act of abusing prisoners to bond among themselves, choosing to fit in (and perhaps to follow the orders of superiors) rather than risk being ostracized from the only peer group available in a remote, alien place.[20] They pretended that the sexual abuse was a joke even when they knew their conduct was causing pain and suffering. In short, they accepted a military realm in which sexual abuse was valued currency.

Crossing the Line: Sexual Play

Homosexual innuendo and sexualized play have been a much more routine aspect of military life than prison gang rape. But like the prison sexual assault recounted above, the sexual play of soldiers and sailors reflected the tension between the military's official stance against homosexuality and the reality of military society, which creates extensive opportunities for same-sex intimacy and bonding. Like Miasel, who characterized the forcible sodomy of his cellmate as a joke, many soldiers kidded each other about homosexual acts and about sodomy in particular. But sodomy was a uniquely reviled crime in the Cold War armed forces. Military courts described sodomy as loathsome, revolting, obscene, abominable, and detestable.[21] They described consensual homosexual acts as "repelling,"[22] "disgusting and repulsive misconduct,"[23] and behavior of a "despicable nature."[24] At trial and on appeal, military lawyers and judges described sodomy as "a morbid sexual passion"[25] and perversion, and repeatedly termed homosexuals "perverts."[26]

As horrifying as sodomy was in the language of the military courts, it was far from unspoken within military culture. Court-martial records suggest broad acceptance of sexual language that included explicit references to sodomy and sexual contact among service members of the same sex. Like service in a combat zone, remote tours of duty and extended deployments at sea created conditions of isolation and deprivation that caused men to seek relief through sexualized teasing and physical interaction.[27] In January 1963, Engineman Third Class Edgar F. Moore was serving on board a U.S. Coast Guard cutter that spent more than seven months each year away from Boston, its home port.[28] After chow one day, during a stint in the ice at McMurdo Sound, Antarctica, some sailors decided to have some fun at the expense of a young man named Ellis in the aviation repair shop, "a small compartment on the main deck." "Purely as horseplay," they grabbed Ellis and took off his dungarees, initiating about fifteen minutes of sexual teasing and roughhousing.[29] The sailors then sent for Moore. When he arrived in the repair shop, four men were holding Ellis, clad only in his thermal underwear, down on the deck. Moore proceeded to expose himself, make "some indelicate remarks and gestures" and pretend to write something on Ellis's backside. "All but the victim were laughing" when Ellis was released. Because a navy lieutenant entered the compartment just as Ellis was pulling up his trousers, this *skylarking*, as the Coast Guard board of review termed it, resulted in Moore's court-martial. Charged with indecent exposure and committing "an indecent and lewd act," Moore was initially sentenced to a bad-conduct discharge. On appeal, however, his sentence was reduced to a loss of grade. The review board considered Moore's offense "quite different" from the sort of conduct contemplated by the *Manual for Courts-Martial*'s description of "lewd acts," which could by punished by a dishonorable discharge and five years' confinement.[30] Moore's act was "a touching in jest," "a mere joke" on Ellis, not a "homosexual touching." To the board of review, "horseplay" was distinct from consensual "homosexual play" and "acts of lust or lechery"; the latter were military crimes, while horseplay was simply part of military life.[31]

The board's decision attempted to draw a line that could be easily erased in the sexual and physical culture of military life. Trying to separate sexualized play from homoerotic conduct was virtually impossible, especially among socially and sexually deprived men. Regardless of military leaders' efforts to distinguish horseplay from sex, case after case revealed how fragile such distinctions were. Sexualized teasing could evolve into intercourse, sometimes consensual, sometimes not.[32] In 1958, two privates described their joint sexual assault on a sleeping serviceman as "just the usual rough, vulgar horseplay" involving nudity and physical abuse typical of servicemen's behavior.[33]

Sometimes horseplay was simply too rough to dismiss as typical behavior. Although underreporting of male-male sexual assaults hinders any effort to gauge the full extent of sexual exploitation among servicemen, military leaders recognized that servicemen were sometimes assaulted by other soldiers and sailors, most of whom considered themselves heterosexual. Like service members' heterosexual encounters, same-sex intimacy was the trigger for a significant number of violent crimes. Servicemen were sometimes convicted at court-martial for forcible sodomy against other servicemen.[34] A steady stream of cases that reached the appellate courts involved assaults on sleeping servicemen.[35] The preponderance of cases involving men who were assaulted while asleep may have been because those victims were more likely to report the incidents than men assaulted under other circumstances. A soldier who was unconscious when a sexual act commenced was better protected against the impression that he consented to the sex act, in addition to the fact that group sleeping arrangements in military barracks provided potential witnesses to corroborate the victim's account of the crime.[36]

Like service members' heterosexual encounters, homosexual connection was often a trigger for intramilitary violence, whether in the communities around military bases or on post. The continuum of hazing, sexual intimidation, and brutal violence was well established in military culture. Long before American military police went too far in Iraq or women in uniform were a common sight, sexual teasing and domination were used to reinforce and sometimes disrupt military hierarchies, especially during the hardships of stressful military duty.

Protecting the Fraternity: Crimes of Intimacy

Because of the intensity of same-sex intimacy that military life encouraged, the Cold War armed forces followed a military tradition of enforcing social and professional distance between officers and enlistees with the threat of criminal prosecution. Officers were expected to avoid becoming so intimate with persons of inferior rank that the senior person's judgment or impartiality might be questioned. Excessive familiarity between officers and enlistees, sexual or not, was of such concern that it was given a special name—fraternization—and prosecuted as a military crime. But rare were the cases so egregious they triggered criminal prosecution in this era of administrative, rather than criminal, sanction. The *Manual for Courts-Martial* did not specify fraternization as a separate offense under the general article until 1984, and the services did not promulgate regulations to clarify its definition until the 1970s.[37] The first official army policy on fraternization was not drafted until 1974, when the army responded to a female officer's relationship with an enlisted man by issuing a regulation defining their relationship as improper.[38]

Part of the military's reluctance to specify fraternization as a crime was its inherent murkiness. Men were expected to be brothers-in-arms when they became part of the military family; the bonds of friendship between service members were often powerful, forged in times of hardship and need. Drawing a line between such intense relationships and the improper associations that could be prosecuted as criminal could be difficult. Clarity about the boundaries of fraternization eluded commanders and judge advocates despite volumes of official guidance issued to try to standardize interpretations of the law from the 1970s through the 1990s.[39] Uncertainty about when fraternization charges were warranted led to few prosecutions for the crime and to tentative opinions from military courts in fraternization cases.[40] Rarely charged at court-martial, fraternization appears infrequently in the appellate record.[41] But when it does appear, the prosecutions were prompted by same-sex, not opposite-sex, relationships.

During the 1950s, 1960s, and early 1970s, fraternization was a gay crime. Its prosecution was triggered by fear that homosexual officers would take advantage of their positions and seduce junior service members, discrediting the armed forces and corrupting the chain of command. Edgar Dauphin Free, a captain in the U.S. Marine Corps Reserve, was the appellee in the first fraternization case to reach the U.S. Court of Military Appeals.[42] The court's 1953 opinion tried to establish a legal standard by which to gauge potentially improper relationships but declined to articulate any rule to divide appropriate from inappropriate conduct. The opinion was light on facts and did not mention homosexuality explicitly. But its description of the conduct that led to the charges reads like an account of an officer on a date: Free drove his companion around while they talked, bought dinner and drinks, and afterward asked his friend to spend the night.[43] The evening apparently ended when Free climbed into bed with his "date"—an enlisted man.[44] The court tried to clarify the boundaries of social interaction in the Cold War military, carefully noting that Free's actions might have demonstrated innocent camaraderie rather than criminal familiarity under different circumstances. Though it accepted that "democratic concepts of social relations" had lessened the social divide between officers and enlistees, the court insisted that fraternization remained a cognizable military crime and that the military's "standards of honor and conduct" were at stake.[45] Refusing to specify a definition for the crime, the court listed examples of what sort of conduct might, or might not be, fraternization—and defended the ability of officers to discern acceptable from unacceptable behavior.[46]

The 2004 case of Private First Class England, pregnant at the time of her trial with a fellow soldier's child, is, of course, not quite the same as that of Captain Free and his companion. Graner, married to another woman while he was involved with England, was charged with adultery as well as other crimes related to his conduct at Abu Ghraib. But marriage and pregnancy aside, the military's concerns with the consequences of sexual involvement between soldiers today are much the same as they were in 1953. Sexual intimacy threatens to undermine the chain of command and the success of military missions, cloud individual judgment, and tarnish the armed forces' public image. Commanding officers faced these problems long before the war against terrorism began in earnest in 2001.

—w→

When scholars review the Abu Ghraib court-martial records, they will find, as we did here, failures of discipline and individual judgment as well as insight into cultural norms and institutional structures. They will see reflections of the armed forces' complex bureaucracy of military grades, occupational specialties, and interactions with civilian intelligence agencies. They will note the mistakes of defense counsel, the limited impact of investigations into detention facilities, the careers of officers derailed but not ended by their roles in authorizing, or at least permitting, the abuse.

They will also be able to assess the results of the national reckoning over the size and shape of the military that has been prompted by the war in Iraq. Because of the increasingly desperate situation, virtually everything about the military is open to reconsideration. Questions abound about who ought to serve and for how long, about how military and government agencies ought to be reconfigured to prevent future intelligence and operational failures, about the role of uniformed and civilian lawyers in the war on terrorism, about whether the United States is bound by the recognized principles of international law.

One proposed solution to the legal and political decisions that made the abuse at Abu Ghraib possible is to eliminate women from some, if not all, of the armed forces. Implementing such a plan would be difficult because of the essential roles that servicewomen play in the contemporary American military. Women now constitute about 15 percent of active-duty military personnel; in 2005, their numbers were roughly equivalent to the 200,000 troops then stationed in and around Iraq. As of 2006, there are 1.7 million female veterans, and more than 140,000 servicewomen in the reserve and national guard.[47]

But even if men could be recruited and trained to perform all the tasks servicewomen currently perform, the problem of sexual abuse in military culture, and the difficulty that military justice has faced in redressing it, will remain. The military's judge advocates enforce "don't ask/don't tell," its commanders accept the limitations on women's service, its judges embrace the military's hierarchy and culture. The military occupying Iraq today is very different than the military that Private Miasel and Engineman Moore and Captain Free served in fifty years ago. But it has not left behind its notions of women as inferior, homosexuality as infectious, or violence as amusing. Until it does, sexualized abuse, within and without military prisons, against enemies as well as comrades, will continue to compromise its effectiveness.

Bitter Fruit:
Constitutional Gender Equality
Comes to the Military

Aziz Huq

The fog of war hides contradictions and ironies. Women in the twentieth and twenty-first century, after long struggle, gained roles on battlefields from Vietnam to Iraq.[1] They overcame what Jean Bethke Elshtain has described as a "Manichean view" of men as "avatars of a nation's sanctioned violence" and women as "beautiful souls," who stay at home and weep.[2] In 1996, the U.S. Supreme Court, after decades of advocacy and litigation by women's rights activists, granted expansive equality rights to women. In the very case in which gender equality norms found full expression, women gained access to prestigious male-only military tertiary institutions in Virginia and South Carolina. The ruling seemed to signal the end of a "military culture ... driven by a group dynamic centered on male perceptions and sensibilities, male psychology and power, male anxieties and the affirmation of identity."[3]

But not so fast. Neither women's inclusion in the enlisted ranks nor their novel admission to privileged officer training institutions has shifted military culture. On the contrary, women's involvement seems to have consolidated prevailing cultural norms. As the involvement of women in torture at Abu Ghraib and other U.S. detention facilities in Iraq, Cuba, and Afghanistan suggests, women have been assimilated into an extant military culture in ways that implicate them in abusive practices central to the war-making enterprise, and that exploit their gender and sexual identity. Women thus have found themselves in morally clouded roles, as both perpetrator and victim in different measures.

In large part, the complexities and cultural nuance of this story remain untold, glimpsed only intermittently in other narratives (albeit important ones concerning the extent and origins of abusive interrogation protocols and confinement conditions). Consider, for example, the narrative of an Iraqi detainee held in Abu Ghraib, as told to reporter Mark Danner: "Two American girls that were there when they were beating me, they were hitting me with a ball made of a sponge on my dick. And when I was tied up in my room, one of the girls, with blond hair, she is white, she is playing with my dick."[4] Danner properly focuses on what one can make of this nightmare from the detainee's perspective. But it is far from clear that there is only one victim here. To condemn a perpetrator, after all, does not mean ceasing to understand and empathize with her, for there may be multiple villains and many victims even in a simple story.

In the absence of her voice, how do we understand and explore the conflicted position of the women interrogator in the Iraqi detainee's story? As rational and modern as the military wants to be, it is deeply steeped in ritual—as are many cultures in which physical danger is proximate and frequent. I examine here one rite of passage involved in *joining* the military, and contrast it with the ritualistic abuse of detainees in Iraq and Afghanistan. In so doing, I hope to disentangle some shades of moral responsibility and some moral complexities of legal change.

—W→

Called on to evoke pain, our "language at once runs dry."[5] Wholly interior, distant, and imperceptible without intermediation, the physical pain of another can be glimpsed only from the corner of an eye.[6] Nevertheless, rituals of initiation and belonging, even in a culture that repudiates tribal thinking and revels in scientific rationalism, can depend and thrive on the physical pain of others. Ritualized, almost sacramental, inflictions of physical suffering are deeply embedded in military culture. And gender has long been implicated in the military's various sacramental uses of pain.

Consider first a rite of initiation. From 1839 to 1996, the Virginia Military Institute (VMI) in Lexington, VA, enjoyed a unique reputation for cultivating the nation's male military elite. The institute supplied Robert E. Lee's Army of Northern Virginia with a third of its field grade officers. More recently, VMI counted Generals George S. Patton and George C. Marshall among its alumni.[7] Like its South Carolina cousin, the Citadel, VMI employed an "adversative method" to train its cadets. Also known as the rat line, the adversative method is "the heart of the military system," as the Rat Bible, a book given to all entering VMI cadets, explains.[8] According to one marine:

> *The entering cadet is termed a "rat" because a rat is probably the lowest animal on earth. Rats endure the "rat line," a yearlong ritual of harsh physical and psychological adversity intended to weed out the unsuited. The "rats" are verbally abused, stripped of previous beliefs and attitudes and instilled with the core values of VMI. Survivors of the first year become "brother rats."*[9]

"Were it not for the 'rat line,' VMI would be just another military school," explains the Rat Bible.

The adversative method finds anchor among VMI's historical roots. In 1862, it was customary for every newcomer at the institute to be called a rat. A recruit mounting resistance was "bucked [cut at] with a bayonet scabbard, his name being spelled on his back side with a lick for every letter and Constantinople for a middle name."[10] In addition, the 1938 comedy *Brother Rat,* starring Ronald Reagan, endowed VMI and its adversative method with the gloss of popular culture mythos.[11]

Through the adversative method, VMI purportedly tried to "produce educated and honorable men, prepared for the varied work of civil life, imbued with love of learning, confident in the functions and attitudes of leadership, possessing a high sense of public service, advocates of the American democracy and free enterprise system, and ready as citizen-soldiers to defend their country in time of national peril."[12] Women, in VMI's view, could not be citizen-soldiers. Since its founding, the institute had been reserved to men. "The very culture of VMI would be changed radically, irretrievably, by the admission of women," explained Josiah Bunting, class of 1963 and superintendent of VMI in 1996, when the United States Department of Justice sued the institution for violation of the United States Constitution's equality provision.[13] According to VMI's expert witness in that lawsuit, Dr. Elizabeth Fox-Genovese, "an advers-ative method of teaching" would be "'not only inappropriate for most women, but counterproductive' because it would be destructive of women's self-confidence."[14]

The ensuing case, *United States v. Virginia,* rose through the federal judicial hierarchy to the U.S. Supreme Court.[15] An advocate who once had led the charge for women's equality, Justice Ruth Bader Ginsburg, penned the court's opinion. Writing for six of eight members of the court participating in the case, she rejected squarely VMI's claim to uniqueness.[16] Historical bars to women in higher education and legal practice, Justice Ginsburg observed, had long been vindicated in terms of women's physical unsuitability—a fear, in the case of Dr. Edward H. Clarke of Harvard Medical School, that too much hard study would harm the feminine reproductive function. Even assuming that the overwhelming majority of women would decline an adversative education,

Justice Ginsburg explained, "the question is whether the Commonwealth can constitutionally deny to women who have the will and capacity, the training and attendant opportunities that VMI uniquely affords." No, was the simple answer. "Inherent differences" might exist between men and women, might even be "cause for celebration," but our culture's fixed and antiquated notions about the proper social roles of women and men could not be hauled up to bar access to educational benefits offered by the state. The case was a landmark in the entrenchment of gender equality as a norm protected by the Constitution's Equal Protection Clause.[17]

For VMI, admission of women was not occasion to revisit its educational modalities. The phrase "brother rats" continued to be used. Nevertheless, in August 1997, the entering class in Lexington included thirty-two women.[18] And in May 2001, more than one hundred years after Justice Joseph P. Bradley of the U.S. Supreme Court had explained that women did not benefit from the equal protection of the law due to the "natural and proper timidity and delicacy which belongs to the female sex,"[19] thirteen women graduated from VMI.[20]

Not only at VMI, but also at Abu Ghraib, the ritualized extraction of pain gave sense and structure to hierarchal relations of social and political power. The adversative method at VMI aimed to make "citizen soldiers" through ritualized shame, degradation, and pain. By contrast, the adversative method applied in 2003 during the night shift at the Abu Ghraib prison aimed to break down noncitizen detainees through ritualized shame, degradation, and pain. The spectacle of Abu Ghraib, evident in the photos released by CBS News and the *New Yorker* in 2004, could be a synecdoche for (and a way of forgetting) a far broader sweep of abusive conduct ranging from Forward

Operating Base in Fallujah to the U.S. Naval Base Guantánamo Bay to the Metropolitan Detention Center in Brooklyn, New York.[21] And somewhat like that former cinematic "rat" Ronald Reagan, the hooded man would become "a certain image of the United States and what it stands for" to ourselves and to others around the world.[22]

Magical thinking, embedded in buried ideas about the transition between social orders, about the establishment of in-groups and others, is apparent in both the rituals of Lexington and Abu Ghraib. While the first assimilates individuals to a social order, the second acts out the exclusion of individuals not only from "society," conceived narrowly in institutional or national terms, but also from humanity. Procedures endorsed from Secretary of Defense Donald Rumsfeld down the chain of command were unequivocally intended to rob detainees of the dignity and self-regard that are fundamental predicates of shared humanity.[23] Through abuse and torture, the military sought to make a detainee *homo sacer*, the condemned man rendered a nullity by his exclusion from the social order.[24]

Women and conceptions of femininity had distinctive places in both the military's ritualized process of inclusion and its hallowed and harrowing procedures for exclusion. For Bunting and defenders of the VMI way of life, female presence on consecrated ground would pollute "the intensity—the ferocity, even" of the institution.[25] For 158 years, women were excluded from VMI's "rat line" and from the ranks of citizen-soldiers.

What was the function of women and femininity, by contrast, in the ritualistic abuse and degradation of detainees in Iraq and elsewhere by U.S. forces? From the early years of global detention operations in the wake of Operation Enduring Freedom and Operation Iraqi Freedom, women soldiers were not excluded from the rituals of detainee abuse. On the contrary, they played an integral part in the humiliation inflicted as part of coercive interrogation. Among techniques authorized for the detainees at Guantánamo, for example, was "invasion of space by a female":[26]

> *[F]emale interrogators smeared red dye, which they told detainees*
> *was menstrual blood, on the bodies of Muslim detainees. . . . female*
> *interrogators sat on detainees' laps and fondled themselves or detainees,*
> *opened their blouses and pushed their breasts in the faces of detainees,*
> *opened their skirts, kissed detainees and if rejected, accused them of liking*
> *men, and forced detainees to look at pornographic pictures or videos.*[27]

As multiple military investigations have demonstrated, tactics used in the Guantánamo facility "migrated" to Iraq through personnel transfers and by Defense Secretary Rumsfeld's decision to send Major General Geoffrey Miller to harden interrogation procedures at Abu Ghraib.[28] Psychologists from the army's Survival, Evasion, Resistance and Escape (SERE) program who helped design interrogation methods also promoted "the notion of using sexual gambits to unnerve detainees."[29]

Women and femininity, in short, were instrumentalities to be taken down from the shelf and applied in the course of ritualistic abuse and torture. The female interrogators participating in "sexual gambits" were assigned functions designed and specified at higher ranks. The U.S. Supreme Court in *United States v. Virginia* ruled that women could not be excluded from military culture, but it did not change the engrained traditional postulates of that culture. Nor did expansion of a female minority in the military alter that culture.

Dissolution of female "stereotypes of fragility and dependence," in short, does not in and of itself entail "men's freedom from stereotypes of aggressor and paterfamilias,"[30] as some scholars and lawyers have argued and hoped. And while it would not be feasible to expect a 1996 legal judgment about officer training to alter culture among the enlisted ranks by 2002, the events at Abu Ghraib are powerful evidence of the military culture's ability to absorb and integrate women and femininity without fundamental challenge to the Manichean logic that underwrites that culture.

—₩→

Official narratives of detainee abuse during the Iraq War are dominated by the "trepanned veteran" and the "dirty girl" that obscure much of what is at stake in the recent assimilation of women into military culture.[31] The media's disproportionate focus on the "dirty girl" (i.e., Private First Class Lynndie England and other women soldiers involved in abuses) reflects a long-standing "media fascination with *bad girls,*" most innovatively and successfully identified by Susan Faludi.[32] In a longer historical perspective, violence by women, who had not been viewed as citizens embedded within a world of juridical relations, was a spectacle because it "was an aberration, an eruption of not wholly disciplined subjects, partial outlaws."[33] The Abu Ghraib courts-martial, moreover, had a "soap opera" subplot, a torrid triangular relationship between three of the soldiers involved in the abuses: Charles Graner, Lynndie England, and Megan Ambuhl. This subplot received disproportionate media attention.[34] Framed as melodrama, it obscured ways in which Graner brought to bear in Iraq a sadism that first found application in his work as a prison guard in Pennsylvania. It also clouded questions about the degree of violence embedded in relations between Graner and either England or Ambuhl. It further eclipses the ambient misogynistic violence of military culture, a culture in which masculine dynamics easily drift into criminality,[35] or within domestic relationships more generally. Tangled skeins of influence and affect at the personal, institutional, and societal levels are difficult to untangle. And ought it not be asked what role "sheer thoughtlessness—something by no means identical with stupidity"[36] played in the metastasis of authorized interrogation tactics into quasiauthorized frolics during the Abu Ghraib night shifts?

It's a short distance between the rat line and the night shift. The stark echoes of abuse and degradation that rebound between them beg questions about the manner in which the military has assimilated women and the manner in which it has constructed men. In his lone dissent to Justice Ginsburg's majority opinion finding against VMI, Justice Antonin Scalia quoted at length "The Code of a Gentleman," a song found in the VMI Rat Bible. This song instructs that a VMI citizen-soldier "does not slap strangers on the back nor so as much as lay a finger on a lady," and "does not take advantage of another's helplessness...."[37] In spite of our remarkable tolerance for cognitive dissonance and high threshold of historical amnesia, does Abu Ghraib—set alongside the accumulating evidence that abuse was authorized, designed, and promoted as a deliberate tool of governmental and military policy—strip bare the glamour from the citizen-soldiers of VMI? At its core, the claim of citizen-soldiers is a moral one, grounded in a sense of noblesse oblige. But after Abu Ghraib, can we frankly sustain the notion that monstrous acts can only be committed by "a foreign nation or a different race," and not by our own citizen-soldiers?[38]

Justice Ginsburg in her majority opinion spoke of the few women with "the will and capacity" to endure the adversative method.[39] But what of the women who became parts of another military narrative pivoted on physical abuse and degradation as a means of establishing command of a situation? What of the female interrogators described by Danner? Women have been assimilated into a ritualized culture of abuse and degradation within the military. While the exclusion of women from VMI sanctified the rat line, the inclusion of women as interrogators provided military leaders with a new tool to use against the enemy. A commitment to legal equality opened the door to women. It did not change the culture on the other side. The female interrogator or soldier asked to deploy her sexuality—in ways above and beyond the manipulation of England and Ambuhl—is placed in a morally cloven position. A woman who stepped up to serve her country, inspired by the ideals of citizenry and patriotism, was asked to betray what most people believe to be elementary moral commitments, asked to turn her body into an instrument to torture, and asked to deploy her sexuality in ways that degraded her and others. At the courts-martial of the Abu Ghraib abusers, military prosecutors argued that "there are two sets of victims" from the abuses: "the men who've had their dignity stripped" and "all the other men stationed in Iraq."[40]

This gendered term, of course, is telling. It signals the omission from the official narrative of the toll paid by women who have chosen to step through the door that the promise of legal equality first opened.

From their exclusion in Lexington to their inculpation at Abu Ghraib, women in the military have traveled a long way. But assimilation has extracted a heavy price. The U.S. Supreme Court in *United States v. Virginia* held out the prospect of equally noble citizenship, a promise that has been eviscerated for a first generation of assimilated women soldiers. As the number of women in the military grows, the pivotal question will be whether the armed services' deeply masculine culture proves malleable, or whether echoes of the rat line will continue to resound in the halls of Abu Ghraib and beyond.

Photography/Pornography/Torture: The Politics of Seeing Abu Ghraib

Laura Frost

A free woman in an unfree society will be a monster.

—*Angela Carter,* The Sadeian Woman: And the Ideology of Pornography

Looking at the photographs of Abu Ghraib is like peeping into someone else's nightmare. The Grand Guignol tableaux evoke the most primal fears and fantasies—incarceration, public nudity, violence, domination, submission. But like dreams, they are also enigmatic. Who are these people? What are they thinking? What does this mean? Most of us were unsure of how to interpret these upsetting images. The photographs are complicated by the way they seem constructed around a number of parodies: of tourism ("wish you were here" postcards), of conquest and trophies (a man as a five-point buck), of national pastimes like sports and cheerleading (the huddle, the pyramid), of macho men of American movies (Lynndie England's dangling cigarette and mugging, the two-thumbs-up pose), and of America's gruesome history of lynching. In the weeks and months after the release of the photographs, another interpretation kept appearing. Both sides of the political spectrum, from Rush Limbaugh to Susan Sontag, read the photographs as pornography. Limbaugh, seeking to minimize the Abu Ghraib abuses, compared the photos to "standard good old American pornography." Sontag saw the images as reflecting an increasing appetite for putting one's sex life on film and for sadomasochistic eroticism; *Guardian* editor Katharine Viner wrote, "The Abu Ghraib images have all the hallmarks of contemporary porn."[1] It's unclear what porn Viner had in mind, but images of naked, hooded Muslim men forced to masturbate by military soldiers bear little resemblance to mainstream porn. At least Limbaugh conceded that the Abu Ghraib images were not drugstore pornography but a specialized variety: "I've seen things like this on American websites. You can find these if you have the passwords to these various porn sites, you can see things like this."[2] How did such strange bedfellows as Sontag and Limbaugh come to similar conclusions about these disturbing images?

The Abu Ghraib photographs seem thematically linked to pornography insofar as they show nudity and charged relationships, some of which have a sexual nature. Whether they function as pornography, an erotic turn-on, and whether that charge was experienced by the actors in the photos or the viewers/consumers, is not so clear. For most critics, having called the images pornographic, the discussion is over. That is, to label the photographs as *pornographic* is to assert that they are, on the one hand, banal and typical or, on the other, deviant and isolated. However, Abu Ghraib's evocation of pornographic style and postures should be the beginning of the discussion rather than the end.

Cultural critic Laura Kipnis eloquently argues that "pornography is revealing. It exposes the culture to itself. Pornography . . . is the royal road to the cultural psyche (as for Freud, dreams were the route to the unconscious)."[3] Both dreams and pornography are propelled by fantasies, fears, and projections. There is always more going on beneath their surface imagery. The way in which the Abu Ghraib photographs were constructed around pornographic citations and, even more so, the way those photographs have been interpreted through the lens of pornography reflect deep-seated confusions that center, in particular, on the camouflaged women in the frame.

Even though women appear in proportionally few of the Abu Ghraib photographs, it is their presence that arguably precipitated the reading of these images (including the ones they weren't in) as sexualized—as pornography. Megan Ambuhl, Lynndie England, and Sabrina Harman, a triumvirate quickly dubbed the "torture chicks," were brought in, one version of the story goes, to break down the Iraqi men since they were susceptible to such humiliation by women. In a *Salon* article with the hackneyed title "How Could Women Do That?" Cathy Hong notes, "[F]or the first time in American history, women are accused of being perpetrators of sexual humiliation against male prisoners of war."[4]

Most critics viewed the women's roles in the photographs in relation to a particular kind of pornography: sadomasochism. In a column called "Torture Chicks Gone Wild," *New York Times* columnist Maureen Dowd comments, "It's like a bad porn movie . . . All S and no M."[5] Barbara Ehrenreich agrees that the Abu Ghraib women are shocking examples of "female sexual sadism,"[6] and Sontag contends that "most of the pictures seem part of a larger confluence of torture and pornography: a young woman leading a naked man around on a leash is classic dominatrix imagery."[7]

There are two points here: One is that the women adopted sadomasochistic postures (of the dominatrix), and the other is that the women exhibited sadomasochistic tendencies (sadism). What's especially puzzling about the photographs is the disconnection between the two. Despite the confidence with which critics describe the women at Abu Ghraib as actors in sadomasochist porn scenarios, the photographs that have been released to date tell another story.

The prototypical dominatrix ("female sadist") was born in the work of the Marquis de Sade. His mad genius at the time of the French Revolution was to imagine a world in which aristocratic libertines threw off the oppressive conventions of society and instead followed the brutal laws of Nature, at the center of which was sexual pleasure and cruelty. Women are cast in two opposing roles in Sade: They are either helpless victims who blindly follow the rules of convention (and pay a high price for it) or daring ladies who seize the reins of sex and power. As Angela Carter remarks, Sade "believed it would only be through the medium of sexual violence that women might heal themselves of their socially inflected scars." Sade's dominatrices "know how to use their sexuality as an instrument of aggression, [and] use it to extract vengeance for the humiliations they were forced to endure as the passive objects of the sexual energy of others."[8]

Private First Class Lynndie England bears little resemblance to the stock female types of pornography: She is neither a Sadean dominatrix nor an impaled victim nor a nymphomaniac. She appears impassive and almost dissociated (as in the leash photographs), or grinning with foolish—and antierotic—glee (in the pyramid photograph). Her dangling cigarette and thumbs-up pose seem blankly detached from the scenario itself. She seems to be imitating a pose, but the affect is wrong. As Linda Williams points out in *Hard Core*, her study of pornography, one of the cardinal rules of porn is that while the man's "money shot" is the proof of the scenario's reality, there is no physical equivalent for women, and hence the woman's burden is to convince the viewer that she is experiencing orgasm otherwise—usually through her expressions.[9] In sadomasochistic pornography, the dominatrix does not usually show orgasmic pleasure but rather coldly cruel delight. Neither is true of the Abu Ghraib photographs. There are no snarls, leers, or postures of intimidation, and none of the slack-jawed ecstasy, eye-narrowing cruelty, or lip-licking excitement of female pornographic types. England's gaze is usually trained on the camera, and when she does look at her victim, it is with complete blankness. Indeed, as Brigadier General Janis Karpinski remarked, "There is little Lynndie

England, looking like some two-bit prison marm with that cigarette dangling out of her throat and her thumbs up. She's looking at Graner."[10] As Karpinski's "two-bit" indicates, England's pose is unconvincing. Her gaze at the camera suggests that we should pay as much attention to what is happening between England and the photographer as between England and the men she is humiliating.

In the photo Sontag singles out, England is holding a prisoner known as Gus on a leash as he crawls out of a cell. There is something forlorn about England's stance and her puffy, passive face registers virtually no affect. The man writhing on the floor is slackly tethered by a limp leash. In all the photos of England, we wonder, who is keeping these men in line? Not England, who is tiny, unarmed, and seems uninterested in expressing dominance. Who is really holding the leash, and who is on the other end?

This questioning of England's "female sadism" began in earnest as soon as the details of her case came to light. Instead of a dominatrix, she was described as a masochistic "woman who loves too much." In early interviews, England shocked many with her cavalier attitude. She reportedly told people, "It was just for fun." She told Brian Maass of CBS, "I was told to stand here, point thumbs up, look at the camera and take the picture. . . . [The photos] were for psy-op reasons, and the reasons worked. I mean, so to us, we were doing our job, which meant we were doing what we were told, and the outcome was what they wanted."[11] This stance became modified over the course of the trial, in which England was portrayed as a voluntary mute, a follower, a slow learner, a compliant personality, and, above all, Graner's dupe. England's counsel encouraged this interpretation:

"Did they order you to do it?"

"It was more or less peer pressure."

"Did they force you to do something you didn't want to do?"

"Yes, sir."[12]

This escalation from "order" to "force" versus England's own "more or less peer pressure" encourages the reading of England as a victim. This is hardly the world of the female sadist, but rather the world of the coerced victim, porn's other type, epitomized by Linda Lovelace, who, after achieving pornographic stardom in *Deep Throat,* claimed that her husband had forced her to perform the acts on film: "There was a gun to my head the entire time." England's lawyers were eager to promote this interpretation of events, which would mitigate England's responsibility. Karpinski also echoed this interpretation of England as a love slave: "It was a relationship based on a kind of bizarre excitement with strong sexual undertones. She wanted to please him. She would do anything he asked her or told her to do."[13]

In the world of literary pornography, this woman is less like the dominatrices of Sade and more like the women found in the works of Leopold von Sacher-Masoch, from whose name the word "masochism" was derived. His classic novel, *Venus in Furs,* features a male masochist who is ostensibly ruled by a splendid, fur-clad dominatrix; in fact, it turns out that the woman is trying to please the man, to fulfill his fantasies by wielding the whip and playing a role of his creation. The dominatrix here is reluctant and only doing what she is told; her pose of power is just that, a pose. If and when the photographs of England having sex with Graner and other soldiers, reportedly in front of prisoners, emerge, her defense probably will be constructed around this interpretation of her participation.

Throughout the depiction of women at Abu Ghraib, the same polarized terms keep recurring: brutal dominatrix or helpless victim. This dichotomy played out starkly in England's initial court case. The lead prosecutor insisted that she "knew what she was doing. . . . She was laughing and joking. . . . She is enjoying, she is participating, all for her own sick humor."[14] England's lawyer responded, "She was a follower, she was an individual who was smitten with Graner. . . . She just did whatever he wanted her to do."[15] While response to the photos keeps breaking down into two categories—the dominatrix "leash girl" versus the love slave—what remains constant is England's centrality to the Abu Ghraib scandal. JoAnn Wypijewski argues convincingly in her article "Judgment Days" in *Harper's* magazine, that England's role was emphasized in the press and in court; even in the trials of other defendants, "it was the photo of the tomboy England that prosecutors repeatedly displayed."[16] This suggests scapegoating and raises the question of why England received a disproportionate amount of attention compared to her Abu Ghraib cohorts.

The men in the Abu Ghraib photographs, particularly Graner and Ivan Frederick, whose demeanors are quite different from those of the women and who are shown physically abusing the prisoners, have received far less press than England. The men's sneers, leers, and macho postures are more in keeping with pornography; they play their roles much more convincingly than the women. Graner is frequently described as a sadist, but the word is used less in the eroticized sense of pornography than in the sense of a sociopath. Of the abusive U.S. soldiers in the photographs, only the women have been subject to eroticized, sexualized readings. (The male soldiers' act of forcing the prisoners to simulate homosexual acts was mainly discussed as a strategy of cultural humiliation and rarely discussed in terms of the homophobia and perhaps disavowed homoeroticism it implies.)

Male aggression is taken for granted; it is "natural." Female aggression is aberrant. A woman in the Abu Ghraib scenario—military and aggressive—is doubly perverse. To think of a woman as a torturer seems impossible—hence, the recourse to extreme pornographic types. Moreover, a reading of a woman as sexualized is more accessible than a reading of her as powerful, whether abusively or responsibly. That is, we can imagine a woman with sexual power (in which case she must be perverse, a dominatrix), but not with military power. As Della Sentilles remarks, "Our idea that female sexuality and power is a form of torture confirms our own fears of female empowerment."[17] This was as true inside Abu Ghraib as out. England seemed to have found it easier to think of herself as a sexual (and in this case, subservient) being than as a figure of authority. The unreleased sex photos will further undermine the notion of these women as figures of authority.

Memoirs from Iraq and other contemporary American military prisons give insight into how the military's assessment of women in power is even more distorted than the civilian view. Kayla Williams's *Love My Rifle More Than You* recounts her time in Iraq as a U.S. Army sergeant in an intelligence company of the 101st Airborne Division. The prologue to the memoir focuses not on what one might expect—e.g., the mission in Iraq or the desire to serve one's country—but on two terms: bitch and slut. "If you're a woman and a soldier, those are the choices you get," she writes, grounding this story of military experience in how she was perceived as a sexual being.[18] The first chapter begins, "Right into it: Sex is key to any woman soldier's experiences in the American military. No one likes to acknowledge it, but there's a strange sexual allure to being a woman and a soldier."[19] A woman, then, is automatically seen (and sees herself) in terms of her sexuality—not in terms of her political mission, her competency at her job, or her position of military authority. In *One Woman's Army*, Janis Karpinski also writes about how femininity and sexuality are a constant concern for women in the military. Erik Saar's *Inside the Wire*, his memoir of serving as a translator at Guantánamo, got considerable attention for its brief account of one female interrogator's tactics of sexually humiliating a prisoner: She wore provocative clothes, rubbed herself against the prisoner, and pretended to wipe menstrual blood on him. After this interrogation, Saar recalls, the interrogator cried. The slide from Sade to Linda Lovelace in a matter of moments suggests the inadequacy of both stereotypes.

Kayla Williams offers one of the most insightful analyses of what is at stake in such interrogations. She recounts an episode in which she screams at and taunts a prisoner:

> *I don't like to admit it, but I enjoyed having power over this guy.*
>
> *I was uncomfortable with these feelings of pleasure at his discomfort, but I still had them. It did occur to me that I was seeing a part of myself I would never have seen otherwise.*
>
> *Not a good part.*
>
> *For months afterward, I think about this episode, minor though it really was. I wonder if my own creepy sense of pleasure at my power over this man had anything to do with being a woman in this situation—the rarity of that enormous power over the fate of another human being.*[20]

Going beyond the stereotypes and dichotomies of bitch and slut that she sets up at the beginning of her memoir, Williams considers the complex arrangement of power in the scenario of female torturers. For her, these acts of abuse are influenced by a woman's preexisting ideas about her ability to be powerful in the world. The dichotomy of bitch and slut, like the pornographic dichotomy of dominatrix and Linda Lovelace, prevents a realistic assessment of women in power, which would require acknowledging how stereotypes fail to capture complex impulses and investments.

The pornographic interpretation of the Abu Ghraib photos was persistent because it reproduced the simpler, more graspable dichotomy of pornography. The images parody a genre that is already itself largely parodic: Pornography's cartoonish version of sexuality and gender encourages the polarization of roles (dominant men and passive women or dominant women and passive men). The military is constructed around the same kind of polarization: a valorization of masculinity and dominance and a contempt for weakness connected with femininity. Williams remarks that the army is "one big frat party." That the insertion of real women into this scenario at Abu Ghraib did not produce a more nuanced reading of women and power but rather reasserted the old polarities demonstrates the tenacity of those stereotypes.

The primacy of the Abu Ghraib photographs themselves, and their ability to subsume the spotlight, is dangerous. The photographs have the effect of anchoring us to the grotesque moments they reference. Their very awfulness suggests that they are isolated and singular, while we know that is not the case. They are by no means as simple as the stark poses we see before us. To view women in positions of authority as pornographic types suggests our failure to accept women as agents of power, for better or for worse. As much as we might want to dismiss Abu Ghraib as a case of a few bad apples or sexual deviants, those photographs make us confront our own limitations. Freud wrote that the dreamer is in every part of the dream; whether we support the policies that led to Abu Ghraib, what we see in those photographs can tell us as much about ourselves and our values at home as it does about what happened in that awful prison a world away.

Gender Trouble at Abu Ghraib?

Timothy Kaufman-Osborn

"It's not a pretty picture," conceded Defense Secretary Donald Rumsfeld in assessing the photographs taken by U.S. military personnel at Baghdad's Abu Ghraib prison complex during the final three months of 2003.[1] Shortly thereafter, en route to Iraq, Rumsfeld contended that "the real problem is not the photographs—the real problems are the actions taken to harm the detainees."[2] This claim is problematic insofar as it fails to appreciate the transformation of these images into so many free-floating weapons deployed to secure partisan advantage on various cultural and political battlegrounds within the United States. This was nowhere more evident than in their mobilization to rehash the struggle over the contemporary import of feminism, especially in light of the cquality/difference debate that has vexed feminists and their opponents for decades.

The initial purpose of this essay, accordingly, is to explain how the mass media flap regarding the Abu Ghraib photographs indicates that gender, understood as a set of mobile disciplinary practices, can sometimes become unsettled, thereby provoking efforts to restabilize heteronormative understandings of what it is to be masculine or feminine. Giving the defense secretary his due, however, I employ my discussion of the domestic reception of these photographs as a preface to asking how we might make better sense of the gendered import of the abuses committed at Abu Ghraib. To answer this question, in the second half of this essay, I argue that much of what appeared so shocking when these photographs were first released can be read as extensions of, but also threats to, the logic of masculinized militarism. The most convenient scapegoat for such "gender trouble," to appropriate the title of Judith Butler's best-known work, is Lynndie England, a military file clerk who was captured by the camera's eye while restraining an Iraqi prisoner at the far end of a dog leash.

Mistaking Lynndie England

Like all photographic images, those taken at Abu Ghraib do not speak for themselves. Henry Giroux explains:

> *Photographs such as those that revealed the horrors that took place at Abu Ghraib prison have no guaranteed meaning, but rather exist within a complex of shifting mediations that are material, historical, social, ideological, and psychological in nature. This is not to suggest that photographs do not capture some element of reality as much as to insist that what they capture can only be understood as part of a broader engagement over cultural politics and its intersection with various dynamics of power. . . . Representations privilege those who have some control over self-representation, and they are largely framed within dominant modes of intelligibility.[3]*

Giroux's point about the framing of photographic meaning in terms of "dominant modes of intelligibility" is well illustrated by the contest to determine what to make of the Abu Ghraib images that include Lynndie England. In addition to the photograph mentioned above, another shows England standing next to a naked Hayder Sabbar Abd, a thirty-four-year-old Shiite taxi driver from Nasiriyah, as a cigarette dangles from her lips, the thumb of her right hand gestures upward in triumph, and her left hand, with forefinger cocked, takes aim at Abd's genitalia, as he is forced to simulate masturbation. Still another depicts England, arm in arm with Specialist Charles Graner, as both grin and offer a thumbs-up sign while perched behind a cluster of seven naked Iraqis piled awkwardly atop one another in a human pyramid.

The general tenor of the mainstream press response to these photographs, which altogether displaced documented reports of the abuse of women prisoners at Abu Ghraib,[4] is indicated by the subtitle of an article written by *Newsweek*'s Evan Thomas in May 2004: "How did a wispy tomboy behave like a monster at Abu Ghraib?" It may well be, as Cynthia Enloe has suggested, that the media's horrified representation of England as a sub- or inhuman creature indicates America's visceral response to her violation of conventional norms regarding the conduct becoming to women;[5] and, as M. S. Embser-Herbert has suggested, the fixation on these particular photographs may well indicate that Americans today are better prepared to see women come home from Iraq in body bags than to see them return as quasisexualized aggressors.[6] There is some truth to both of these readings; and it is equally true that the media's preoccupation with the photographs portraying women involved in "abnormal" conduct facilitated the Bush administration's interest in representing what transpired at Abu Ghraib as the "disgraceful conduct by a few American troops who dishonored our country and disregarded our values,"[7] and so as an anomalous departure from established military doctrine. That noted, neither Enloe nor Embser-Herbert fully captures the ways in which these photographs were mobilized, especially during the months immediately following their release, in the service of larger domestic political and cultural agendas. This proved most strikingly so when the proponents of various right-wing agendas seized on England to advance a reactionary backlash aimed at reversing whatever advances women have made in the military, under the banner of gender equality, since termination of the all-male draft in 1972.

Three examples, all published in May 2004, less than two weeks after the Abu Ghraib photographs initially aired on CBS's *60 Minutes II*, suffice to illustrate this appropriation. First, the president of the Center for Military Readiness, Elaine Donnelly, asserted that the photograph of England with leash in hand "is exactly what feminists have dreamed of for years." She represented England's conduct as an articulation of the dispositions displayed by those feminists "who like to buy man-hating greeting cards and have this kind of attitude that all men abused all women. It's a subculture of the feminist movement, but the driving force in it in many cases, certainly in academia."[8] On this basis, which figures feminists as so many would-be dominatrices afflicted by a burning desire to transform men into obsequious lapdogs, Donnelly argued that the U.S. military should abandon its unofficial gender quotas, aimed at enlisting more women, and return to basic training segregated by sex. Arguing on behalf of the same counterreforms, Peggy Noonan, columnist and contributing editor of the *Wall Street Journal*, claimed that before basic training became coeducational, women "did not think they had to prove they were men, or men at their worst. I've never seen evidence to suggest the old-time WACs and WAVES had to delve down into some coarse and vulgar part of their nature to fit in, to show they were one of the guys, as tough as the guys, as ugly at their ugliest."[9] On this reading, England is a young woman whose turn to the dark side can be explained by her desire to be embraced by her brutish counterparts, with the implication that she never would have acted as she did had she been excluded from their crass company. Finally, in a screwy twist on much the same narrative, the president of the Center for Equal Opportunity, Linda Chavez, suggested that England's participation in the abuse at Abu Ghraib can be explained by the mounting "sexual tension" that has accompanied "the new sex-integrated military." Because that stress produces hormone-crazed soldiers, which in turn undermines "discipline and unit cohesion," we should not be unduly surprised when those in uniform occasionally release their pent-up passions by sexually abusing their captives.

What Donnelly, Noonan, and Chavez share is the conviction, expressly articulated by George Neumayr, columnist for the *American Spectator*, that the conduct of Lynndie England "is a cultural outgrowth of a feminist culture which encourages female barbarians."[10] Their concern that women are "losing their femininity" requires that an unambiguous masculine identity be refortified and sharply distinguished from the equally unambiguous gender identity of women (e.g., by reconfining GI Janes to suitably ladylike roles on the sidelines of the military in accordance with their customary roles as civilizers of beastly men). Such claims presuppose an uncritical conception of gender, one which includes a dyadic conception of sexual identity, the naturalness (as well as the apparent irresistibility) of heterosexual desire, and stereotypical, if not essentialized, conceptions of masculine and feminine conduct. Lest there be any doubt on this latter score, also in May 2004, the president of the Eagle Forum, Phyllis Schlafly, asserted that "the picture of the woman soldier with a noose around the Iraqi man's neck" demonstrates "that some women have become mighty mean, but feminists can't erase eternal differences."[11]

Unfortunately, many readings of the Abu Ghraib affair advanced by mainstream liberal feminists are similar to the interpretations proffered by the right wing. Embracing the construction of these photographs as a referendum on feminism and its commitment to the equality of women, these readings have demonstrated the stubborn persistence of conceptions of gender, which, though not wedded to the reactionary political agendas advanced by Schlafly and her ilk, are nonetheless quite problematic. This sort of appropriation is best illustrated by Barbara Ehrenreich, whose 2004 *Los Angeles Times* article, "Feminism's Assumption Upended," is reprinted as the foreword for this book.

"As a feminist," Ehrenreich begins, the Abu Ghraib photographs "broke my heart. I had no illusions about the U.S. mission in Iraq—whatever exactly it is—but it turns out that I did have some illusions about women." These illusions were based on the belief that women are "morally superior to men," whether because of "biology," "conditioning," or "simply the experience of being a woman in a sexist culture." On this basis, Ehrenreich "secretly" entertained the hope "that the presence of women would over time change the military, making it more respectful of other people and cultures, more capable of genuine peacekeeping." These illusions were shattered when Ehrenreich first saw the image of England, her Iraqi prisoner in tow: "A certain kind of feminism, or perhaps I should say a certain kind of feminist naiveté, died in Abu Ghraib. It was a feminism that saw men as the perpetual perpetrators, women as the perpetual victims, and male sexual violence against women as the root of all injustice." But now, having witnessed "female sexual sadism in action," Ehrenreich rejects as "lazy and self-indulgent" any form of feminism that is "based on an assumption of female moral superiority." "A uterus," in sum, "is not a substitute for a conscience."[12]

In retrospect, Ehrenreich confesses, she should not have been so shocked to learn that "women can do the unthinkable," for, unlike her right-wing opponents, she "never believed that women were innately gentler and less aggressive than men." But the very fact that she was so shocked by England's conduct, as well as the fact that this response was situated at the far edge of comprehensibility ("the unthinkable"), indicates the deep-seated tenacity with which, too often, we cling to a vision of the world that neatly distinguishes between powerful men and powerless women, between those who are guilty of acts of sexual violence and those who are their victims. This vision of the world presupposes the self-evident intelligibility of the category of "women," as well as their fundamental differences from the equally self-evident category of "men"; and it presupposes problematic stereotypes about women, including, in Ehrenreich's case, the belief that because they "do most of the caring work in our culture," they are less inclined "toward cruelty and violence."[13] As such, and despite their very different political agendas, there are unsettling points of convergence between the conception of gender that Ehrenreich embraced before Abu Ghraib and the conception Schlafly and her cohorts continue to promote after Abu Ghraib.

Ehrenreich is to be commended for the intellectual honestly that prompted her to question this conception of gender (although she does not advance any adequate alternative). It remains true, however, that she accepts her opponents' construction of the England affair as a referendum on feminism and its quest for gender equality. That, though, is a misguided enterprise. It is problematic when the revulsion provoked by these photographs is predicated on retrograde gender representations, and it is pernicious when it animates an antifeminist backlash that seeks to resituate women in a world where they are compelled to live out those odious stereotypes. Moreover, this construction encourages sterile repetition of unproductive and arguably unanswerable questions (e.g., are women really different from men?); and it plays into the hands of feminism's detractors by inviting them to assert that the ultimate import of the quest for gender equality is revealed in the conduct of England. This is not to suggest that we discard the category of gender in thinking about what happened at Abu Ghraib, but rather that we turn away from the conception that is presupposed whenever someone asks, "How could women do that?"[14] Instead, I would urge that we think of gender as something constructed through engagement in a complex set of performative practices, including the abusive techniques deployed at Abu Ghraib, and that we ask how those practices engender persons in ways that are not readily reducible to what Ehrenreich or her adversaries mean when they uncritically speak of "women" and "men."

Technologies of Emasculation at Abu Ghraib

The official investigative reports issued in the wake of Abu Ghraib do not themselves offer a more nuanced account of its gendered import. Read in light of a more adequate understanding of gender, however, they provide clues toward such an account. The principal documents include the Taguba and Fay-Jones reports, both of which were commissioned by Lieutenant General Ricardo Sanchez, commander of Coalition Ground Forces in Iraq; the Mikolashek report, conducted by the army's inspector general; and the Schlesinger report, issued by an independent panel chartered by the secretary of defense. Though conceding certain failures of leadership in higher (but not too high) ranks, all reports explain what happened at Abu Ghraib in terms of the pathological and/or criminal conduct of a handful of rogue soldiers.[15] The Schlesinger report, for example, concludes, "The events of October through December 2003 on the night shift of Tier 1 at Abu Ghraib prison were acts of brutality and purposeless sadism."[16] In much the same vein, according to the "psychological assessment" appended to the Taguba report, the events at Abu Ghraib were the work of "immoral men and women" who engaged in "sadistic and psychopathic behavior," including "abuse with sexual themes."[17] Finally, the Fay-Jones report determines that "the primary cause of the most egregious violent and sexual abuses was the individual criminal propensities of the particular perpetrators."[18]

These readings will not do. They decontextualize the deeds, rendering them so many transgressions enacted by a few unruly anomalies. Once Abu Ghraib is defined in these disingenuous terms, the soldiers, including Lynndie England, can all too easily be assigned the role of patsies whose service to the military now includes distracting attention from the institutional forces that breed and sanction such exploitation. These readings also will not do because they occlude the ways in which gender is in fact constitutive of what happened at Abu Ghraib. The representation of these events as "sexual abuse" does not adequately specify the particular form of degradation involved here. That degradation is trivialized when James Schlesinger, former secretary of defense and lead author of the report bearing his name, refers to Abu Ghraib as *Animal House* on the night shift."[19] To compare what happened on Tier 1 to so much reprehensible behavior on the part of intoxicated undergraduates at a fraternity bash is to confound the distinction between sexual abuse, on the one hand, and acts of imperialist and racist violence that mimic sexual exploitation, on the other. It is, moreover, to fail to ask *why* so much of the abuse meted out at Abu Ghraib, as the reports make abundantly clear, trafficked in gendered stereotypes, as well as what that might teach us about how gender operates as a complex vector of power within the context of masculinized militarism.

The acts of principal concern to me in this section are a subset of the larger group that exhibited sexualized dimensions. Although the distinction is admittedly problematic, I will primarily confine my attention to those that traded on misogynistic understandings, as opposed to those that were patently homophobic as well as arguably homoerotic (e.g., forcing prisoners to masturbate while being photographed; compelling prisoners to engage in simulated fellatio; and sodomizing a prisoner with a phosphorous light stick).[20] My chief concern is with incidents such as the following: compelling otherwise-naked men to wear women's underwear, often red and often on their heads; having a servicewoman apply red ink to the face of a prisoner after she placed her hand in her unbuttoned pants and informed him that she was menstruating; forcing men to remove their clothing and then stand before women service personnel; and, lest we forget Lynndie England, placing a leash around a naked prisoner's neck while posing with him for a snapshot.[21]

How are we to make sense of these incidents? Loosely following the lead of Judith Butler,[22] I propose that we think not about men and women in the unreflective sense in which all the authors discussed in the previous section employ these terms, but, rather, about complex disciplinary practices that engender bodies by regulating, constraining, and constituting their conduct in ways that prove intelligible in light of the never entirely stable or coherent categories of masculine and feminine. "Men" and "women," in other words, are constantly being gendered as they participate in practices mandated by cultural norms of masculinity and femininity, which are themselves contingently related to anatomical equipment: "When the constructed status of gender is theorized as radically independent of sex," Butler argues, "gender itself becomes a free-floating artifice, with the consequence that *man* and *masculine* might just as easily signify a female body as a male one, and *woman* and *feminine* a male body as easily as a female one."[23] If this is so, then what we should be exploring at Abu Ghraib is the differential production of masculinity and femininity, as well as the ways in which specific performances sometimes unsettle foundational illusions about the dependence of gender on sex. This redirection of inquiry suggests that much, but certainly not all, of what happened at Abu Ghraib can be understood in terms of what I will call the "logic of emasculation," where the aim of disciplinary techniques is to strip prisoners of their masculine gender identity and turn them into caricatures of terrified and often infantilized femininity. What this implies for our reading of Lynndie England is the question taken up in this essay's conclusion.

In applying this performative account of gender to Abu Ghraib, it is useful to begin by doing precisely what the Fay-Jones report (which insists that "no policy, directive or doctrine directly or indirectly caused violent or sexual abuse"[24]) discourages us from doing: to relate the exploitation at Abu Ghraib to the U.S. military's approved techniques regarding the treatment of those detained during combat. For present purposes, the directive of principal concern is *Field Manual 34–52*,[25] which officially governed the treatment of those imprisoned at Abu Ghraib.[26] It is my contention that many of the practices commended in this manual, whether employed in the context of formal interrogations or in conjunction with efforts to "soften up" prisoners as a preface to such interrogations,[27] trade on specific conceptions of masculinity and femininity. One of the principal virtues of the Abu Ghraib photographs is the way they render visible this implicit content.

"Unless this publication states otherwise," *Field Manual 34–52* affirms, "masculine nouns or pronouns do not refer exclusively to men."[28] Because *34–52* is formally neutral, revelation of its gendered content must be a matter of plausible inference. An intimation of that content is provided by the Central

Intelligence Agency's 1963 manual titled *Counterintelligence Interrogation*, which, according to a correspondent for the *Atlantic Monthly*, "remains the most comprehensive and detailed explanation in print of coercive methods of questioning."[29] Unearthed in 1997 through the Freedom of Information Act, the document, which came to be known as the *KUBARK Manual*, is refreshingly candid in specifying the summum bonum of disciplinary techniques applied to the incarcerated:

> *It is a fundamental hypothesis of this handbook that these techniques ... are in essence methods of inducing regression of the personality to whatever earlier and weaker level is required for the dissolution of resistance and the inculcation of dependence. ... [T]he circumstances of detention are arranged to enhance within the subject his feelings of being cut off from the known and the reassuring, and of being plunged into the strange. ... Control of the source's environment permits the interrogator to determine his diet, sleep pattern and other fundamentals. Manipulating these into irregularities, so that the subject becomes disorientated, is very likely to create feelings of fear and helplessness.*[30]

A 1983 revision of *KUBARK*, titled *Human Resource Exploitation Training Manual*, states,

> *Throughout his detention, subject must be convinced that his "questioner" controls his ultimate destiny, and that his absolute cooperation is essential to survival. This can be achieved by radically disrupting the familiar emotional and psychological associations of the subject. Once this disruption is achieved, the subject's resistance is seriously impaired. He experiences a kind of psychological shock, which may only last briefly, but during which he is far more open and far likelier to*

*comply. . . . Frequently the subject will experience a feeling of guilt. If
the "questioner" can intensify these guilt feelings, it will increase the
subject's anxiety and his urge to cooperate as a means of escape.*

For those familiar with feminist literature on battered women, it
is difficult to read these passages without recalling accounts of abusive
relationships in which men seek to secure the wholesale subordination of
women by isolating and terrifying them either through violence or threats
of violence. Such compliance is best secured when a woman, consumed
by fear, determines that her situation is helpless, and, still more perfectly,
when she concludes that she is ultimately culpable and thus guilty for the
abuse to which she is subject. In this light, consider the claim, advanced
in *KUBARK,* that well-designed interrogation techniques strip those
undergoing questioning of all vestiges of autonomy, thereby transforming
them into creatures who are "helplessly dependent on their captors for the
satisfaction of their many basic needs, and experience the emotional and
motivational reactions of intense fear and anxiety."[31] If such techniques
harbor tacit gendered baggage, as I believe they do, then arguably the effect
of their application is to emasculate subjects by dismantling the qualities
conventionally associated with masculinity and replacing them with a
hyperbolic incarnation of the qualities stereotypically associated with
femininity: obedience, passivity, depression, anxiety, and shame.

Although certain of the harshest techniques prescribed by *KUBARK* in
1963 were deleted from its 1983 revision, and are no longer present in either
the original 1987 version of *Field Manual 34–52* or its 1992 revision, there is
little reason to believe that the basic logic of these disciplinary practices has
changed in any significant way;[32] and there is every reason to believe that the
latent gendered content of that logic announced itself at Abu Ghraib. Consider,
for example, the tactics identified as "futility," which aims to demonstrate that
resistance of any sort is hopeless, and "pride and ego down," which attacks

"the source's sense of personal worth. Any source who shows any real or imagined inferiority or weakness about himself, loyalty to his organization, or is captured under embarrassing circumstances, can be easily broken with this approach technique."[33] How the general terms of these tactics were to be translated into practice at Abu Ghraib, as the Fay-Jones report acknowledges, left "certain issues for interpretation."[34] How those issues were resolved says much about the conceptions of masculinity and femininity, which, by and large, remain predominant within the U.S. military; and, although I will not deal with this issue with the care it deserves, it also says much about the possibilities of emasculating those who are already effectively infantilized, if not feminized, in virtue of their identity as colonized and racialized "others."

Consider, for example, the stripping of male prisoners, who were then forced to stand before American servicewomen. In addition to offending cultural sensitivities, especially those dictated by Islamic law regarding proper attire, this technique emasculates prisoners by exposing them in a way that is familiar from representations of women, including but by no means limited to those conventionally labeled "pornographic." What one sees here, in inverted form, is a sort of enforced vulnerability joined to a fantasy of absolute sexualized power. Much the same logic is apparent in the practice of smearing prisoners with red ink said to be menstrual blood; here, emasculation is a function of staining the male body with that which is taken to mark women's bodies as distinctively female and, as such, a source of degradation. Finally, with the requirement that some of those imprisoned at Abu Ghraib wear women's underwear on their heads for hours, days, and even weeks, the logic of emasculation achieves its consummation in drag. In each of these cases, misogyny is deployed as a tactic to humiliate prisoners, where the term "humiliation" can be translated as "treat like a woman." That this aim often succeeded is confirmed by Dhia al-Shweiri, who, several months after his release from Abu Ghraib, was quoted as follows: "They were trying to humiliate us, break our pride. We are men. It's okay if they beat me. Beatings don't hurt us, it's just a blow. But no one would want their manhood to be shattered. They wanted us to feel as though we were women, the way women feel, and this is the worst insult, to feel like a woman."[35]

This process, whereby the gendered import of formally gender-neutral disciplinary tactics becomes explicit, achieved its official confirmation when, in mid-2005, the U.S. Army released the results of an investigation, conducted by Lieutenant General Randall Schmidt of the U.S. Air Force, into the treatment of those imprisoned at Guantánamo Bay.[36] Making clear that many of the abuses now associated with Abu Ghraib were put into play in Cuba and later "migrated" to Iraq, Schmidt codified these techniques under the rubric of "gender coercion," which, on his account, includes authorizing servicewomen to "perform acts designed to take advantage of their gender in relation to Muslim males." Specifically, in late 2002, two "high-value" but resistant prisoners were subjected to the following actions in accordance with *34–52*'s "pride and ego-down" as well as "futility" provisions: "The subject of the first Special Interrogation Plan [Mohamed Qahtani, the alleged twentieth hijacker in the September 11 attack] was forced to wear a woman's bra and had a thong placed on his head during the course of the interrogation"; had his face marked with alleged menstrual blood; had a leash clasped around his neck, after which he was led around the interrogation room "and forced to perform a series of dog tricks"; and, during a strip search, was "forced to stand naked for five minutes with females present."

Concluding his investigation, Schmidt reported that "the creative, aggressive, and persistent" questioning of this prisoner, especially in light of his solitary confinement for 160 days, as well as his subjection to eighteen- to twenty-hour interrogations over a period of forty-eight of fifty-four days, constituted "degrading and abusive treatment." However, because "every technique employed" by the interrogation team at Guantánamo Bay "was legally permissible under the existing guidance," Schmidt found no evidence "of torture or inhumane treatment at JTF-GTMO" (Joint Task Force–Guantánamo Bay). Accordingly, when Schmidt recommended that the commander at Guantánamo Bay, Major General Geoffrey D. Miller, be "admonished,"[37] he did so not because the specific techniques employed violated policy, but because Miller had failed to supervise the interrogation process adequately. That Miller was not in fact disciplined by General Bantz Craddock, head of the U.S. Southern Command, is telling, as is the fact that Miller was subsequently dispatched by the Pentagon to improve the quality of intelligence extracted from those imprisoned at Abu Ghraib.

The Schmidt report makes clear that interrogation taking the form of sexualized exploitation was conducted prior to the invasion of Iraq, and that the abuse perpetrated at Abu Ghraib was not an aberration. It is not implausible, therefore, to contend that the conduct of England and Graner, like that of Miller, was wholly within the parameters of the techniques specified in *Field Manual 34–52*. Indeed, Graner stated that when he ordered England to remove a prisoner from a cell using a leash, he was employing a legitimate cell-extraction technique;[38] and England informed military investigators that forcing prisoners to crawl, while attached to dog leashes, was a "humiliation tactic" intended to facilitate formal interrogations.[39] In this regard, Graner and England were not unusual; many of the personnel at Abu Ghraib believed that their actions were entirely consistent with established military doctrine. As a warden in Tier 1 stated, "It was not uncommon to see people without clothing. I only saw males. I was told the 'whole nudity thing' was an interrogation procedure used by military intelligence, and never thought much of it."[40] That these scenes were so often photographed, absent any concerted effort to hide the evidence, may say more about the banality of officially sanctioned evil than it does about the "sadistic and psychopathic" impulses of England and her cohorts: "We thought it looked funny," England stated matter-of-factly, "so pictures were taken."[41]

Cynthia Enloe is quite correct to claim that we will not completely grasp what happened at Abu Ghraib until we fully explore the culture of masculinized militarism, and, more particularly, "the masculinization of the military interrogators' organizational cultures, the masculinization of the CIA's field operatives and the workings of ideas about 'manliness' shaping the entire political system."[42] Obviously, it is beyond the scope of this essay to offer what Enloe rightly calls for. That said, because it offers insight into the specific form assumed by certain of the abuses at Abu Ghraib, I close this section by citing one factor that contributes to the culture of masculinized militarism in the United States.

Some have suggested that the exploitation at Abu Ghraib articulates American servicepersons' knowledge of Muslim culture, as well as its alleged taboos and phobias.[43] With Enloe, though, it seems equally plausible to ask whether American military police and their military and CIA intelligence colleagues might have been guided by their own masculinized fears of humiliation when they forced Iraqi men to go naked for days, to wear women's underwear, and to masturbate in front of each other and American women guards. That is, belief in an allegedly "exotic," frail Iraqi masculinity, fraught with fears of nakedness and homosexuality, might not have been the chief motivator for the American police and intelligence personnel; it may have been their own homegrown American sense of masculinity's fragility . . . that prompted them to craft these prison humiliations.[44]

But where and how might Graner and his cohorts have learned this fear of emasculation, which was then arguably incorporated into various techniques aimed at "softening up" his charges at Abu Ghraib? Though not a complete explanation,[45] this question can be answered in part by pointing to the hazing techniques that remain so prevalent in basic training. Consideration of these techniques requires that, albeit incompletely, I reconnect the misogynistic and homophobic elements of the exploitation at Abu Ghraib, which, to this point, I have separated for analytic purposes, although they are clearly joined in many of the incidents recounted in the investigative reports and depicted in many of the photographs.

In a striking recapitulation of the central premise of *KUBARK* (and, by extension, of *Field Manual 34–52*), a former head drill instructor explained that the key purpose of basic training is to "break [the recruit] down to his fundamental self, take away all that he possesses, and get him started out in a way that you want him to be. . . . Tell him he doesn't know a damn thing, that he's the sorriest thing you've ever seen, but with my help you're going to be worthwhile again."[46] Techniques employed to achieve this end, explains Carol Burke in a study of Australia's equivalent of West Point, include stripping recent recruits of their clothing; requiring them to run a gauntlet while those in their second and third year slap them with towels, belts, and suspenders; forcing them to sit naked on a block of ice, which is sometimes electrified in order to produce a shock; handcuffing and hooding cadets before their pants are pulled down and a vacuum cleaner hose is applied to their genitals; and the performance of Reverse Vienna Oysters, in which one freshman is required to lie on his back while another, atop him, performs push-ups in a simulation of heterosexual intercourse.[47]

That these are not Australian idiosyncrasies is made evident when Burke, anticipating one of the more infamous Abu Ghraib photographs, explains how, at the U.S. Naval Academy once a year, a twenty-one-foot obelisk is greased with lard, and all members of the outgoing freshman class, stripped to their underwear, "scramble to construct a human pyramid secure enough to raise a midshipman to the top more quickly than any preceding first year class." While the occasional woman cadet joins in this ritual, she will "never get far up the pyramid before her male counterparts toss her off, for no class wants to be the first to send a woman to the top of Herndon."[48] Furthermore, Susan Faludi, in her study of basic training at the

Citadel, which erupted into mass-media frenzy when Shannon Faulkner became the first woman to be admitted, found much the same logic at work. Specifically, one of Faludi's respondents explained how in basic training under same-sex conditions, upperclassmen play the role of men, while "knobs" play the role of women, "stripped and humiliated." "Virtually every taunt," Michael Lake confessed, "equated him with a woman. . . . They called you a 'pussy' all the time, or a 'fucking little girl.'" And when Lake showed fear, he was typically asked, "Are you menstruating?" "According to the Citadel creed of the cadet," he summarized, "women are objects, they're things that you can do with whatever you want to."[49]

Obviously, unlike what happened at Abu Ghraib, where the aim was to emasculate in order to subjugate, the aim of hazing techniques employed in basic training is to destroy deficient forms of masculinity, then to replace these with a construction built on what R. Claire Snyder has aptly characterized as an "unstable masculine identity predicated on the denigration of femininity and homoeroticism."[50] This combination is uneasy because it requires suppression of any "feminine" impulses soldiers may have harbored prior to enlistment, but also the very homoeroticism that is cultivated during basic training.[51] Coping with this tension requires that the well-disciplined serviceman perpetually reiterate what Snyder calls the ideal of "armed masculinity": "He must constantly reestablish his masculinity by expressing his opposition to femininity and homoeroticism in himself and others. The anger, hostility, and aggressiveness produced in the process of constituting armed masculinity get channeled into a desire for combat against [or, I would add, abuse of] the enemy."[52] In short, the exploitation at Abu Ghraib is perhaps best understood as an externalized projection of the anxieties bred by a masculine identity that cannot help but subvert itself.

—W→

What about Private First Class Lynndie England? Is she or is she not a source of gender trouble? Given my representation of gender as a malleable signifier, and given my claim that women's bodies can act as vectors of patriarchal norms, whether as victims, as perpetrators, or as something more vexing than this binary categorization suggests, the answer must be yes and no, depending on the contingencies of the context in which her deeds were first enacted, as well as the contexts into which those deeds subsequently entered via various cultural and media appropriations, domestic as well as foreign.

Within the context of Abu Ghraib, one might argue that England conducted herself in exemplary accordance with pathologized norms of feminine submissiveness. Located in the midst of an institutional culture predicated on the ideal of masculinized militarism, England found herself obliged to play by the rules of the game, which, in this case, included doing what she was ordered to do by her superior officers: "I was instructed by persons in higher ranks to stand there and hold this leash. . . . To us, we were doing our jobs, which meant doing what we were told."[53] This reading is reinforced by the testimony of a psychologist who, during England's court-marital, argued that her "overly compliant" personality rendered her incapable of making an independent judgment about participating in the exploitation at Abu Ghraib, thereby justifying a defense on the grounds of "partial mental responsibility."[54] This characterization would appear to be cemented by the fact that, according to one of her defense attorneys, her love for Graner, who allegedly has a history of abusing women and is the biological father of the child with whom England became pregnant while at Abu Ghraib, rendered her inordinately susceptible to bad influences: "She was an individual who was smitten with Corporal Graner, who just did whatever he asked her to do. Compounding all this is her depression, her anxiety, her fear."[55]

Yet this reading becomes problematic when we recall that England was at the same time participating in abusive conduct aimed at emasculating Iraqi prisoners, who were thereby reduced to something akin to the sort of submissiveness she apparently displayed in her relationship with Graner. If, as Snyder's analysis implies, Graner must perpetually seek to bolster a troubled conception of masculinity by transforming the targets of his abuse into so many incarnations of a despised conception of femininity, then England's conduct surely complicates this task. That a woman who appears more master than slave is the means of propping up that identity, in other words, would appear to spell gender trouble for Graner (which, although this is entirely speculative, may partly explain why he ultimately left England in favor of another, but less calumniated, of the women of Abu Ghraib). Graner's conundrum, moreover, may be ours as well. As Zillah Eisenstein suggests, England and the other women in the Abu Ghraib photographs are, in effect, "gender decoys" who "create confusion by participating in the very sexual humiliation that their gender is usually victim to."[56]

I do not intend to choose between these rival readings of Lynndie England. Instead, I want to suggest that the apparent tension between them will begin to dissipate only when we abandon the conception of gender discussed in the first section of this essay and embrace that commended in its second section. On the latter account, what is significant about the Abu Ghraib photographs is not whether the perpetrators of such abuse are anatomically male or female, nor whether Lynndie England is a woman or some sort of gender-bending monster. Rather, what is significant are the multiple ways in which specifically gendered practices are deployed as elements within a more comprehensive network of technologies aimed at disciplining prisoners or, more bluntly, at confirming their status as abject subjects of U.S. military power. In the photographs of principal concern here, gender as a complex structure of asymmetrical power relations has been detached from human bodies, and, once detached, deployed as something akin to so many weapons, weapons that can be employed by and against anyone, male or female. What we see here, in sum, are so many scripted practices of subordination that achieve their ends through the manipulation of gendered stereotypes, all of which work precisely because degradation, weakness, and humiliation remain very much identified with matters feminine. If Barbara Ehrenreich is shocked by Lynndie England, I would maintain, it is not because she is not a "true" woman, but because her conduct reveals the artificiality of normative constructions of gender, as well as the untenability of any essentialized account that insists on its rootedness in anatomical equipment. Whether Phyllis Schlafly and her kin can recapture England in a way that deflects her revelation of the way in which gender performances can sometimes simultaneously reinforce and trouble heteronormative strictures remains to be seen.

What I have offered in this essay is a modest first step toward making better sense of certain of the Abu Ghraib photographs. This reading does not, however, capture much of the complexity of the gendered permutations at work in the Abu Ghraib photographs. It does not, for example, explore the irony implicit in the fact that the military continues to employ techniques saturated with misogynist stereotypes, even as the Bush administration highlights the alleged gains for women in Afghanistan and Iraq as a result of U.S. military intervention. Nor does this essay adequately consider the virulent homophobia among U.S. military personnel (although it does imply that when these assaults appear to assume the character of homosexual acts, what is salient is not the imputed sexual orientation of any of the participants but, rather, the fact that the abused are once again forced, at least in the minds of the perpetrators, to assume the position of those on the receiving end of sexualized violence). Nor, moreover, does this reading adequately grasp the complex interplay of race and gender in these photographs and the incidents they depict; we must not forget that the three U.S. women who appear in the Abu Ghraib photographs, Megan Ambuhl, Sabrina Harman, and Lynndie England, are all white women, and that those they abuse are all brown men. Nor, finally, does this essay adequately explicate the larger political logic, that of neocolonialism and imperialism, from which these practices derive much of their sense.

Mark Danner was certainly correct when he contended that "officials of the Bush administration . . . counted on the fact that the public, and much of the press, could be persuaded to focus on the photographs—the garish signboards of the scandal and not the scandal itself."[57] Saying so, he effectively indicated the strategic foolishness of Rumsfeld's contention that "the real problem is not the photographs—the real problems are the actions taken to harm the detainees." From the vantage point of the Bush administration, far better to encourage a single-minded fixation on these photographs since that, in a culture too much saturated by obscene (which should be distinguished from pornographic) imagery, cannot help but depoliticize what happened at Abu Ghraib. To overcome such depoliticization, we ought to ask how these photographs expose the tangled strands of racism, misogyny, homophobia, national arrogance, and hypermasculinity, as well as how these strands inform the U.S. military's adventure in Iraq. What we ought not to ask is whether or how these photographs should be read as a referendum on the feminist quest for gender equality.

Is That the Pose of a Liberated Woman?

Elizabeth Maddock Dillon

What should we make of the smiling face of Private First Class Lynndie England? How much does it matter to viewers of the Abu Ghraib photos that it is a *woman* who holds the leash around the neck of a naked man forced to grovel beside her—a *woman* whose insouciant grin has come to stand for the specter of an American arrogance, lawlessness, and inhumanity exercised in the occupation of Iraq?

The sexual politics of the photos seen round the world should not be ignored. In England's free and easy stance, her tomboy haircut, army fatigues, and James Dean cigarette, we see the pose of a liberated woman—a woman unconstrained by the codes of traditional femininity. American women are in the army now, in this war more than ever before, and in the United States, this has been seen as an indication of increased gender equality. Indeed, were it not for the naked male bodies around her, it would be easy to imagine England as the centerpiece of a photo essay on the new face of the American military. Yet surrounded by the bodies of Iraqi prisoners—men made to pose in sexualized and dehumanizing positions—we must ask how femininity, in its liberated American mode, is operating in this picture.

The icon of the liberated body of the American woman soldier has significance in the current war in part because it is implicitly counterposed with the figure of the veiled Muslim woman. At the policy level, the Bush administration has identified the fight to liberate Iraq and Afghanistan with a fight to liberate women. Removing the veil becomes symbolic of freeing women from patriarchal oppression as well as, perhaps, from the imputed primitivism of Islamic law.

But what kind of liberation and what kind of sex are Americans so eager to export? In the United States, sexuality is often linked to autonomy and freedom: Sex is the arena where we enact our most private and personal desires and thus where we are *free* to be ourselves. Historically, however, our very private sex lives have been circumscribed and scripted by both culture and law. For instance, while sex in the bedroom between husband and wife has been a legally protected act of privacy, sex in the private home of two men was only in the last year granted the status of a private act by the U.S. Supreme Court. Sexual freedom in the United States has never been entirely free: It has, at the very least, had strings attached.

One might argue that Americans are obsessed with sexuality because it is at once the space of freedom and remarkable constraint: It finds us at our most private and finds us most tangled up within cultural norms. Public displays of sexuality replicate this conundrum. Ask a teenage girl, for instance, if imitating the dress and gyrations of Britney Spears is an act of empowerment or disempowerment.

If Americans want to remove the veil of Iraqi women, what will appear in its place? Will women be empowered to own and exercise their desires, or will they be more easily subjugated to the desires of men? There is no easy answer to this question: Desire is never simply private (never simply our own) since it is always formed in relation to the images we absorb from the culture around us, our history, and the dynamics of power between men and women, or bosses and workers—even between prisoners and guards.

In the photos from the Abu Ghraib prison we can certainly discern a script in which sexuality is not liberating. The piles of nude male bodies clearly are designed to evoke homosexuality (and hence an absence of heterosexual masculinity), and placing a man on a leash takes away his very humanity. England's smiling face affirms that the prisoners are lorded over by a woman and thus utterly lacking in masculine authority. The figure of the liberated American woman here plays into and reinforces an implicit logic of homophobia and racism, and suggests that women's authority will occur at the cost of men's sexual prowess.

England is a disturbing figure because she seems so powerful and free, and yet what she does with this freedom and authority is reprehensible. How free is she, if this is what freedom amounts to? The prison photos are potent and disturbing because they expose the workings of abusive forms of power in very bare terms, and gender is obviously central to the calculus of power at work in the photos. We should *see* gender at work in these pictures and ask, as we see it, how we might imagine alternative pictures of American and Iraqi women's freedom.

Feminism as Imperialism

Katharine Viner

"Respect for women . . . can triumph in the Middle East and beyond!" trilled the leader of the free world to the UN last week. "The repression of women [is] everywhere and always wrong!" he told the *New York Times,* warming to his theme that the West should attack Iraq for the sake of its women.

Just as he bombed Afghanistan to liberate the women from their burqas (or, as he would have it, to free the "women of cover") and sent out his wife, Laura, to tell how Afghans are tortured for wearing nail varnish, now Bush has taken on the previously unknown cause of Iraqi women—actually, look at the quotes, it's women everywhere!—to justify another war. Where next? China because of its antigirl, one-child policy? India because of widow-burning outrages? Britain because of its criminally low rape conviction rate?

At home, Bush is no feminist. On his very first day in the Oval Office, he cut off funding to international family-planning organizations that offer abortion services or counseling (likely to cost the lives of thousands of women and children); this year he renamed January 22—the anniversary of *Roe v.*

Wade, which permitted abortion on demand—National Sanctity of Human Life Day and compared abortion to terrorism: "On September 11, we saw clearly that evil exists in this world, and that it does not value life. . . . Now we are engaged in a fight against evil and tyranny to preserve and protect life."

However, this theft of feminist rhetoric is not new, particularly if its function is national expansion; in fact, it has a startling parallel with another generation of men who similarly cared little for the liberation of women. The Victorian male establishment, which led the great imperialistic ventures of the nineteenth century, fought bitterly against women's increasingly vocal feminist demands and occasional successes (new policies allowing women to enroll in universities; new laws permitting married women to own property). At the same time, across the globe, they used the language of feminism to acquire the booty of the colonies.

The classic example of such a colonizer was Lord Cromer, British consul-general in Egypt from 1883 to 1907, as described in Leila Ahmed's seminal *Women and Gender in Islam.* Cromer was convinced of the inferiority of Islamic religion and society, and had many critical things to say about the "mind of the Oriental." But his condemnation was most thunderous on the subject of how Islam treated women. It was Islam's degradation of women, its insistence on veiling and seclusion, which was the "fatal obstacle" to the Egyptian's "attainment of that elevation of thought and character which should accompany the introduction of Western civilisation," he said. The Egyptians should be "persuaded or forced" to become "civilised" by disposing of the veil.

And what did this forward-thinking, feminist-sounding veil-burner do when he got home to Britain? He founded and presided over the Men's League for Opposing Women's Suffrage, which tried by any means possible to stop women from getting the vote.

Colonial patriarchs like Cromer believed that middle-class Victorian mores represented the pinnacle of civilization, and set about implementing this model wherever they went—with women in their rightful, subservient place, of course. They wanted merely to replace Eastern misogyny with Western misogyny. But, like Bush, they stole feminist language in order to denounce the indigenous culture. Ahmed writes that feminism thus served as a "handmaid to colonialism. . . . Whether in the hands of patriarchal men or feminists, the ideas of western feminism essentially functioned to morally justify the attack on native societies and to support the notion of comprehensive superiority of Europe."

The thieves of feminist language couldn't (and can't) even be bothered to pretend they actually care about women in the colonized or bombed countries. In Egypt, Cromer actively ensured that women's status was not improved; he raised school fees (preventing girls' education) and discouraged the training of women doctors. And "feminist" George Bush has abandoned the women of Afghanistan. Where is his concern (or Laura's, or Tony Blair's, or Cherie Blair's, who was also wheeled out by her husband) for the many Afghan women who live in fear of the marauding mujahideen who now run the country and are in many ways as repressive as the Taliban? Where were their protests when Sima Samar, Afghanistan's women's affairs minister and one of only two women ministers in Hamid Karzai's Western-installed government, was forced from her job this summer because of death threats?

This cooption of feminism without a care for the women on the ground is not without consequences—although, predictably, it is not the colonizers who suffer. Ahmed writes: "Colonialism's use of feminism to promote the culture of the colonisers and undermine native culture has . . . imparted to feminism in non-western societies the taint of having served as an instrument of colonial domination, rendering it suspect in Arab eyes and vulnerable to the charge of being an ally of colonial interests."

Indeed, many Muslim women are suspicious of Western-style feminism for this very reason, a fact that is crucial for feminists in the West to understand, before they do a Cromer and insist that the removal of veils is the route to all liberation. The growing Islamization of Arab societies and the neocolonial impact of the war on terror, according to academic Sherin Saadallah, have meant that "secular feminism and feminism which mimics that of the west is in trouble in the Arab world."

Just because Arab women are rejecting Western-style feminism doesn't mean they are embracing the subjugation of their sex. Muslim women deplore misogyny just as Western women do, and they know that Islamic societies also oppress them. Why wouldn't they? But liberation for them does not encompass destroying their identity, religion, or culture, and many of them want to retain the veil.

Reflecting this, a particular brand of Muslim feminism has developed in recent years that is neither Westernized and secular nor Islamist and ultratraditional. Instead it tries to dismantle the things that enforce women's subjugation within the Islamic framework. Increasingly relevant and influential, Leila Ahmed and Fatema Mernissi are the most significant theoretical voices.

And in the West, feminists are left with the fact that their own beliefs are being trotted out by world leaders in the name of a cause which does nothing for the women it purports to protect. This is nothing less than an abuse of feminism, one that will further discredit the cause of Western feminism in the Arab world, as well as here. When George Bush mouths feminist slogans, feminism loses its power.

But such a theft is in the spirit of the times. Feminism is used for everything these days, except the fight for true equality. It is used to sell trainers, to justify body mutilation, to make women make porn, to help clear men of rape charges, to ensure women feel they have self-respect because they use a self-esteem-enhancing brand of shampoo. No wonder it's being used as a reason for bombing women and children too.

The "Sex Interrogators" of Guantánamo

Kristine A. Huskey

On December 26, 2004, I flew to Guantánamo, the U.S. military base in Cuba. During my first visit, my colleague and I did not question our clients, assuming they had been through countless interrogations. We merely explained who we were, and said that our purpose was to help them. They were skeptical and mistrusting for good reason. I have been to Guantánamo a dozen times since, and every visit has revealed more and more shocking information: that they had been subjected to abuse and torture, that they had been deprived of the most basic medical and dental care, that they were given little exercise and no reading materials other than the Koran, that letters from their families were withheld by interrogators until they "cooperated," that the interrogation techniques were "excessive." And all of the conduct had been done in the name of the United States of America.

It wasn't until we had visited several times that I began to learn the detail and full extent of just how twisted and depraved those techniques were. They went beyond coercion and were infused with sexual depravity, relying on the use of females as manipulative "sex tools" and "sex objects" to intimidate the detainees. Sexual intimidation did not stop at interrogation. The general treatment of the detainees was similarly rife with physical and mental sexual abuse in which American women played a key role.

During the last year and a half, I learned that my clients—devout Muslim men—have been subject to sexual harassment and abuse both in and out of interrogation. They have been forced to strip naked in front of female guards; some have had their private parts touched and squeezed; some have been offered sex in exchange for cooperation; some have been threatened with rape. One of my clients told of an interrogator pulling out a condom and threatening to use it on him unless he "cooperated." Another client was forced to lie across a table with his legs spread while a female pulled his pants down.

Over the course of their detention, two of my clients were repeatedly subjected to excessive sexual abuse and mistreatment by a particular female interrogator, named Megan. She apparently made a habit of wearing tight, revealing clothing to interrogations. Her shirt—transparent—was unbuttoned very low. She wore heavy makeup and "full lipstick." On several occasions she put her chair close to the detainee, and giggled and flirted in a manner so clearly sexually aggressive that one of my clients said he felt "embarrassed for her." To add insult to injury, Megan reminded this man more than once that his lawyers were "Jews" and "Jews have always betrayed Arabs."

Megan also played a role, albeit unknowingly, in instigating what became known as the Hunger to Death, a mass hunger strike that began in August 2005. Using sexually provocative tactics—such as tight clothing—Megan continually harassed one of my clients. For sixteen months, in addition to using the "sexual intimidation lite" described above, she also went so far as to blow cigarette smoke in his face, rub his neck, call him handsome, "talk dirty" by speaking of sexual acts, make sexual sounds, and take her shirt off so my client could see her breasts and nipples. Sometimes during his interrogation, there was more than one "sex interrogator"; two to three females would engage in similar tactics at the same time. When he refused to react to the clothing and dirty talk, Megan taunted his masculinity and said she would make him like women. When my client got angry, Megan laughed and left him shackled for several hours without allowing him to use the toilet.

This client sadly relayed to me that such tactics had been occurring for a long time but that he had been afraid to tell me because of fear of retribution. Abusive interrogation methods ramped up substantially during the summer of 2005 to the point that my client just had enough. One day when the guards informed him he had a "reservation" (the term for an interrogation session), he refused to go. He explained to me quite simply, "I would not let my own two feet take me to abuse." He did not mind the interrogation but could no longer take the harassment. The Immediate Reaction Forces (IRF) team showed up and beat him, and physically forced him out of his cell to his interrogation. News of the beating spread quickly though the detention camp. That event, coupled with a beating by the IRF team of another detainee, set off a widespread hunger strike that lasted until January 2006. At the height of the hunger strike, over a hundred detainees were protesting their treatment and indefinite detention by attempting to starve themselves. Up to twenty-five to thirty detainees participating in the strike were eventually force-fed for several months through tubes running up their noses and into their stomachs. The strike ended when medical personnel began using the "restraint chair" to tie detainees down for hours at a time, forcing so much Ensure and laxatives into their systems that they vomited and defecated on themselves. Because the government refuses to release any medical information on the hunger strikers, the extent of damage caused by their prolonged force-feeding is unknown. My client, whom Megan had taken a liking to, joined the hunger strike for periods at a time. Fortunately, he was released back into the custody of Kuwait in November 2005 and did not continue the strike.

As shocking as they are, the sexual interrogation techniques are but part of the bigger picture that is Guantánamo. The overall treatment of the detainees there is a concerted effort by the government to "break them." Perhaps this goal, in theory, would be laudable or at least somewhat acceptable to most Americans if, in fact, these individuals had information that would prevent future attacks. But, as high-ranking U.S. officials have admitted, many were brought to Guantánamo by mistake and have no connection to terrorism. Even if we assume the detainees are connected to terrorism, their treatment went beyond breaking them in a manner we might consider to be legal or even valid interrogation for known criminals. The detainees' treatment relied on sex and the use of women in coercion techniques that not only insult our women in uniform, but vastly undermine the role women play in the military and armed conflict. We would never condone Megan's actions if she were a man interrogating a female suspect, because the imbalance of power too clearly crosses the line into sexually threatening as we know it. Given the detainees' vulnerability and utter dependence on their captors, the sex tactics used by Megan and her cohorts should be appreciated no differently. Yet, the government allowed, indeed likely encouraged, our women to engage in such activity.

There is a consensus among the detainees that the sexual terrorization started after Major General Geoffrey Miller (of Abu Ghraib infamy) took over operations at Guantánamo. Given what we know about Abu Ghraib and how little we know about Guantánamo, it is frightening to think of the possible ways in which the men there have been mistreated. The American public should require an accounting of how our country treats individuals— human beings—in custody, even those suspected of terrorist acts.

Women in the Interrogation Room

Riva Khoshaba

He had been captured during a night raid on the home he shared with his wife, parents, and three children. Like others taken under similar conditions, he had been thrown on the floor, his hands tied behind his back, a dark, rough hood pulled over his head. The American soldiers spoke in English, but their words were translated by a foreign translator—perhaps an Arab by birth, but for whom Arabic had become a second language.

And yet this Iraqi man was most traumatized by his interaction with an American interrogator he encountered after his capture. Why was her exposing herself and making suggestive gestures the most threatening thing that happened to him, despite the severe beatings and threats he endured? Why was his interaction with her the most traumatic part of his detention? I believe this man's trauma resulted from the contrast between the American woman and himself—because her presence and role as an interrogator contrasted with his own subjugation as a prisoner, and her open sexuality inverted the Iraqi ideal of a chaste woman. In short, this man's trauma was the result of two inversions—that of the proper male and female roles and their relationship to one another; and that of the idealized chaste Iraqi woman.

He would become one of a disturbingly large number of Coalition Provisional Authority prisoners to be abused in Abu Ghraib, the dreaded prison, transformed from an Iraqi detention and torture site to an American detention and torture site. During his imprisonment, he was kept in a windowless room with black walls, floor, and ceiling. He was stripped naked. He was beaten with fists and furniture, doused with cold water, and left shivering for hours during the cold night. He was hung by his arms from the ceiling and made to believe his father was being tortured, abused, and perhaps killed in a room nearby. But despite the horror of all these experiences, he was most traumatized by his interaction with female interrogators. He breaks down in tears when he describes how a woman made gestures suggestive of sexual intercourse and sometimes bared her breasts. It was then, he relates, that he was *truly* afraid. He feared she would rape him.

It seems unusual, perhaps farfetched, that the worst moments in this man's detention in Abu Ghraib came when women participated in his interrogation. He never stated that they touched him in any way—although torture survivors often leave off the worst parts, describing how close they came to rape and denying they were indeed ever raped. But this story did not seem incomplete to me—I believed that all these women had to do to strike fear in this man, in hopes of coercing a confession or eliciting more information, was enter the room, make suggestive gestures, and perhaps remove some of their clothing. The most jarring and painful experiences for this man were not the beatings, the nights left shivering and wet, or even the times he was literally knocked unconscious; they were when the unknown women caused him humiliation and fear so profound that he cried when he told his story to several lawyers and journalists.

Listening to his story, I am struck by how an experience many American young men would describe as a fantasy realized was for this Iraqi man the pinnacle of horror. To understand why, we have to understand something about women and Iraqi society. As an Iraqi-born American, I am familiar with the strict boundaries and hierarchies that define the role of men and women in Iraqi society. Many of the boundaries are defined by the increasingly fundamentalist character of the Iraqi brand of Islam. My family is part of the ever-dwindling number of Iraqi Assyrians—non-Arab, Iraqi Christians whose numbers continue to shrink through pogroms, persecution, and diaspora. The boundaries separating men and women observed in Iraqi Assyrian society were not as strictly delineated as those of mainstream (Muslim) Iraq. Our men and women mingled more often, polygamous marriages were not permitted, and our women tended to be highly educated—often becoming doctors and engineers. Assyrian women in Iraq were full participants in the public sphere, aptly symbolized by their uncovered heads and Western clothing.

Despite being Westernized and, in American terms, "liberated," Assyrian families like my own are nevertheless influenced by the gender boundaries enforced back "home." Even though we live in the United States, our *Iraqi* roots are evident in the litany of things young women in my community are not allowed to do—date, go clubbing, wear certain types of clothing. Straddling the worlds of Assyrians in Iraq and in America, I knew the profound impact the presence of women played in the torture survivor's story.

To say that women in Iraq are simply "unliberated" versions of American women would be to drastically oversimplify the situation and to fail to recognize the nuanced role of women in a society that, through constant warfare and oppression, has been largely woman-centric. Indeed, the role of women in Iraqi society reveals a paradox between the ideal, subordinated status of women and the reality of a highly educated female population with many female-headed households. Iraq is often cited as having the most highly educated female population in the Middle East. This in part is because Saddam Hussein, who was fiercely secular, used Iraq's oil wealth to create a state-funded education system open to everyone. A darker reason is tied to

Iraq's almost continuous state of war during Hussein's rule; it decimated the nation's population of young men, leaving potential husbands in short supply and rendering many young women widows. Without the security of marriage to ensure their economic future, and with the availability of college education, many women earned degrees and entered the workforce as accountants, attorneys, engineers, teachers, and doctors. In addition, the exodus of men to war, many of whom did not return, left many government administrative positions open to women.

Iraqi women in the 1980s and 1990s not only assumed prominent roles in the public sphere, they were also forced into more expansive roles at home. Many women became the primary breadwinners when their husbands went to war. Women were forced into the position of sole household protectors, often caring for children without the aid of a husband or male relative.

Despite the reality of women's lives in Iraq—or perhaps because of it— Iraqi society remained male-dominated. After the first Gulf War, women's status deteriorated as a once-secular Saddam Hussein turned to religion, believing it would give him greater support in the Arab world. The dictator, who had once been photographed in a defiant stance with firearm in hand, now was photographed praying. Hussein's change of heart marked a corresponding shift in the Iraqi populace—and perhaps in the Arab world. As society grew more conservative, women's roles became more circumscribed. Western fashions that had once been the norm were replaced by traditional head coverings and even full abayas. Women drivers were increasingly harassed, so much so that younger women no longer bothered to learn to drive.

With the Iraq War and the increasing Islamization of Iraqi society, women have experienced significant changes in their daily life and their role in society commensurate with their social and economic subjugation. Some women still work—indeed, some are forced to work because of economic realities. But many have had to quit their jobs because of the danger and unrest that have destabilized their communities. Others have stopped going to school as the security situation in their region destabilizes. The longer the war drags on, the further behind in education these girls and young women will fall, risking a future generation with fewer educated women capable of participating in the public sphere. While social pressures have idealized a retreat into the household, the realities of warfare have resulted in a literal retreat into the home. As women are driven back into the private sphere, they take on an increasingly idealized role that epitomizes female virtues (modesty, chastity or fidelity, submissiveness) and this role in turn takes on increasing social significance. Put differently, as women are forced out of the public sphere and onto a pedestal, they are stripped of the social and political advances they have made and forced into the restrictive mold of the idealized submissive and silent woman.

Women in Iraq epitomize family honor, which is ultimately defined in sexual terms. Women are idealized as virgins, and many of the rules regarding social interaction are designed to police female sexuality. Accordingly, women do not date. Social interaction between men and women is closely guarded by a woman's male relatives. Even mixed groups are discouraged without the presence of a chaperone. A woman's behavior reflects not only on herself, but on her family. Accordingly, the penalty for violating these rules can be severe, up to and including murder. These ritualized, and legalized, murders are designated as "honor killings" because they are committed to restore a family's honor. The U.S. State Department reports that at the end of Hussein's regime, at least four hundred women were murdered every year in so-called honor killings.

The salient thread here is that women are at once the source of a family's honor and the greatest threat to it. Through the most casual action, a woman can cast her family into despair. Men are therefore protectors of women and of family honor. Protecting women's honor necessarily entails protecting (or ensuring) their sexual virtue—abstinence, if unmarried, and fidelity, if married. But this arrangement begs the questions, *Who exactly are these women being protected from? Who is it that poses a threat?* Ultimately, it is every man who is not a relative. Men protect their own women, but nevertheless pose a threat to other, unrelated women. Equating women's honor with family honor, and giving men responsibility to guard it, creates a culture in which every man is both protector and predator. Either role, however, casts the man as actor, with the woman as object.

The status and significance of Iraqi women stand in stark contrast to that of American women. The feminist movement, the advent of birth control, and other cultural trends have dramatically redefined the American woman's role. In the United States, women have increasingly sought meaningful work outside the home and have gained access to political power, with increasing numbers of women occupying prominent positions in federal, state, and local governments. They have raised their profile in the professional sector, becoming executives, attorneys, and physicians.

Women in the United States have gained control over their private family lives as well. Many continue to enjoy the "traditional" family role of wife and mother; but an increasing number of women, by choice or circumstance, have decoupled those two identities and enjoy one without feeling obligated to undertake the other.

Women's broad entrance into the public sphere and control of their own agency in the private sphere are clearly demonstrated in their increasing participation in the military. Coincidentally, the general in charge of Abu Ghraib when the scandal broke was a woman.

The convergence of the idealized image of the Iraqi woman and the reality of the American woman in Abu Ghraib's black room created more fear for one man than any other event he encountered during his detention. The agony of the situation was not caused by contact with a woman, but by the inversion of roles. In effect, he was denied the traditional agency he enjoyed in Iraqi society as protector or otherwise. In the black room he was denied any ability to act; his roles had been usurped by a woman. He was made an object, while the woman was the actor. The situation in effect feminized him—an inversion he unconsciously realized through his fear of being raped.

The woman's presence in the interrogation room, where he had been beaten and abused for days, in itself created a threatening cast. She was wearing an American military uniform and entered a room where men in American military uniforms had been abusing him. By virtue of her presence, she became a threat, further magnified because of its psychological effects. Women in virtually all societies are viewed first and foremost as nurturers. Bringing a woman into the black room created another inversion—a nurturer recast as a tormentor.

But he did not fear the women or what she would do to him. He feared what she symbolized. Iraqi perceptions of the United States, although tinged with some envy for our affluence, is primarily marked by horror at what they view to be a largely atheistic and sexually promiscuous society. Whether warranted, American women in particular are viewed as "loose." In Iraq, where premarital sex is so stigmatized, there are virtually no births outside of wedlock. Thus, unmarried women are very unlikely to become pregnant, and once pregnant, very likely to have secret abortions or risk a terrible fate at the hands of their families. By contrast, American movies, televisions, and magazines reflect a society that is tolerant and accepting of premarital sex and out-of-wedlock births.

The presence of the female soldier in the black room, participating in the interrogation, underscored the detainee's sense of his own horrific, helpless status. It confirmed his perception of American culture as being alien, unnatural, and, ultimately, abhorrent. That women were willing to make suggestive movements at all, especially in front of him and their own male colleagues, reflected his sense of a society in which women are unrestrained by social convention or notions of family or personal honor. Further, that their male colleagues would permit and perhaps encourage them to act this way signified that American men have no shame. Not only did the men tolerate it, but the state itself condoned it, reifying the Iraqis' notion of the United States as a soulless place. Finally, to even include women in the military in the first place exemplified the failure of American men to police the sexual behavior of "their" women and the relinquishing of the traditional male role of "protector." Indeed, if they are sending their women to fight, what, after all, are they fighting to protect?

The United States (unknowingly, I'm convinced) projects a certain image when it uses women in this manner during interrogations. Doing so reifies all the perceived differences between American and Iraqi societies—differences many Iraqis believe need to be maintained. All American women are lascivious and impulsive. By making them the social equals of men, men have relinquished any responsibility for protecting women or the home. Introducing women into the interrogation room ultimately confirms for Iraqi detainees the perception of American culture as being decadent and representing everything they reject. It also convinces them that this war is not about protecting the American homeland. (Iraqis never have been swayed by the homeland-defense argument, firmly believing they had no connection to September 11.) Instead they see the war as a way of projecting American values or more precisely valueless society into their own culture. It shows a disordered culture where women act like men, and men allow it.

As an Assyrian from Iraq, I understand the detainee's social expectations regarding women; as a human, I commiserate with his profound fear and suffering; as an American woman, however, I am unable to escape the fact that his fear is inextricably intertwined with his misogynistic expectations of what a "good" woman should be and do. The presence of women in interrogation rooms would not be particularly effective or unusual if it weren't for the profound fear these men have of women and of their own contact with them. These fears grow out of a society that teaches that the worst thing you can do to a man—even worse than killing him—is confront him with a naked, suggestive woman. The loss of agency on its own is not the reason for the deep torment—indeed, the detainee was in a similarly passive role when only male soldiers were beating him. Nor is it sexuality alone; after all, protecting a woman's honor in Iraqi society would not be necessary if it weren't for the potential threat other men pose. A woman's sexuality is not to be feared as long as a man controls it—whether through domination or protection (ultimately, two sides of the same coin, and better characterized as benign-versus-malicious domination—and sometimes not even benign, as when the protection devolves into an honor killing). It is the confluence of these two strains—the lack of agency and the confrontation with women's sexuality—that brings about the fierce psychological strain, thus making the use of women in the interrogation room a particularly traumatizing phenomenon.

Women's Role in Mob Violence: Lynchings and Abu Ghraib

LaNitra Walker

In 1929, NAACP leader Walter White published his book *Rope and Faggot: A Biography of Judge Lynch,* a searing indictment of the practice of lynching. In the preface, White wrote, "Mobbism has inevitably degenerated to the point where an uncomfortably large percentage of American citizens can read in their newspapers of the slow roasting alive of a human being in Mississippi and turn, promptly and with little thought, to the comic strip or sporting page."[1] Americans, White argued, had become so used to reading about lynching and racial violence that the two were inexorably woven into the nation's cultural and political fabric. Lynching was so prevalent that Americans could easily digest it along with the rest of the daily news; even after White's book was published, it would still take several years and the publication of dozens of gruesome photographs to draw national attention to the nation's worst acts of domestic terrorism.

In 2004, American soldiers and contractors were accused of raping and torturing Iraqi prisoners thousands of miles away in the Abu Ghraib prison in

Baghdad. The accusations caused mixed reactions, mostly drawn along liberal and conservative political lines. Like African Americans during the pre–Civil Rights era, many Iraqi prisoners were arrested and detained with little or no evidence that they had committed a crime. And like the more than 4,700 African Americans who were lynched in America, the prisoners' systematic physical and sexual abuse was documented in photographs.

Since the Abu Ghraib photographs emerged in 2004, the images of prisoner abuse and torture have been analyzed, dissected, reproduced, and condemned. They have been compared with images of torture and violence committed during previous wars and, most frequently, with lynching photographs. Although great debates have raged in the nation's most prominent newspapers and magazines about the Abu Ghraib photographs and their relationship to our nation's history of torture, little has been said about how the conspicuous presence of women in the images raises questions about women's ability to commit violence, specifically in a racial context.

What does it mean to see American women prominently participating in the torture of Arab men in an Iraqi prison? In this essay, I argue that the complicated relationship between race and gender in the images of torture from the Abu Ghraib prison was already part of America's visual vocabulary through the legacy of lynching photography. Both sets of images depict how gender roles reinforce perceptions of racial superiority; and by comparing them, it is possible to see how white American women have moved from the background to the foreground in committing politically motivated acts of violence. Although decoding this aspect of lynching photography is crucial to understanding its social function, an understanding of the cultural forces that define women's visual presence in lynching photography is also critical.

Whereas the spectacle of lynching photography was used as a deterrent to prevent sex across the color line, the Abu Ghraib photographs demonstrate how white female soldiers exploited power relationships and transgressed gender roles to reinforce American political and cultural dominance in a Muslim country. Female soldiers played a large role in torturing Iraqi detainees. They are pictured not only grinning and giving the "thumbs-up" sign while they admire their barbaric handiwork, but they also participate in the prisoners' sexual humiliation. In recent years, the struggle for women's rights in the American military has included demands that women be able to participate equally in combat. In the Abu Ghraib photographs, women appear to be equally culpable in the prisoners' abuse, which raises the question, *Is this what women meant by gender equality?*

"This Is Her First Lynching": Women's Roles in Mob Violence

The Bush administration, as *Nation* writer Naomi Klein argues, did not invent state-supported torture.[2] In fact, America's founding fathers also struggled to prevent terrorism on American soil. The torture of prisoners at Abu Ghraib recalls the original intent of lynching as described by Colonel Charles Lynch of Bedford County, Virginia, who many historians believe ordered the first lynchings in America. Even after America gained independence from Britain, the new nation was still infested with British spies and soldiers who wanted to destabilize the new government. In a series of letters to Virginia politicians and military officials in 1780, including then-governor Thomas Jefferson, Lynch referred to the British as "insurgents" and argued that they did not need to be prosecuted according to American law.[3] Instead, Lynch suggested that extrajudicial torture and executions be used to punish Tory insurgents who were caught spying. His suggestions resulted in the torture and execution of dozens of insurgents, which led him to recommend "Lynchs Law too for Dealing with the negroes."[4]

Lynching became a method of political and social control of blacks after Reconstruction. White men searched for ways to maintain a system of racial oppression in slavery's absence. If blacks exercised their newly bestowed rights, they conceivably could socialize across the color line and have sexual relations with white women, an idea that was threatening to white male conceptions of masculinity.[5] It is no coincidence that the women's suffrage movement also intensified at the same time that lynchings and racial violence reached an apex in the late nineteenth century—both groups were struggling to break free from white male oppression. However, since many of the most vocal suffragists were also frustrated abolitionists, they began to see their struggle to achieve voting rights for women and for blacks as mutually exclusive and irreconcilable pursuits.[6]

The number of lynchings steadily decreased during the twentieth century, though they became more violent and more public. Local authorities justified their right to allow lynch mobs to murder blacks under the cover of defending the purity of white womanhood. In many states, mostly in the South, raping a white woman was a capital offense. Talking to or even looking at a white woman could easily send a black man to the gallows. As women's studies scholar Robyn Wiegman observes, inventing the persona of the black male as a sexual predator allowed white men to act outside the boundaries of the law to protect their women: "The white woman serves, in the ethos of the nineteenth century racialism, as a pivotal rhetorical figure for shaping the mythology of the black male rapist."[7]

Although some may be surprised to see women committing acts of torture and sexual humiliation, women, specifically white women, were at the center of debates about the practice of lynching. They are documented as both accusers of black men and as participants in lynchings.[8]

In lynching photographs, women and girls are frequently pictured as part of the crowds pointing at the hanged body, smiling with excitement, or posing for the camera. After a woman made her accusation of rape (or the accusation was made for her), her work as conspirator in the lynching was finished, and she could join the crowd to witness the event. A 1934 *New Yorker* cartoon titled "This Is Her First Lynching," for example, is critical of women's involvement in lynchings. The cartoon shows a white woman with a young girl hoisted above her so she could view the lynching.[9] The lynching is not depicted, but the soft glow of a large bonfire in the distance alludes to the sinister activity taking place. The cartoon implies, disapprovingly, that participating in a lynching is a rite of passage for a woman, her initiation to the racial and gendered hierarchies that define what it means to be a Southerner and an American.

Female Soldiers and Torture at Abu Ghraib

Women have played important roles during wartime even when they were not allowed to fight on the front lines. Clara Barton dodged bullets to deliver medical care to wounded Civil War soldiers. During World War II, thousands of women replaced men in domestic factories to produce the vital supplies and weaponry for the American military. Women fought bravely on the front lines during the first Gulf War, and Congress began repealing laws banning them from participating in combat.

If the Abu Ghraib photographs are any indication of how women's roles in the military are changing, there are many reasons to be concerned. The photos show female soldiers being visibly transformed from cautious participants into complicit perpetrators of acts of torture. In early photos, for example, Private First Class Lynndie England appears to participate reluctantly. In press interviews, she maintained that she was just following orders. "I was instructed by persons in higher rank to stand there and hold this leash and look at the camera," she stated in her first television interview after the scandal emerged.[10] In later photographs, however, she appears to be increasingly comfortable with her role as torturer, sporting a broad smile and a casual stance as she stands in front of the naked prisoners.

As the *New Yorker* reporter Seymour Hersh describes in his May 2004 article "Torture at Abu Ghraib," which exposed the abuses at Abu Ghraib, the violations of Islamic codes that call for gender separation and the shielding of male nudity were part of U.S. torture methods.[11] Like Col. Lynch, Bush administration officials argued that national security interests trumped concerns about human rights violations. According to Hersh, senior military personnel encouraged the abuse, and the prison had a history of problems that had been reported to Brigadier General Janis Karpinski, who was responsible for managing the military prisons in Iraq.[12] Karpinski was not prepared to handle the large-scale prison system; as Hersh writes, she was "the only female commander in the war zone who had served with the Special Forces and in the 1991 Gulf War, but she had never run a prison."[13]

Group Photos: Documenting Acts of Torture

The soldiers in the Abu Ghraib photos, specifically the women, seemed to act without fear of repercussions. Like the women who proudly posed in front of lynched men in the twentieth-century photographs, the female soldiers at Abu Ghraib did not expect to have to account, much less atone, for their actions.

The photographs of female soldiers at Abu Ghraib are disturbing because they destroy the stereotype that women do not have the same capacity to commit violence as do men. In addition, traces of the American visual vernacular of race and gender that code lynching photography are also present in the Abu Ghraib photographs, creating a historical link that exposes the fault lines in America's democratic values.

In one of the earliest photographs published by the *Washington Post*, England is shown leading a naked prisoner on a leash.[14] With her masculine haircut and military fatigues, England towers over the prisoner who is being dragged across the floor. The leashed prisoner is being subjected to sexual, political, and racial domination. Being photographed in this position is also humiliating; but most important, the photograph draws a line between England and the male Muslim prisoner. She is human, but the prisoner is not. In fact, if the photo is rotated to the right, one sees that the leashed prisoner's head is unnaturally bent like that of a lynched man.

A photograph aired on *60 Minutes II* shows England standing in front of a row of naked, hooded prisoners while she gives the thumbs-up sign with one hand and points her finger in a gun position at a prisoner's genitals. Boasting a wide smile, she appears to be having more fun than she was when she was leading the prisoner on a leash. This photograph is loaded with visual references that connect it to lynching photography. England's jovial facial expression resembles the wide grins that adorned the proud faces of men and women who had just witnessed a lynching. The act of pointing at the prisoner's genitals draws the viewer's attention to them. But England's fingers are shaped like a gun. Is she merely trying to make us look, or is she gesturing as if she were going to shoot at the genitals? Her gesture recalls the act of castrating black men during lynchings. Castration was a common part of the lynching process, with the ritual emasculation manifested in stripping a man of his sexual and political power.[15] Methods of castration included cutting or shooting, as England's hand gesture suggests in the photograph. Photographing the event or simulated event connotes further social and emotional humiliation of the individual and the community, demonstrating their powerlessness in stopping the torture.

In another photo, England and Specialist Charles Graner stand behind a pile of naked prisoners. With their arms on each other's shoulders, England and Graner sport wide smiles and thumbs-up signs while the prisoners' buttocks face the camera. Visibly proud of their work, their convivial pose contrasts directly with the visible physical pain the prisoners are suffering in the human dog pile. Their smiles and glee make them look like the thousands of men and women who gathered under trees to witness lynchings, which many Southerners considered to be festive events that should be memorialized by professional photographers. England and Graner pose for the camera in that same way.

Specialists Sabrina Harman and Graner pose for a similar photo in which naked prisoners are stacked in a human pyramid and the word "RAPEIST [sic]" has been written on one of the prisoner's legs. This photograph exposes the close relationship to lynching photographs more than the others. As they stand behind a pile of mangled bodies, Harman and Graner demonstrate

U.S. political power by literally positioning themselves at the top of the social pyramid. However, Harman kneels to pose slightly above the prisoners, while Graner stands fully upright, towering above Harman and the prisoners. As a female soldier and an American woman, Harman exerts her power over the prisoners; but it is clear from Graner's body language that as an American male, he is at the top of the social hierarchy.

Misspelling the word "rapist" in the photograph not only reveals the participating soldiers' ignorance, it recalls the ways that poor, uneducated Southern whites used rape accusations to incite lynch mobs as a means of confirming their racial superiority and reasserting political control over the black population. Some lynching photos also labeled blacks as rapists as part of the torture process. For example, on the back of a professional photograph of George Meadows taken in Pratt Mines, Alabama, in 1889, the printed title on the back of the image reads, "George Meadows, Murderer and Rapist. Lynched on the scene of his last crime."[16] In the context of nineteenth-century Alabama, labeling Meadows as a rapist was enough to justify his punishment and to erase any traces of guilt or sympathy that a white person might have after viewing the photograph. The "RAPEIST" photograph at Abu Ghraib is intended to function in the same way, by encouraging the viewer to accept the soldiers' word as the truth. It implies that if some of the prisoners are rapists, then viewers should not be critical of how soldiers treat them, illustrating how easy it is to commit torture in the absence of ethical and judicial boundaries.

Photography, Violence, and the American Way

What lessons can we learn from looking at the Abu Ghraib photos in the context of lynching photography? As Susan Sontag points out in a 2002 *New Yorker* essay that advises against invading Iraq, the process of viewing disturbing photographic images conjures moral and psychological responses designed to bring us closer to understanding the origins of such violent and sadistic behavior:

[S]ubmitting to the ordeal should help us to understand such atrocities
not as acts of "barbarism" but as a reflection of a belief system, racism,
that by defining one people as less human than another legitimizes
torture and murder.[17]

America's shameful indulgence in the practice of and in condoning lynching has moved out of the shadows of history and into sharp focus thanks to groundbreaking exhibitions of lynching photography, including Without Sanctuary: Lynching Photography in America. If the Abu Ghraib photographs, like the lynching photographs, had been tucked away in photo albums, it might have taken another fifty years before we discovered the atrocities that occurred in Iraq. But the medium of digital photography and the speed of the Internet brought the photos to our inboxes instantaneously, and it is clear that the political and social climate that allowed Americans to participate in lynchings and collect souvenir lynching postcards still exists—it's just been reshaped by twenty-first century technologies.

In the 1930s, the Communist Party USA successfully recruited new African American members by criticizing the United States government for its unwillingness to stop the practice of lynching. Similarly, the inhumane treatment of the Abu Ghraib prisoners also undermines America's ability to promote democracy around the world. When military officials authorized soldiers to bypass the principles outlined in the Geneva conventions, they compromised America's ability to convince other countries to adopt our democratic values, making autocratic and theocratic alternatives seem more attractive.

England and Harman's participation in the torture at Abu Ghraib is a reminder that race and gender still have an uncomfortable relationship in American society. Both women grew up in states where at least fifty lynchings were recorded (West Virginia and Virginia, respectively).[18] Lynching photography and the Abu Ghraib photos demonstrate how gender roles reinforce perceptions of racial superiority, and the images' power comes from their ability to illustrate the consequences of submitting to the mob mentality. Both sets of photographs reveal women's crucial roles in committing racial violence and challenge us, the viewers, to think critically about the underside of what is meant by *liberty and justice for all.*

Pawn, Scapegoat, or Collaborator? U.S. Military Women and Detainee Abuse in Iraq

Barbara Finlay

Many people were shocked at the reports of torture and abuse coming out of the Abu Ghraib prison in April 2004, but one of the most stunning elements of the stories was the participation of women in the events. How could women, who are supposed to be the gentler sex, have participated in these degrading and sadistic actions? What's more, the photos depict them not just participating, but seemingly *enjoying* themselves while doing so. Though the photos should have demolished still-popular notions of essential gender difference, many people have the ability to maintain favored ideas in spite of evidence to the contrary. In fact, the photos and the events they depict reinforce what most feminist scholars have been arguing for decades—that there is little difference in the essential makeup between men and women. Given the right circumstances, women have as much capacity for inhumanity as men.

Since the incriminating photos were published, more evidence of U.S. military women's involvement in torture and abuse has become public, although without the graphic imagery the impact has not been as great. In fact, most U.S. citizens seem blissfully unaware of the ongoing widespread abuse perpetrated by their military against civilians and detainees in various places around the globe; and many have apparently accepted official claims that the Abu Ghraib photos represented the aberrant actions of "a few bad apples" who have now been brought to justice. Yet, the question of women's involvement in inhumane and degrading treatment demands analysis, if only to counter these erroneous assumptions.

The Military Context for Women

The abuse of military detainees in Iraq and elsewhere cannot be understood apart from the context in which it occurs—the contemporary military world in the midst of the so-called war on terror. Soldiers in places like Iraq and Afghanistan can easily become numb by the brutality of a war in which "the enemy" is difficult to identify and civilian casualties are dismissed as "collateral damage." The extent of damage to the psyches of U.S. soldiers is only now being recognized in the high rates of post-traumatic stress disorder being reported in returning veterans, especially in women.[1] For both men and women, seeing one's friends killed and wounded can engender an intense hatred of the enemy and anyone who looks like the enemy. U.S. soldiers frequently come to resent all Iraqis, even though they are the very people the soldiers were supposedly sent to "liberate." In such an environment, soldiers in charge of prisoners of war must be highly trained, supervised, and held to strict limitations, if prisoners are to be treated according to international and U.S. military standards.

Women in the military face additional challenges. One cannot understand the behavior of women involved in prisoner abuse without taking into account the general context in which they find themselves. The military is a dominance-based, hierarchical organization that encourages a devaluation of women and all things feminine. A successful soldier must learn to go along with a culture that glorifies dominance, masculinity, and aggression, and motivates hostility against "the enemy" in part by depicting "him" as weak and unmanly. Traits valued more than ever during times of warfare include toughness, aggressiveness, willingness to endure harassment and to maintain a code of silence. For women, military service in a war zone also means living in a hostile environment and experiencing harassment, sexist stereotyping, female-devaluing language, and even sexual assaults from fellow soldiers. A recent Amnesty International report puts it this way:

> *Military culture typically prizes aggression and reinforces male stereotypes, while devaluing attributes traditionally associated with women. Armed forces encourage male bonding and expressions of virility so that soldiers trust each other and resist any display of weakness in front of their peers, which is derided as "feminine." Male aggression towards women is often tacitly tolerated, or even encouraged, as raw recruits are turned into hardened "warriors" through a brutalizing training regime.[2]*

Women in such a quintessential patriarchal milieu are never fully integrated. To survive, they tend to take one of three general approaches. Some try to fit in, to be "one of the guys," as manly and aggressive as the men, enduring sexist behavior in silence and participating in or complying with the misogynistic culture and harassment of other women. This is the only way a woman can actually be accepted and promoted. She may be quite successful, trading in her humanity for a veneer of toughness in order to succeed and "belong." Even these women, however, are never as safely ensconced in the system as are men; their status as honorary men can come into question quickly if their identity becomes "spoiled" by feminine behavior or "weakness."

Other women survive by isolating themselves and trying to go it alone. They work hard to prove themselves and show themselves and others that they are fit members, doing their best to avoid situations of conflict. They do not participate in harassment, nor do they defend others who are harassed; they simply try to survive, mind their own business, and tough it out. Out of fear of reprisal, they seldom complain when harassed. Both this group and the first resent it when other women make waves and complain to officers about ill-treatment. They believe these complaints will only result in increased harassment of women.

The least likely approach taken by military women involves confronting the system of devaluation, registering complaints, and trying to stand up for themselves and others and for the rules. Women who follow this path are the least likely to be accepted and the most likely to experience retaliation and further harassment.

According to many reports, women deployed in Iraq and elsewhere suffer harassment, rape, sexual threats, and a general atmosphere of misogyny.[3] Most are afraid to report these incidents. When they do, they are more often than not told to keep silent, and nothing is done to the offending men. A recent example is U.S. Army Specialist Suzanne Swift, who refused to return to Iraq because of the serious sexual harassment and retaliation by her sergeants she experienced while stationed there. "When you are over there, you are lower than dirt, you are expendable as a soldier in general, and as a woman, it's worse," she said.[4] Low-ranking military women in a foreign deployment in an unpopular war, overwhelmingly outnumbered by men and living in this environment of sexism and harassment, find it difficult to refuse to go along with, much less oppose, abusive actions by their peers or unlawful orders by superiors.

Wide-Scale Abuse of Detainees in Iraq

By now there is ample evidence of widespread torture, abuse, and inhumane treatment in U.S. military engagements and detention centers,[5] but little public outcry has resulted except in the case of the Abu Ghraib scandal. There, the shocking photos were impossible to ignore, and public outrage demanded corrective action. Yet, in the absence of photos, and with consistent public claims that the United States "treats detainees humanely," there seems to be much less concern about frequent and credible reports of torture and abuse of prisoners by the U.S. military in Iraq, Afghanistan, and Guantánamo. Soldiers and officers who have engaged in or promoted abusive treatment of prisoners have rarely been disciplined or called to account.

Indeed, the few who complain or express doubts about the mistreatment of detainees are warned into silence. Denials and cover-ups appear to be more common than serious attempts to confront abuse and demand compliance with international law or standard U.S. military codes of conduct.[6] A recent report concludes that "detainee abuse was an established and apparently authorized part of detention and interrogation processes in Iraq for much of 2003–2005," and that those who tried to report it "faced systemic obstacles." Moreover, no adequate measures have been taken to stop reported abuses, nor have such cases been properly investigated, especially when they involve "officers who allowed abuses to occur on their watch."[7]

The fate of a few MPs at Abu Ghraib within this context seems to indicate that they were singled out not because of their actions, but because the distribution of the photographs made it impossible to maintain the pretense that such actions were not occurring. Widespread public outrage and disgust demanded a response. The high-profile prosecution of seven low-ranking MPs thus made it possible for the army to claim that it does not condone torture or approve inhumane treatment, and that these were just "a few bad apples" involved in an isolated case. Nevertheless, mistreatment of detainees has continued in this and other locations.[8]

Torture as Bonding Ritual

It's significant that of the seven soldiers convicted in the Abu Ghraib scandal, three were women. These women were all involved in less abusive behaviors than at least some of the men, and less abusive tactics than those that studies have documented are broadly used in Iraq, Afghanistan, and Guantánamo.[9] Most of the women involved in the actual tormenting of detainees at Abu Ghraib served mainly as *instruments* of masculine aggression, pawns in the game, responding to orders and encouragement by men who often held positions of authority over them. The prosecuted women acted primarily as "props," assistants, bystanders—taking photos or posing, acting as taunters, seducers, or observers in male-designed sexual humiliations of male detainees. Only occasionally and in relatively minor ways did the women join in the physical abuse, and there is no evidence that they were the instigators or directors of the abuse. Yet they were punished for going along, for being caught in the photos. It is certain that most—and the most serious—abusers in detainee centers are men, and that most of them have not been held accountable. Nor are their actions always disapproved by their ranking supervisors.

Women who willingly participate in such activities are, for the most part, attempting to join in a macabre male-bonding ritual, in which cohesion is established through acts of violence and humiliation toward "the other," in this case dehumanized prisoners of a despised race, culture, and language. Ironically, these misogynistic rituals were acted out in a way that depended on the devalued status of women, as male detainees were humiliated in part by being treated "as women"—sodomized with objects and forced to wear women's underwear. The victims' experience of being under the power of women, who could taunt them, observe them in sexually humiliating poses, and lead them about on a leash, was rendered even more degrading by their assumption that women are properly beneath men in status and authority. For the low-ranking women, their participation allowed them access to the inner circle of masculine solidarity and power, at least for a time. They were momentarily allowed into the game, in a survival strategy used by powerless women who hope to share in the status and camaraderie of their male friends. The degree to which they were eager participants rather than coerced by virtue of their lesser position in the rank order is unclear. Nevertheless, women who engage in this type of male-identified behavior are guilty of complicity in abhorrent dehumanizing and abusive actions, leaving them vulnerable not only to long-term feelings of remorse and shame, but to scapegoating and prosecution if their actions become known by the "wrong" people.

Perhaps the most famous and memorable photograph from the Abu Ghraib scandal is that of Lynndie England, cigarette held jauntily in her mouth, smiling and pointing to the genitals of a naked Iraqi man. This photo is impressive and shocking and helps obscure the reality behind it—that she was asked to pose, that she was not the one who directed the man to undress, that she did not beat him or threaten him with further physical abuse if he did not do as he was told. The photo provides a strong, emotional symbol of a perverse, out-of-control woman, who easily became a scapegoat for an entire system over which she had no control. As with the other women in the Abu Ghraib scandal, England was a minor actor, but she became the poster girl for the claim that these bad apples had to be punished.[10]

The participation of these women and men in their unit's atrocities did not occur in isolation, but was aided and abetted by permission and encouragement from higher authorities to "soften up" the detainees; by the widespread racist and dehumanizing attitudes of U.S. soldiers toward Iraqis in general; by the labeling of all Iraqi prisoners as terrorists; by the stress and anger at having to live under the harsh and demoralizing conditions of warfare in Iraq; and by the very banality of evil—once such actions begin taking place, they become routine, so are no longer shocking. As England said, sometimes prisoners were roughed up and humiliated "for fun."[11]

Senior Women as Collaborators

Senior women in the officer corps are in a very different social position from the lower-ranking women who were prosecuted, and similarly their relation to the practice of torture has been different. As women in powerful positions, senior officers with careers to protect usually rose up through the ranks by adopting the masculinist philosophies and practices of military culture. They help to plan, implement, and support the domination-based, abusive system. These women rarely make waves or question the actions or policies of their (mostly male) superiors and peers who decide to ignore the Geneva conventions or similar military rules about prisoner treatment. Their motivations to participate in the promotion of abusive practices may vary from a desire to protect their own privileged status as a member of the club of officers to a genuine belief that they are protecting "freedom" and opposing terrorism. Of course, their cooperation enhances the possibility of future promotion, and they may put their own careers at risk if they dare refuse to be a team player. By the time these women earn their higher positions, they usually identify strongly with the institution. Even if they should feel uncomfortable with the mistreatment taking place, they are also concerned with protecting the institution from embarrassment or disapproval. Thus, like their male peers, they are willing to engage in cover-ups and denials of activities that go against the rules, while seeking to silence any protest or publicity about questionable practices. On the other hand, in many cases, they appear to have few qualms about allowing the assault and humiliation of detainees in the interest of gaining "intelligence."

Two senior women have been strongly implicated in the harassment and abuse of detainees in Iraq and Afghanistan: Major General Barbara Fast and Captain Carolyn Wood. Fast was the head of military intelligence in Iraq during the period of most of the worst abuses (late 2003–2004). A 2006 Human Rights Watch report documents continuing brutality and abuse occurring at various locations in Iraq, much of which took place *after* the Abu Ghraib scandal. The report provides strong evidence that Fast had received credible reports of detainee abuse, had been warned to correct it, but had taken no action (or inadequate action) to do so.[12] Despite ample evidence of her awareness of the situation, Fast has received little attention from military investigators.[13] Rather than being held accountable, she has

been promoted "for her work in Iraq" and now serves as commander of the
U.S. Army Intelligence Center at Fort Huachuca, Arizona, helping to train a
new generation of soldiers in interrogation techniques.[14]

Wood was the chief military intelligence officer in Afghanistan during a
period in which serious prisoner torture and abuse took place, resulting in the
deaths of two detainees. A recent army investigation concluded that she lied
to investigators about the purposes of some of the more cruel and dangerous
practices.[15] In the fall of 2003, Wood was transferred to Abu Ghraib, where,
working with Lieutenant General Ricardo Sanchez, she helped draft the rules
of engagement for interrogators that contributed to the abuses at that prison.
Wood was strongly criticized by some investigations, but was not disciplined
for her role in prisoner abuse. Instead, she received two bronze stars for her
service in Afghanistan and Iraq, and later taught at the training facility for
army interrogators at Fort Huachuca.[16]

Who Gets Rewarded, Who Gets Punished?
The Politics of Scapegoating

The Bush administration and military leaders viewed the publication of the
now-infamous Abu Ghraib photos as a huge public relations debacle (an
image problem rather than a human rights issue). Someone had to take the
blame. There had to be the appearance of accountability and correction. So
who would take the fall? Not the military intelligence officers who directed
the low-ranking MPs to use harsh techniques. Certainly not higher-ranking
officers who developed guidelines that encouraged the use of dogs, sleep
deprivation, stress positions, and humiliation, and who maintained that the
Geneva conventions were not applicable. Instead, the low-ranking group,
the youngest and least educated, was singled out for blame, because of its
relatively powerless position and inability to resist.

Of the higher-ranking officers, only Army Reserve Brigadier General
Janis Karpinski has been punished, by demotion to the rank of colonel, even

though there is ample evidence of more direct involvement by other officers. Karpinski, who was in charge of detention centers in Iraq at the time, was unaware of the abuse at Abu Ghraib and unable to observe it, since it took place at night when travel to the facility was restricted. Moreover, her authority over the unit had been taken over by military intelligence. As a woman and a reservist, she was not part of the inner circle and was thus a convenient target for blame. Even the army inspector general's investigation admitted that she was not directly involved in the abuses and probably was unaware they were happening.[17] The investigators found her in "dereliction of duty" but also concluded that "no action or lack of action on her part contributed to the abuse of detainees at Abu Ghraib." Yet Karpinski would be the only senior officer punished in any way for the Abu Ghraib events. As her attorney commented, "They're saying she's the only senior leader that had any part in this, but they're saying she didn't have any direct part in it."[18]

The higher officers, responsible for formulating or promoting policies that encouraged abuse, on the other hand, were never punished; instead, many have been rewarded with promotions and other honors. Even more disturbing, when Bush administration representatives were asked about documented reports of inhumane and illegal practices, instead of denying or condemning them, they sometimes tried to *justify* them by labeling the detainees as "terrorists" or "very bad people," the implication being that such people deserve no rights.[19] In official pronouncements, the military continues to portray abuse cases as exceptional and abusers as independent "bad apples," in spite of "evidence that military intelligence officers and higher-echelon military and civilian leaders knew about or even authorized abusive techniques."[20] Their denials and obfuscation have stood in the way of attempts to hold violators accountable and to stop the abuse.

Among the higher-ranking officers and civilian officials most closely implicated in the torture of detainees, the majority has *not* been held accountable and has, in fact, been rewarded. Two examples are Major General

Geoffrey Miller and Lieutenant General Sanchez. Originally in charge of interrogations at Guantánamo, Miller is credited with introducing dogs and other abusive tactics to Abu Ghraib, which he helped set up in September 2003. More recently, it has been reported that many of the techniques for which the Abu Ghraib MPs were prosecuted had previously been used at Guantánamo while Miller was there, further evidence that the Abu Ghraib guards did not make up their procedures on their own.[21] Miller was never punished for his actions, despite a recommendation by Pentagon investigators that he be disciplined.[22] Instead, he was placed in charge of detention operations in Iraq in April 2004 and later accepted a Pentagon post. In August 2006, he was awarded the Distinguished Service Medal by President Bush. This honor, given for "exceptional and meritorious service to the government" beyond the call of duty, was scathingly condemned by a *New York Times* editorial in view of Miller's questionable record.[23]

Sanchez, who oversaw detention centers in Iraq, was strongly criticized in Pentagon investigations for his mishandling of interrogation procedures and policies, among other failures of leadership. He authorized a number of interrogation techniques used at Abu Ghraib, including intimidation by dogs, the use of stress positions, and isolation, going well beyond standard acceptable practice. As with Miller, no disciplinary action was taken despite harsh criticism of his conduct. Instead Sanchez was awarded a fourth bronze star and now heads the army's V Corps in Europe.[24]

The list of officers and civilian leaders who have been implicated in prisoner abuse in Iraq and other U.S. military sites is vast. The lack of accountability in these cases, as compared to the plight of the few prosecuted in the Abu Ghraib scandal, supports the conclusion that the Abu Ghraib defendants and Karpinski were scapegoats for a system that continues to promote abuse and illegal detentions. That women were more likely to be punished than the many men more directly and seriously involved exposes the still-tenuous role of women in the military.

There is evidence that some (both men and women) are able to resist requests to participate in unlawful and abusive actions. For example, Specialist Kayla Williams, who wrote of her experiences in her book, *Love My Rifle More Than You*, participated in one interrogation in which she was directed to sexually humiliate an Iraqi prisoner. Unaware of what her role would be when she entered the interrogation room, she became very uncomfortable with what happened. Williams refused to participate in any more interrogations. But socially, she was in a different place than the women of Abu Ghraib. She was asked, not ordered, to participate; she was not assigned to MP duties; and she had more personal resources with which to refuse: She was older, a college graduate, a military intelligence specialist, and generally a more independent and assertive person who was aware of her rights.[25]

—⟶

Women in the military are in a highly dominance-oriented, hierarchical institution that engenders and reinforces sexism, misogyny, and harassment of those who are perceived as different. The conditions in military detention centers and prisons encourage dehumanization, much of it intentional and part of the system as planned by higher-ranking officers in the interest of obtaining "intelligence." The entire system generates and relies on an atmosphere of racism and sexism. In this context, some women, in order to survive and fit in, become willing participants in misogynistic and racist actions against prisoners. They become the instruments of masculine aggression toward others; they become helpers and assistants whose role is to increase the suffering and humiliation of the male "enemy."

Other women, at higher levels, buy into the culture and participate because that is where the rewards are. They have become part of the military culture and thus are useful to the male officer corps, which can then claim that they are inclusive. Their careers can be enhanced by their participation in these operations, and they maintain clear consciences by redefining abusive techniques as necessary to the larger goal of intelligence, toughness, protection of the institution, and defeat of the terrorists.

Finally, when public embarrassment due to exposure occurs, some people will be singled out for public punishment to show that the military "takes these things seriously." The men who are punished are typically at the bottom of the system, including not only low ranks but typically reservists rather than regular soldiers. Yet the MPs at Abu Ghraib, as well as those in many locations in Iraq and elsewhere, consistently say they were following orders and the techniques they employed were allowed, approved, and demanded by those in higher ranks. The evidence bears them out. Meanwhile, those who designed the procedures have been left untouched. Women of lower status and rank may be most likely to be singled out for punishment, but women at *any* rank may be vulnerable.

Just as men can become torturers given the "right" conditions, so can women. But women in the military are in a more powerless position, more vulnerable to pressures to conform, and more likely to suffer negative consequences if caught. The most sadistic and physical abuse is still carried out by men, while women are usually involved as coparticipants in sexual harassment, humiliation, and other less central roles, usually under the direction of men. It's still a man's army, and women who join are caught in a web of misogyny where only the very strongest can survive unscathed.

The problem of women engaged in these abuses highlights the problem with so-called liberal feminism, which calls for equality for women and men without examining the institutions in which women are to be integrated. Many feminists in recent decades have recognized this, calling for justice not only for gender-related issues, but also in terms of nation, race, class, and other dimensions of social inequality. Many women have pressed for better treatment of women in the military. However, under current conditions, I could not in good conscience encourage any woman (or man) to join this institution, which promotes and condones torture, abuse, and deception in the pursuit of questionable goals. In the final analysis, militarism itself is the root problem—the entire notion that it is heroic to use violence and massive force against a government-defined enemy. In its essence, militarism is always associated with abuse, racism, misogyny, heterosexism, short-sighted patriotism, and objectification of "enemy" nations.

Many people have commented on the negative impact prisoner abuses have had on the image of the United States in the world and, in light of our ignoring the Geneva conventions, on the potential danger to our soldiers should they become prisoners of war in the future. But a more immediate issue for Americans is the potential impact that the torture, degradation, and humiliation of other human beings will have on young soldiers themselves. What will be the impact on their families, their communities, and our nation when they return having learned to practice extremes of cruelty and violence? Will men who have treated others (including some women prisoners) savagely come home to be kind, gentle lovers, husbands, and fathers; or will they believe that violence is a legitimate way to deal with others? Will they believe that women's sexuality is a tool to be used for men's purposes, as it has been in the prisons of Iraq? Will the constant atmosphere of misogyny and homophobia on which much of the humiliation is based become ingrained permanently in their minds? At the very least, both men and women who participate in these horrors will carry the images in their minds throughout their lives, with unknown consequences for their mental, spiritual, moral, and physical well-being and that of those around them.

Lynndie England in Love

Janis Karpinski (as told to Tara McKelvey)

Lynndie England arrived at Abu Ghraib in late October. It was still warm outside. She came in a carload of about twenty soldiers, and on their way to the prison, they hit an Improvised Explosive Device. It didn't hurt them. But it was a real "Welcome to Baghdad" moment. We first met in the battalion headquarters. It was a room with high ceilings. All the windows were blown out. I said hello. They had this wide-eyed, scared look—as if they were saying, "Oh, do you realize we just hit a bomb on the way here?"

That's when I met England. I shook her hand. I remember that her hand was very small. She was small, you know. Not assertive or aggressive. She seemed nondescript. Honestly, she was young and innocent. And I know those words don't seem to apply to those pictures she was in. When I touched her, I felt fear. I could just feel it. There was a tension in her and in all the people in the group—even the men. They had this need for physical touch. You want someone to comfort you. You want to say, "Make this stop. It's making me crazy."

I tried to reassure them. "Conditions are improving every day," I said.

I know she's from West Virginia. She was working the night shift in a chicken-processing plant. That was her future unless she found a way out. She joined the army reserve for the college money. She went through basic training. Then she went back to the orderly unit in the United States. She was very quiet while she was there. She didn't know anybody at the time. She probably felt inferior because she was working alongside military police. They seemed more important than she did. Also, she recognized her own mental limitations. I don't mean she's retarded. But she's slow.

Enter Charles Graner. Their paths cross for the first time. He's thirty-two. And he's full of himself. He's just got that kind of personality. He comes into the room and says, "England? Are you from England?"

She is blown away. He is joking around with her. She feels like someone is talking to her. Paying attention. He seems far more experienced and worldly than anyone she knows. It only takes a few short conversations. She is enamored of him. Two weeks after they meet, they spend a long weekend together and get drunk. "Take off your clothes and we'll take some pictures," Graner tells her. She does it. Everybody knows about it, and they deploy them anyway.

She ends up at Abu Ghraib, and they send for Graner. They tell him to work in Cellblock 1A on the night shift. Why? Because they know he'll be a willing participant when interrogators say, "Do this. Do that."

One of the unfortunate things I've seen is that young female soldiers are often not equipped or trained to face these kinds of things in the military. The first thing they'll look for is a protector—a senior male, let's say, who's sitting in a vehicle with her. She says, "I'm really afraid." And he says, "Don't worry." This closeness starts to develop. It's intentional on the male's part. And unintentional or naive on the part of the female. England is small. Graner is a big, hunky guy. He can probably put his arms around her and touch his shoulders. Does she feel safe with him? Yes. And all she has to do is be sexually wild with him. Someone catches them in England's room. They're both asleep on the cot. They are reminded that they are supposed to stay away from each other. She has been told not to fraternize with Graner. But she doesn't care if she loses her rank. One night in early November, some people in the hard site decide they are going to take pictures. They'd heard about the female interrogators at Guantánamo Bay.

Someone says, "Do you know any women we can get to do this stuff?"

And Graner says something like, "I know just the person."

Graner tells England to come over to Cellblock 1A. She is an administrative person. Not an MP. There is no reason for her to be in the hard site. But they send a vehicle over to get her from her quarters. Someone tells her, "Graner says to come over. He has something for your birthday."

"I have something for your birthday," he says.

She goes over there and they ask for her help. "Give us the thumbs-up," they say. "Give us a smile."

I first saw the photos in my office at Camp Victory in Baghdad. A colonel came to my office with a folder. When I opened it, the first thing I saw was a human pyramid with England. I was shocked. I felt like the whole world was caving in on me. I remember feeling absolutely cold. There is little Lynndie England, looking like some two-bit prison marm with that cigarette dangling out of her throat and her thumbs up. She's looking at Graner.

Why did she do it? You have to understand that it builds to a crescendo. They're away from the flagpole. She'd been working in a chicken factory, where she saw blood and guts all the time. Now they're at Abu Ghraib—the most terrible place. You're drained of every bit of compassion you have. Especially if you're a female. You breathe dust and broken concrete all the time. It's hot. You feel dehumanized. You're being mortared every night, and then these people come in their dark T-shirts, spouting authority from Washington, D.C.

She did it because she wanted to come back from this godforsaken war and say, "This is what we did. We did this for the spooks. We did this for the

FBI." That's what she and Graner had been told: "We have this authority from the highest levels of the U.S. government." She was made to believe that this was of such importance to national security. It was, you know, *You stick with me, kid, and you might even win a medal.*

Then they told her they needed pictures. You're in a different frame of mind.

Also, she wanted Graner to be happy. It was a relationship based on a kind of bizarre excitement with strong sexual undertones. She wanted to please him. She would do anything he asked her or told her to do. She thought, *Graner would never tell me the wrong thing. I'm sleeping with him. I trust him.* She was thinking, *I'm a modern woman because I'm not afraid to deal with my sexuality and to do all these things Graner asks me to do.* And it somehow made her less afraid. Maybe those are characteristics people would normally associate with men. I guess she was envious of a person like Graner. He's bold and belligerent and sexually aggressive, and she wanted to pattern herself after this guy.

I didn't feel sorry for her when I first saw her in the pictures. I didn't feel sorry for anybody in those pictures except for the Iraqis. But now I do. It's grossly unfair that these soldiers were labeled "seven bad apples" and tried in the world court. How dare Bush reduce this scandal to seven bad apples. She's now serving three years. She probably wonders herself today why she did that stuff.

The Military Made Me Do It: Double Standards and Psychic Injuries at Abu Ghraib

Lila Rajiva

And these American prisoners of war—have you people noticed who
the torturers are? Women! The babes! The babes are meting out the
torture. You know, if you look at—if you, really, if you look at these
pictures, I mean, I don't know if it's just me, but it looks just like
anything you'd see Madonna or Britney Spears do onstage.

—Rush Limbaugh [1]

Rush Limbaugh was not alone in whitewashing the "babes of Abu Ghraib."
The icon of right-wing talk radio was joined by other conservatives, including
a feminine troika—Ann Coulter, Peggy Noonan, and Linda Chavez. They
too saw the young women caught taunting naked Iraqi men on camera not
as individuals doing something wrong but as the products of culture—and in
that sense victims.

The Female Gaze

Victims of what? Integration of the military, it turns out. And for a mix of reasons, each of which—like a Rorschach test—seems to say more about the pundit offering it than about the prison scandal in Iraq.

For Coulter, never one to pass up rhetorical shrapnel, Abu Ghraib proves the failure of integration, and the primary reason is because "in addition to not being able to carry even a medium-sized backpack, women are too vicious."[2] It says something about the responses to the torture that this is actually one of the more coherent arguments.

On the other hand, Republican speechwriter Peggy Noonan has no problem with women in the military provided they stay in traditional roles—supporting the men, but keeping their distance: "[Lynndie England] looks coarse, cruel, perhaps drunk. And as I looked at her I thought, 'Oh, no. This is not equality but mutual degradation.' Can anyone imagine a WAC of 1945, or a WAVE of 1965, acting in this manner? I can't. Because WACs and WAVEs were not only members of the American armed forces, which responsibility brought its own demands in terms of dignity and bearing; they were women. They apparently did not think they had to prove they were men, or men at their worst. I've never seen evidence to suggest the old-time WACs and WAVEs had to delve down into some coarse and vulgar part of their nature to fit in, to show they were one of the guys, as tough as the guys, as ugly at their ugliest."[3]

Substituting a few words here and there, this deliciously loaded argument—that it is mostly men who make women bad—would have been summarily dismissed as fringe radicalism had it come out of the mouth of a progressive feminist like Barbara Ehrenreich. As a matter of fact, in a piece included in this anthology, Ehrenreich herself confesses that it was just this sort of naiveté about women's innate morality that died at Abu Ghraib.

Still, at least Noonan's women do have some coarse and vulgar part to them, even if they have to role-play that they don't or have to delve down deep to get at it; even if, as usual, boys will be boys; and even if Noonan has no problem characterizing what that means—tough and ugly. Men—tough and ugly. That's how far cultural conservatism has strayed from the tradition of the gentleman—a tradition that began with the knights *sans peur et sans reproche* of the Round Table and puttered out, I suppose, in Edwardian England with *The Code of the Woosters.*

In contrast, Noonan's men are only brutes doing what brutes do best, and the women ought to have known better and played Florence Nightingale from a genteel distance.

Stay remote. Keep busy. Never ever get too familiar. Call it "The Rules" for Abu Ghraib.

Linda Chavez, syndicated columnist and FOX News Channel political analyst, goes one better. It's not that women ought to have distinct and separate roles. It's that they shouldn't even be there at all.

> But one factor that may have contributed—but which I doubt investigators will want to even consider—is whether the presence of women in the unit actually encouraged more misbehavior, especially of the sexual nature that the pictures reveal. . . . Take a look at the faces of those soldiers again, especially the female soldiers. . . . They look like they're showing off at some wild party, trying to impress everybody with how "cool" they are.[4]

Here "mutual degradation" has gone the full route. The presence of men has reduced the women to moral idiots. But the opposite is also true. The men also are just showing off. It's sexual tension that stirs up trouble for both men and women. The problem isn't simply the integration of the military. It's the integration of the sexes.

I don't know if Chavez realizes the implication of what she is saying—which is that left to their own devices with no women looking on, men would never cut up. On their own, they would never tear walls down. It's women watching that causes the trouble.

Where this novel theory of the female gaze leaves all the raping and pillaging that have accompanied the males-only wars that dominate human history is something she doesn't address, needless to say. Was there really a Helen looking on behind every one of them? And what does that do to the usual conservative argument about the civilizing effect of women on men? Is Chavez really arguing for military burqa?

Meanwhile, some male commentators go even further and point the finger beyond the baneful influence of the military, at feminist culture in general. Thus, George Neumayr, managing editor of the *American Spectator:*

> *The image of that female guard, smoking away as she joins gleefully in the disgraceful melee like one of the guys, is a cultural outgrowth of a feminist culture which encourages female barbarians.*[5]

Female barbarians: Ah, now there we have the real engine of the defense-industrial complex.

What is most remarkable is to hear these cultural conservatives, who never fail to argue for individual responsibility in other contexts, offer such a range of excuses for the actions of the women in the pictures. There is nothing remotely similar said in defense of the men. Instead, they are instantaneously dismissed as a few rotten apples, with no indictment at all of the culture that produced them.

Apparently conservatives—like radical feminists—think women are inherently more moral than men, inherently more peaceful, inherently more considerate of others, inherently less capable of coarseness as well as of cruelty . . . and yet also inherently less responsible than men.

Two Faces of Eve

Among conservatives, this argument for women's simultaneous moral superiority and moral imbecility is of course assumed to be derived from religion. The major religions, according to traditionalists, demand that we hold women to higher supernatural standards—but to lower natural ones. Women stand on pedestals . . . not because they climbed up there themselves, but because they were placed there by God . . . or men . . . or both. And one of the two will have to answer for it if women ever clamber down . . . or fall off.

Now, of course there has always been a rich treasure of imagery in religion and mythology glorifying the female moral nature. Of course there are countless myths about the innate purity, the supernal and selfless character of women. In the West, we have Beatrice lighting the way to Dante's heaven and faithful Penelope waiting silently at the hearth for Ulysses to return; in the East, there is Sita whose chastity withstands fire and Savitri whose love withstands death.

The trouble with looking to religion for an explanation of female nature is that for every text that idealizes women, one can find a counter-text that denigrates them. For every loyal Ruth, there is a treacherous Jezebel.

"Where women are honored, there the gods are pleased; but where they are not honored no sacred rite yields rewards," says the Manu Smriti III:56 of Hinduism.

But then there is the Tulasi Ramayana, Aranya Kanda 5:AB, also a Hindu scripture: "A woman is impure by her very birth; but she attains a happy state by serving her lord (husband)."

Thus, among Jewish texts, the Bereshit Rabbah 17:2 states, "It was taught: He who has no wife dwells without good, without help, without joy, without blessing, and without atonement."

But the Avodah Zarah 36b, in the Judaic Torah, has this: "The daughters of the [heathens] should be considered as in the state of niddah [filth] from their cradle. . . ."

In a revolutionary act in sixth-century-BC India, Buddha founded an order for nuns as well as monks. But he taught that a woman could never become a fully enlightened being. "A woman's heart is haunted by stinginess . . . jealousy . . . sensuality," says the Anguttaranikâya iv:8, iv:10.

While Jesus included women among his disciples and talked to them as equals, both the Old and the New Testaments have their misogynistic moments: "Give not thy strength unto women," counsels Proverbs 31:3, while I Peter 3:7 refers to women as "the weaker vessel."

Likewise, Islam, despite its relatively enlightened attitude to female property rights, contributes this gem:

> *The Prophet said, "I looked at Paradise and found poor people forming the majority of its inhabitants; and I looked at Hell and saw that the majority of its inhabitants were women."*[6]

It would be convenient to see in these contradictory texts the source of the schizophrenic polemics that both denounced and exculpated the female torturers of Abu Ghraib, but on closer examination, the link between dogma and social practice turns out to be much more complicated and tenuous.

Take for instance something that most people do not immediately associate with the pornographic barbarism at Saddam's old prison—the practice of female feticide, or the selective killing of unborn girls. Female feticide is so rampant in India that the female-to-male ratio there is the lowest in the world. One might call it a regressive social evil, not a crime; comparing it to Abu Ghraib might be misleading, true, but this does not prevent feticide from also being a form of torture, one in which women figure both as victims and perpetrators. Placing the torture in Iraq in the continuum of such cruelty helps one see that it makes little sense to look to religious notions to condemn or excuse female behavior.

While it might at first be plausible to blame female feticide on Hinduism, skewed sex ratios are also a severe problem in China, which has no equivalent religious dogma. Furthermore, while feticide is generally more prevalent among Hindus than among Buddhists and Christians, it seems more closely connected to other social practices among Hindus than to specific religious requirements. It is widely practiced, for instance, among warrior tribes, where the prestige of having sons derives from the ethos of fighting men; and the stigma of bearing daughters derives from the burden of hypergamy—the practice of marrying women into a higher social class, which requires that their families give them huge dowries.

Like those other forms of torture—infanticide and dowry killing—in which females are often both victims and perpetrators, feticide is more closely linked to illiteracy and poverty than anything else.

Ergo, both radical feminists and conservatives might want to rethink any facile linking of religion and social practice. Progressives might begin to see that religion has provided a convenient post hoc rationalization for oppression or even murder, but that the crimes themselves are rooted in power relations, not merely dogma. And conservatives might note that when women are elevated in religious texts, it is usually only after they have already won some independence and equality to men in the real world first. So, it really won't do for conservatives to appeal to the female ideal they find in religion, without first encouraging the behavior that makes that ideal possible.

Barbie/Barbarella

Female empowerment is the prerequisite for feminine idealization, not its outcome. And accepting responsibility for one's own actions is the first step toward empowerment. To fault Lynndie England, Megan Ambuhl, and Sabrina Harman for failing to live up to their ideal female selves while at the same time absolving them of any responsibility for that failure is to demand cherubs on one hand and outlaw wings on the other. The truth is that the feminine ideal of the religious texts—the woman whose moral strength is a beacon to those around her—has to grow from more fertile soil than the eyelash-batting "belle" of Noonan's nostalgia or the lewder-than-thou "guy" of Chavez's fears. Or even the "mean queen"—the spiteful, narrow-minded shrew—of Ms. Coulter.

And yet, what is it about Coulter's sardonic barb that seems to break down the belle and the barbarian, Barbie and Barbarella, the rules follower and the rule breaker? That seems much more authentic than either?

Very simply, it's this: Both the belle and the barbarian are ultimately driven by the dance of the sexes. The belle's poses are struck to snag a husband, the barbarian's to tease a playmate. While the belle withholds sex to manipulate, the barbarian pours it on to overpower. One uses subtle fraud; the other uses outright force. One undermines resistance to pursue long-term security; the other overwhelms resistance to pursue short-term pleasure. One is socially approved, the other socially derided. Conservatives at least would see the first as socially productive and the other as socially destructive.

But ignore for the moment the moral or social implications of the behavior of belle and barbarian, and it's clear that each is pursuing the same thing—power over the male, only through different strategies. The belle sacrifices short-term for long-term power; the barbarian sacrifices the long term for the short term.

In contrast, Coulter's contemptuously self-reliant shrew surely displays a form of autonomy. It may not be the best kind, but at least it's one that escapes the mating game altogether. The shrew neither stalks a husband nor provokes a sex partner. Even if she might only be the product of curdled sex, the curdling is salutary, for it throws her back on her own resources. Rooted in separateness, her spitefulness at least has the potential to eventually move her into her own moral center. But that potential is completely lost to the others, who feed on the power of sexuality and pay the price by losing their autonomy.

Virtual Violence

It is to that loss of autonomy that conservative critics react instinctively. It is why they find excuses for the women soldiers so readily, ignoring the fact that it was the women themselves who had forfeited their autonomy in favor of sexual power play, in which they were not victims at all but willing and equal participants. Indeed, if the expressions on their faces are to be believed, they held the upper hand.

But conservatives translate lack of autonomy into diminished culpability. The fault is not the women's but that of feminism, for enslaving the women to their own sexual appetites.

At the other end of the political spectrum, many progressives, focusing only on the women's lowly status in the military, make another sort of mistake. They misattribute the sexual misbehavior to the masculine hierarchy of the military. Progressives translate lack of female institutional power into diminished culpability. It is not the fault of the women but of the patriarchy, for subjecting women to masculine sexual appetites.

But neither feminism nor male chauvinism is to blame. What conservatives and progressives fail to see is that the women soldiers of Abu Ghraib were not merely impressing the men around them unconsciously, but consciously reveling in their power. That they were young and few in number was not a mark of weakness at all but of the considerable status they enjoyed among men deprived of family life and female companionship. Our female torturers were clearly not reluctant ciphers, but willing and enthusiastic participants.

And their age is no defense. To the contrary, it has usually been young people who have been more idealistic, not adults. Joe Darby, who slipped a CD of the pictures under a superior's door in January 2004, is young; Rachel Corrie, who was killed while peacefully protesting the demolition of homes in Palestine, was twenty-one. As young and lowly as they are, the female torturers of Abu Ghraib cannot be passed off as victims.

But we fail to see this because we continue to think of sex in terms of male domination and female submission, male culpability and female victimhood. Having been conditioned to think of sexuality in terms of genitality and a specific model of genitality—one characteristic of the young male—we think in terms of penetration and conquest and see women as its victims. Sex, even "normal" sex, is still something done to women. And aggression or rape is the underlying model—something evident from vernacular or slang terms for the act. Perhaps trying to compensate for the harshness of traditional society toward transgressive female sexual behavior, progressives especially have come to see women as perpetually victimized. And when one considers sex crimes such as trafficking, rape, and domestic abuse—in which it's mainly women who suffer the worst physical consequences—or considers regressive social practices such as honor killing and female genital mutilation, it may, in fact, seem as if women are always the cardinal, and even sole, victims of sexual offenses.

This is a serious error. And I suggest that it is an error caused by an assumption in modern Western culture that only tangible physical harms merit the status of real injuries, an assumption, moreover, applied with great inconsistency. On some subjects, of course, there's an educated consensus that there are real injuries that are psychic or emotional. The Geneva conventions, for instance, considers extreme humiliation, religious persecution, and sexual taunting to be real injuries. Under UN human rights protocols, the destruction of culture—through attacks on language, ethnic customs, and heritage—is even considered to be a form of genocide. And some types of racial or sexual baiting have become completely unacceptable, at least in polite society. Nonetheless, the popular feeling is that such sensitivity is, at best, political correctness and not worthy of serious inquiry and, at worst, zealotry and a form of censorship. To illustrate this, consider how many severe mental illnesses have only recently been given the same level of attention as physical illnesses.

Ironically, on this matter, the CIA is far ahead of popular understanding. Through its Cold War research into behavior modification and interrogation methods, it long ago proved that psychic injury, verbal abuse, and other forms of "no-touch torture" are actually more deeply traumatic and long-lasting than more common types of physical brutality. Because they tend to be invisible, these techniques are also more acceptable and more effective for the purposes of an intelligence service in a democracy—where public opinion is crucial. Yet, the CIA also believes that no-touch torture ("torture lite") is far more deeply antihuman in its premises than conventional torture, because it attacks the very identity of the individual and denies one access to one's own consciousness, volition, and moral sense.

Admit the seriousness and reality of psychic injury, and we can no longer see women as only victims and men as only perpetrators in sex-related or family crimes. It is generally true that men do the most physical damage in such cases, but that is mainly because they are far stronger physically and more protected socioeconomically, and not because of any monopoly they have on malice. In fact, even physical altercations can be initiated by women. And as far as emotional or psychological abuse goes, women can do as much damage, given their well-established superiority in verbal and relational skills.

More pertinent to Abu Ghraib, admitting the reality of psychic injury allows us to see that women can also use sex as a weapon as often as men, although in different ways. A whole range of behaviors, then, no longer seems completely harmless, as free speech fundamentalists would have us believe, and those who perpetrate them no longer seem completely innocent. In short, it becomes impossible to pass off Abu Ghraib as simply "good old American pornography," as Rush Limbaugh did.

What happened in the detention cells was, of course, pornography, American, and "old"—in the sense of well-worn—but there was nothing good about it. And when we see it ripped out of the frame of entertainment and inflicted on people not conditioned by nonstop exposure to accept it as healthy fun, when we see it with the glossy mask ripped off its face, with each coarse smirk, pout, and gesture in ugly relief, we see it for what it is—vicious and intended to hurt and degrade. If people still feel the need to defend the perpetrators, it is only because the victims were men, and Arab men at that. It is only because the injury is seen as mostly psychic and therefore—in our still-shoddy understanding of the psyche—trivial or even laughable. Reverse roles and imagine Iraqi men torturing foreign women in that way and you immediately understand the real nature of what happened. (Of course, a strong argument could be made that that is precisely why we have never seen pictures of women being tortured at all. The outcry would be far too great and whatever humanitarian rationale remains for the Iraq invasion would be shredded for good.)

Ultimately, we are compelled to admit that it was not because they were powerless that the women acted as they did, but because they were exulting in their power—exulting both in the voluntary submission of their fellow soldiers to their sexual power (witness the sex videos of Lynndie with numerous partners) as well as in the coerced submission of the male prisoners. The triumph of the women lay in eliciting a response from men who did not want to give it. It was just this reduction of human beings to objects without their own wills that made them gloat. And their gloating made what they did at Abu Ghraib pornographic in essence and not merely in incidentals. Much as we might find a reason to excuse these women torturers because their superiors had set the tone and policy, the fact remains that they could have exhibited their moral autonomy and refused to obey criminal orders. That, instead, these young women chose to participate in criminal behavior and did so with glee tells us that they were enjoying the exercise of their unfettered power on those weaker than they. That makes them not victims . . . but victimizers, bearing as much moral guilt as the male guards around them.

Afterword

Cynthia Enloe

"Women Mud Wrestling Tonight!" What is there that is so enticing about women engaging in either real or faux violence? *Enticing*, of course, shouldn't be confused with *intellectually thought-provoking*. The analytical essays you've just read in this collection seriously address three issues: first, popular culture's inordinate (one might say unseemly, sometimes obscene) fascination with women who engage in physical violence; second, the causal dynamics and consequences of particular women taking part in particular acts of violence; and third, the relationship between the two. It's these thinkers' determination to explore these connections that makes this a distinctly *feminist* conversation.

We each read and think within history. I've been reading and mulling over this feminist conversation about women as wielders of violence during a time when a tsunami of human-perpetrated violence seems to have been sweeping over the globe. Every day during these last few weeks, as I've been digesting these provocative essays, there has been an emergent civil war in

U.S.-occupied Iraq. Reporters have been making the Baghdad city morgue a regular stop on their daily beat. The numbers of civilians being wounded and killed has risen in Afghanistan as armed violence there has escalated. Military commanders in Afghanistan were dismissing as "inevitable" American pilots' "friendly fire" killing and wounding Canadian soldiers on the ground. In Sri Lanka, a fragile ceasefire has been coming unraveled, perpetuating a twenty-five-year war. The equally tenuous ceasefire between the government of Israel and the forces of Lebanon-based Hezbollah remained untested seriously. The Kurdish communities in southeastern Turkey have also been living the lives of people caught in the never-never land of an unstable ceasefire. In Colombia, the Congo, and Chechnya, violent clashes have continued to displace thousands of civilians.

And, during all this time, as I was preparing for my new fall seminar, talking with graduate students, writing manuscript reviews, and taking these essays to read at my favorite Cambridge café, women with their dependent children continued to risk death, wounding, and sexual assault in Darfur, the besieged southern province of Sudan, at the hands of government troops, aircraft, and allied militias.

Yes, one's brain goes numb even trying to stay attentive while reading such paragraphs. Still, one of the stunning common threads running through these current horrors is that virtually all of the immediate wielders of militarized violence here—in Sudan, Congo, Colombia, Chechnya/Russia, Palestine, Turkey, Lebanon, Israel, Sri Lanka, Iraq, and Afghanistan—are male. So why create—and, as a reader, join in—a feminist conversation now about women's relationships to the wielding of violence? Isn't feminists' attention more productively focused on militarized masculinities?

Yet that's always been the distracting argument, hasn't it? Why pay attention to the handful of women bankers when most bankers are men and the culture of local and global banking is so masculinized? Why pay attention to the scattering of women in the construction trades when most construction workers in most countries are men? Why pay attention to the 2 percent or 14 percent or even 27 percent of women elected to their countries' legislatures when the majority of the world's legislative bodies remain so stubbornly male-dominated? Are women acting in deeply masculinized roles interesting in the way Dr. Johnson dismissively said a dancing dog is interesting—just as a curiosity, a freakish sideshow?

Here is what feminist analysts have found: Taking women in male-dominated and/or masculinized settings seriously yields significant explanatory rewards. By investing genuine curiosity in women as a minority, even as the "first" or the "only," in any sociopolitical arena, makes visible the men-as-men there.

When there are only men in the proverbial landscape (or when one glibly imagines that there are only men there), one often only sees race, ethnicity, generation, class, nationality, or partisan attachments. Seeing these dynamics at work, of course, is itself demanding. In fact, studies of all-male groups and arenas rarely delve into the possible workings of all of these dynamics. Since gender—the workings of masculinities (often rival masculinities) and femininities (and fears of feminization)—has been even easier to overlook, taking women seriously in a male-dominated setting has the great advantage of making men and their presumptions visible.

Feminist analysts have also taught us that devoting time and thought to women in spaces and in roles "unbecoming for a woman" makes clear how much effort has been expended to keep women out of those spaces and roles. Most of the padlocks of the patriarchal doors have been hard to discern. In business, feminists have tried to capture this phenomenon of the hard-to-see exclusionary barriers by coining the phrase "glass ceiling." These structures—and their complementary practices and rituals—of masculinized exclusion are far more likely to be seen and thus examined when a few women pick the lock or, surprisingly, are invited into the exclusivist room. It is then that one is more likely to ask what the padlock was made of, who designed it, who kept its machinery oiled, and why hadn't more women long ago tried to pick it, or just dig under the door?

It is then, too, that "tokenism" is likely to be taken seriously as an object of exploration. It is then that women's agency is most likely to be thoughtfully weighed: Are these women (in the masculinized state military, in the masculinized paramilitary or militia, in the masculinized insurgency) only imagining that they are carving out wider spaces in which to enact their own commitments, while in reality their presence is part of a conscious strategy crafted by the still-controlling masculinized leadership? How can we tell? Or maybe there will ensue a tug-of-war between the masculinized strategists and their feminized tokens, with unexpected consequences for everyone.

Reading all of these essays together—avoiding the temptation to just cherry-pick among them—confirms and adds nuance to a third feminist revelation. That is: Making women in masculinized spaces and roles the objects of genuine curiosity can serve to underscore the complexity in the politics of femininities. Yes, *femininity* in the plural. Theorists and observers of women's marginalization have made explicit the diversity and the downright tensions between women—women of the imperialist and the colonized societies, women on opposite sides of political borders when state-vs.-state wars break out, women of the poor, debt-ridden rural regions, women of the working classes in the smoky industrializing towns, women of the emergent aspirant middle classes, and women of the cloistered but cushioned landed aristocracy, with their country estates and town mansions—all under the same state authority but relating to it (and being maneuvered by it) in quite distinct ways.

Feminist scholars of India, Japan, Britain, Egypt, the U.S., Canada, Mexico, Chile, Morocco, Poland, Germany, France, Turkey, the Philippines, Israel, Brazil, Korea, Bangladesh, Iran, and South Africa have given us libraries full of lively, nuanced studies of how these differences and tensions have played themselves out in state policies, state debates, state transformations, nationalist movements, social reform and cultural movements, peace movements, suffragist movements, labor movements, human rights movements, and pro-democracy movements.

Of course, there have been times when the yearning for solidarity among women has become so intense (or seemed so urgently needed), or when the evidence of localized or globalized misogyny has become so stark, that these differences and tensions among women have been underestimated. But the overwhelming body of feminist literature has served to open our eyes to these differences and their resultant tensions.

So, when we read here of women's diverse relationships to the wielding of violence, we should not be surprised. States and insurgencies have long needed diverse femininities to make systematic violence "work." And to achieve this, there have had to be complementary (though not allied) plural femininities. Just start a list of all the diverse notions, standards, and practices of femininity it takes today, for instance, simply to maintain any one state's military base: the femininity constructed by and for those civilian working-class (and racialized or ethnicized?) women canteen and laundry workers keeping the base personnel fed and clean; the femininity of the nurses in the base hospital; the femininity of the military wives of enlisted men; the femininity of the wives of the male officers; the femininity of the women enlisted soldiers; the femininity of the women officers; the femininity of women as mothers of the male and the female soldiers, trying to keep their sons and daughters engaged with them despite their remote lives; the femininity of the local civilian women working in the bars and discos outside the base; the femininity of the middle-class civilian women of the base town. It is keeping this plurality of femininities working in and around the wieldings of violence that encourages us to follow the bread crumbs between the women so thoughtfully analyzed here and other women.

One of the Guys is a book for our times. It is also a book intended by its contributors and editor to foster a conversation with the smart feminist thinking that has gone before and prepared us as readers. And it is more than a book. It is a conversation. By reading attentively, we join this feminist conversation.

Cynthia Enloe is research professor of international development and women's studies at Clark University in Massachusetts. Among her books are *The Curious Feminist: Searching for Women in a New Age of Empire, Maneuvers: The International Politics of Militarizing Women's Lives,* and *Bananas, Beaches, and Bases: Making Feminist Sense of International Politics* (all from University of California Press). Her newest book is *Globalization and Militarism: Tracking the Connections Between Them with a Feminist Lens* (Rowman and Littlefield, 2007).

Notes

Introduction

1. Transcript of Girman army hearing obtained by American Civil Liberties Union in litigation against Department of Defense and other government agencies under the Freedom of Information Act. see www.aclu.org/torturefoia/released.

2. Dan Rather, "Camp Bucca, Iraq; Soldier's Video Diary and Two Ex-Soldiers Reveal Problems in Prison Camps," *60 Minutes II*, CBS, May 12, 2004.

3. Dave Janoski, "A Long, Lonely Battle: POW Accusations Haunt Ex-Reservist," *Wilkes-Barre Times Leader*, May 23, 2004.

4. Ibid.

5. Ibid.

6. Transcript of Girman army hearing.

7. Transcript of Girman army hearing.

8. Staff and wire reports, "Girman Accused of Being 'Vigilante'; Reservist Denies Claims by Commander of the Ashley-Based 320th That She Took Revenge on POWs for Raping Jessica Lynch," May 12, 2004.

9. Janoski, "A Long, Lonely Battle."

10. Ibid.

Sexual Coercion, Prisons, and Female Responses

1. Angela Davis, *Abolition Democracy: Beyond Prison, Torture and Empire* (San Francisco: Seven Stories Press, 2005), 64.

2. Ibid.

3. Ibid., 64–65.

4. Ibid., 65.

5. Ibid., 66.

6. Ibid., 63–64.

7. Ibid., 65–66.

The Women of Abu Ghraib

1. 14.6 percent is the exact number. Original data comes from the Department of Defense. The proportion deployed is an estimate, as DoD does not release current statistics on active missions. The *Washington Post* reported, "One in every seven troops in Iraq is a woman." (Linda Wertheimer, "Wounded in War: The Women Serving in Iraq," *Washington Post*, September 15, 2006.) By this account, the number would be 14 percent for Iraq (not Iraq and Afghanistan together), and it is still an estimate.

Shock and Awe:
Abu Ghraib, Women Soldiers, and Racially Gendered Torture

1. "Red Cross Saw Widespread Abuse," BBC News, May 8, 2004, http://news.bbc.co.uk/2/hi/americas.

2. Susan Taylor Martin, "Report Steers Clear of Interrogators' Boss," *St. Petersburg Times,* May 8, 2004.

3. David Finkel and Christian Davenport, "Records Paint Dark Portrait of Guard: Before Abu Ghraib, Graner Left a Trail of Alleged Violence," *Washington Post,* June 5, 2004.

4. Ilene Feinman, *Citizenship Rites: Feminist Soldiers and Feminist Antimilitarists* (New York: New York University Press, 2000), 202.

5. Carol Cohn, "Clean Bombs and Clean Language," in *Women, Militarism, and War: Essays in History, Politics, and Social Theory*, eds. Jean Bethke Elshtain and Sheila Tobias (Lanham, MD: Rowman & Littlefield, 1990).

6. Melissa Herbert, *Camouflage Isn't Only for Combat: The Management of Sexuality Among Women in the Military* (New York: New York University Press, 1998); Mary Fainsod Katzenstein, *Faithful and Fearless: Moving Feminist Protest Inside the Church and Military* (Princeton: Princeton University Press, 1998); see note 4 above.

7. Department of Defense, 2002, www.defenselink.mil/prhome/poprep2002/chapter2/.

8. Department of Defense, "Active Duty Military Personnel by Rank/Grade 2004," http://siadapp.dior.whs.mil/personnel/MILITARY/Miltop.htm

9. Carol Mason, "The Hillbilly Defense: Culturally Mediating U.S. Terror at Home and Abroad," *NWSA Journal* 17, no. 3 (Fall 2005): 223–31.

10. Anthony Taguba, *Taguba Report: Article 15–6 Investigation of the 800th Military Police Brigade,* March 2004.

11. Carol Burke, *Camp All-American, Hanoi Jane, and the High and Tight* (Boston: Beacon Press, 2004).

12. Feinman, *Citizenship Rites,* 149–50, 207–10.

13. Herbert, *Camouflage Isn't Only for Combat.*

14. Seymour Hersh, *Chain of Command* (New York: Harper Perennial, 2004), 38–39.

15. Raphael Patai, *The Arab Mind* (New York: Scribner, 1973).

16. Luke Harding, "The Other Prisoners," *Guardian,* May 20, 2004.

17. Kristen McNutt, Association of Humanitarian Lawyers, "Sexualized Violence Against Iraqi Women by U.S. Occupying Forces" (paper presented to UN Commission on Human Rights, March 2005), www.uruknet.info.

18. Tara McKelvey, "Unusual Suspects," *American Prospect,* February 1, 2005.

19. Cynthia Enloe, "The Right to Fight: Feminist Catch-22," *Ms.,* July–August 1993, 87.

20. Taguba, *Taguba Report.*

Gender and Sexual Violence in the Military

1. Josh White, "Abu Ghraib Tactics Were First Used at Guantánamo," *Washington Post,* July 14, 2005. An estimated 70–90 percent of detainees in Abu Ghraib were wrongfully imprisoned.

2. "Sex Used to Break Muslim Prisoners: Women Allegedly Wore Thongs, Touched Guantánamo Detainees," Associated Press, January 27, 2005.

3. Seymour Hersh, "Torture at Abu Ghraib," *New Yorker,* May 10, 2004.

4. Jasbir K. Puar, "Abu Ghraib: Arguing Against Exceptionalism," *Feminist Studies* 30, No. 2, 2004: 523.

5. Catherine Lutz and John Elliston, "Domestic Terror," *Nation,* October 14, 2002.

6. Amy Herdy and Miles Moffeit, "Betrayal in the Ranks," *Denver Post,* 2004.

7. Human Rights Watch, *Leadership Failure: Firsthand Accounts of Torture of Iraqi Detainees by the U.S. Army's 82nd Airborne Division,* September 2005.

8. Seymour Hersh, "The Gray Zone," *New Yorker,* May 24, 2004.

9. Erik Saar, *Inside the Wire* (New York: Penguin Putnam, 2005).

10. "Sex Used to Break Muslim Prisoners."

11. www.tomdispatch.com, June 2, 2004.

12. See note 7 above.

13. White, "Abu Ghraib Tactics Were First Used at Guantánamo."

14. Hersh, "Torture at Abu Ghraib."

15. Ibid.

16. Department of the Army, *Field Manual 35–42: Intelligence Interrogation,* September 28, 1992, 1–9.

17. Tony Lagouranis, interview, *Frontline,* PBS, October 18, 2005.

18. John T. Parry, "'Just for Fun': Understanding Torture and Understanding Abu Ghraib," *Journal of National Security Law and Policy* (2005): 3–5.

19. Jasbir K. Puar, "Abu Ghraib: Arguing Against Exceptionalism," *Feminist Studies* 30, no. 2 (2004), citing Joe Crea, "Gay Sex Used to Humiliate Iraqis," *Washington Blade,* May 7, 2004.

20. Ibid.

Women Soldiers and Interrogational Abuses in the War on Terror

1. 3rd Military Police Group, *CID Report of Investigation,* July 5, 2004.

2. Michael Fuoco and Cindi Lash, "Abuse No Secret to Many in Iraq," *Pittsburgh Post-Gazette,* June 27, 2004.

3. Gail Gibson, "Other Abuses at Prison Recounted," *Baltimore Sun,* August 6, 2004.

4. Kate Zernike, "Only a Few Spoke Up on Abuse as Many Soldiers Stayed Silent," *New York Times,* May 22, 2004.

5. Sabrina Harman, First Sworn Statement (January 14, 2004), *Taguba Report*, Annex 25, 26.

6. Lynndie England, First Sworn Statement (January 14, 2004), *Taguba Report*, Annex 25, 26.

7. U.S. Army, 10th Military Police Detachment, 3rd Military Police Group. CID Report of Investigation-Final (C)0031-03-CID519 621479j/5C1N/ 5X/15Y2D/5Y2G. June 8, 2003, Taguba Annex 34.

8. T. Wright, 320th MP Battalion. MP soldiers and allegations of maltreatment of Enemy Prisoner of Wars. September 15, 2003, 8090–92.

9. Karen J. Greenberg and Joshua L. Dratel, eds. *The Torture Papers: The Road to Abu Ghraib* (New York: Cambridge University Press, 2005), legal brief on proposed counter-resistance strategies, 233–35.

10. Ibid., 237.

11. Tim Golden, "In U.S. Report, Brutal Details of Two Afghan Inmates' Deaths," *New York Times*, May 20, 2005.

12. Tim Golden, "Army Faltered in Investigating Detainee Abuse," *New York Times*, May 22, 2005.

13. Greenberg and Dratel, *The Torture Papers*, 1037.

14. Barbara Fast statement, July 20, 2004, DOD 00654-70.

15. Article 32 investigation, *United States v CW2 Williams, SFC Sommer, and SPC Loper*, December 2, 2004.

16. Lynndie England Sworn Statement (January 15, 2004), *Taguba Report*, article *15–6* Investigation of the 800th Military Police Brigade. Annex 25, 26.

17. See note 6 above.

18. *Army Regulation* 15–6: *Final Report: Investigation into FBI Allegations of Detainee Abuse at Guantánamo Bay*, April 1, 2005, amended June 9, 2005.

19. James Yee, *For God and Country* (New York: PublicAffairs, 2005), 117–26.

20. Greenberg and Dratel, *The Torture Papers*, 466–67.

21. *Army Regulation 15-6: Final Report*.

22. www.supportmpscapegoats.com.

23. Greenberg and Dratel, *The Torture Papers*, 1122.

24. *Army Regulation 15-6: Final Report.*

25. Greenberg and Dratel, *The Torture Papers*, 1116–17.

Women and the Profession of Arms

1. Lory Manning, *Women in the Military: Where They Stand,* 5th ed. (Washington, D.C.: Women's Research and Education Institute, 2005), 10.

2. Erin Solaro, *Women in the Line of Fire: What You Should Know About Women in the Military* (Emeryville, CA: Seal Press, 2006).

3. The distinction between dying in childbirth and of a complicated pregnancy or childbirth is primarily one of time. Since the Ninth Revision of the International Classification of Diseases (ICD-9) in 1977, the time frame for calculating maternal deaths was extended to 42 days after termination of a pregnancy, regardless of the length or site of pregnancy; in 1993, ICD-10 recognized late maternal deaths between 43 and 365 days after delivery. Like automobile accidents, childbirth may kill you outright, or it can damage you so badly that it kills you later alone, or in conjunction with a disease that on its own would not be fatal.

4. Howard H. Peckham, ed., *The Toll of Independence: Engagements and Battle Casualties of the American Revolution* (University of Chicago Press, 1974), 130–31; Statistical Information Analysis Division, http://siadapp.dior .whs.mil/personnel/CASUALTY/WCPRINCIPAL.pdf.

5. Genesis 3:16.

6. An infantry battalion generally includes three infantry (or rifle) companies, a weapons company, and a headquarters company.

7. "Women at West Point? 'Silly' to Westmoreland," *The New York Times,* May 31, 1976; cited by Sandra L. Bateman, "'The Right Stuff' Has No Gender," *Aerospace Power Journal* (Winter 1987–88), www.airpower .maxwell.af.mil/airchronicles/apjlapj87/bateman.html.

8. Frederick J. Kroesen, "Women in Combat," *Army,* May 2006.

Guarding Women: Abu Ghraib and Military Sexual Culture

1. See http://Guantánamobile.org/blog/archives/ and http://jurist.law.pitt.edu/ hottopics/abughraib.php.

2. See Eric Schmitt, "Army Moves to Advance 2 Linked to Iraq," *New York Times,* June 29, 2005; Eric Schmitt, "4 Top Officers Cleared by Army in Prison Abuses," *New York Times,* April 23, 2005; for Karpinski, other officers' administrative punishments, see National Security Archive, www.gwu.edu/ ~nsarchiv/; for officers escaping criminal censure while subordinates court-martialed, see James W. Smith, "A Few Good Scapegoats: The Abu Ghraib Courts-Martial and the Failure of the Military Justice System," *Whittier Law Review:* 27 (2006): 671.

3. See commentary of Elaine Donnelly and Linda Chavez; Mary Leonard, "Abuse Raises Gender Issues, Women Soldiers' Role Debated," *Boston Globe,* May 16, 2004; Richard Ostling, "Southern Baptist Blames Women in Military for Iraq Prison Scandal" (Associated Press), *Grand Rapids Press,* June 19, 2004; Kathleen Parker, "Why Are Women There Anyway?" *Daily Press* (Va.), June 1, 2004. See generally Diane Richard, "POW Catch-22: Is the risk of rape worth keeping women from the frontline?" *Contemporary Sexuality* 37, no. 7 (July 2003).

4. Gail Gibson, "Added Combat Issue: Pregnancy Relations," *Baltimore Sun,* May 16, 2004.

5. Martha Chamallas, "The New Gender Panic: Reflections on Sex Scandals and the Military," *Minnesota Law Review* 83 (1998): 305, 310–16; Elizabeth L. Hillman, "The 'Good Soldier' Defense: Character Evidence and Military Rank at Courts-Martial," *Yale Law Journal* 108 (1999): 879.

6. William H. McMichael, *The Mother of All Hooks: The Story of the U.S. Navy's Tailhook Scandal* (New Brunswick, NJ: Transaction Publishers, 1997); Jean Zimmerman, *Tailspin* (New York: Doubleday, 1994); Richard Chema, "Arresting 'Tailhook': The Prosecution of Sexual Harassment in the Military," *Military Law Review* 140 (1993).

7. See Chamallas, "The New Gender Panic."

8. Julie Yuki Ralston, "Geishas, Gays and Grunts: What the Exploitation of Asian Pacific Women Reveals About Military Culture and the Legal Ban on Lesbian, Gay, and Bisexual Service Members," *Law & Inequality* 16 (1998): 661–62; Chalmers Johnson, "The Okinawan Rape Incident and the End of the Cold War in East Asia," *California International Law Journal* 27 (1997): 389; Derek van Hoften, "Declaring War on the Japanese Constitution: Japan's Right to Military Sovereignty and the United States' Right to Military Presence in Japan," *Hastings International and Comparative Law Review* 26 (2003): 289, 302.

9. Carie Little Hersh, "Crossing the Line: Sex, Power, Justice, and the U.S. Navy at the Equator," *Duke Journal of Gender & Law Policy* 9 (2002): 277; Carol Burke, *Camp All-American, Hanoi Jane, and the High and Tight* (Boston: Beacon Press, 2004).

10. See www.sldn.org/binary-data/SLDN_ARTICLES/ (detailing gay-bashing occurrences under "don't ask/don't tell" policy).

11. Madeline Morris, "By Force of Arms: Rape, War, and Military Culture," *Duke Law Journal* 45 (1996): 651.

12. Katharine H. S. Moon, *Sex Among Allies: Military Prostitution in U.S.–Korea Relations* (New York: Columbia University Press, 1997); Saundra Pollock Sturdevant and Brenda Stoltzfus, eds., *Let the Good Times Roll: Prostitution and the U.S. Military in Asia* (New York: New Press, 1992); Elizabeth Rho-Ng, "The Conscription of Asian Sex Slaves: Causes and Effects of U.S. Military Sex Colonialism in Thailand and the Call to Expand U.S. Asylum Law," *Asian Law Journal* 7 (2000): 103; Emily Nyen Chang, "Engagement Abroad: Enlisted Men, U.S. Military Policy and the Sex Industry," *Notre Dame Journal of Law, Ethics and Public Policy* 15 (2001): 621; Gwyn Kirk and Carolyn Bowen France, "Redefining Security: Women Challenge U.S. Military Policy and Practice in East Asia," *Berkeley Women's Law Journal* 15 (2000): 229.

13. Linda K. Kerber, *No Constitutional Right to Be Ladies: Women and the Obligations of Citizenship* (New York: Hill and Wang, 1998).

14. R. Jeffrey Smith, "Sexual Assaults in Army on Rise," *Washington Post*, June 3, 2004.

15. Peter J. Mercier and Judith D. Mercier, *Battle Cries on the Home Front: Violence in the Military Family* (Springfield, IL: Charles C. Thomas, 2000); Stephen J. Brannen and Elwood R. Hamlin II, "Understanding Spouse Abuse in Military Families," in *The Military Family: A Practice Guide for Human Service Providers*, eds. James A. Martin, Leora N. Rosen, and Linette R. Sparacino (Westport, CT: Praeger, 2000), 169–83. See also Miles Foundation website, http://hometown.aol.com/milesfdn/; 3rd Military Police Group, CID Report of Investigation, July 5, 2004, DODDOACID-00482-51.

16. Elizabeth L. Hillman, *Defending America: Military Culture and the Cold War Court-Martial* (Princeton, NJ: Princeton University Press, 2005).

17. *United States v. Cockram*, 15 C.M.R. 199 (A.B.R. 1952); *United States v. Barker*, 13 C.M.R. 472 (A.B.R. 1953); *United States v. Young*, 18 C.M.R. 729 (A.F.B.R. 1955); *United States v. Martin*, 24 C.M.R. 156 (1957) and 22 C.M.R. 601 (A.B.R. 1956). On homosexuality in military prisons, *United States v. Parrish*, 24 C.M.R. 345 (A.B.R. 1957); *United States v. Smith*, 28 C.M.R. 782 (A.F.B.R. 1959); *United States v. Matthews*, 38 C.M.R. 430 (1968).

18. *United States v. Miasel*, 24 C.M.R. 184 (1957). The other cases were not reported, but were referred to in the court's opinion. See also *United States v. Miasel*, 22 C.M.R. 562 (A.B.R. 1956).

19. Victim's testimony corroborated Miasel's claim, but also described being sodomized by three prisoners who had been part of Miasel's "joke" during a later assault without Miasel. Board of review reversed Miasel's conviction (confirmed by Court of Military Appeals) because evidence of later assault was admitted into evidence at trial, thus prejudicing Miasel's court-martial panel with information irrelevant to his guilt.

20. The cost of taking a stand against abuse at Abu Ghraib was evident from the army's reassignment, to prevent reprisals of soldiers who reported incidents

to higher authorities. See Barbara Ehrenreich, "Honor the Resisters," *Milwaukee Journal Sentinel*, July 16, 2004.

21. *United States v. Parker*, 33 C.M.R. 111, 112–13 (1963).

22. *United States v. Warren*, 20 C.M.R. 135 (1955).

23. *United States v. Bennington*, 31 C.M.R. 151 (1961).

24. *United States v. Parker*, 33 C.M.R. 111, 13 (1963).

25. *United States v. Doherty*, 17 C.M.R. 287 (1954).

26. *United States v. Bennington*, 31 C.M.R. 151 (1961).

27. Same-sex harassment was recognized as actionable under Title VII in a case involving sexual teasing and abuse on an oil rig. See *Oncale v. Sundowner Offshore Services, Inc.*, 118 S.Ct. 998 (1998).

28. *United States v. Moore*, 33 C.M.R. 667 (C.G.B.R. 1963).

29. Ibid., 668.

30. The dissent takes issue with this definition of "indecency," arguing that if mere exposure of Ellis's buttocks constitutes a crime of indecent exposure, then forcibly restraining Ellis and pretending to mark his exposed body must also be a crime of indecency.

31. See Burke, note 9 above; see Hersh, note 9 above.

32. In 1957, two army privates were court-martialed for their role in abusing and sodomizing a GI. Both tried to prevent others from testifying against them, revealing the depth of peer pressure to hide this sort of behavior. *United States v. Hayes*, 24 C.M.R. 440 (A.B.R. 1957).

33. *United States v. Marcey*, 25 C.M.R. 444 (1958). Members of the court-martial disagreed with the assessment and sentenced the men to five years' confinement and dishonorable discharges. Not a unique argument; see *United States v. Polak*, 27 C.M.R. 87 (1958).

34. Army soldiers predominate this category of offenders whose cases reached appellate records. (See air force case *United States v. O'Connell*, 18 C.M.R. 881 [A.F.B.R. 1955].) Other army cases of forcible sodomy against men, apart from prosecutions of officers discussed below: See *United States v.*

Williams, 13 C.M.R. 438 (A.B.R. 1953); *United States v. Jones,* 13 C.M.R. 420 (A.B.R. 1953); *United States v. Morgan,* 24 C.M.R. 151 (1957); *United States v. Bonnell,* 32 C.M.R. 608 (A.B.R. 1962); *United States v. Greene,* 33 C.M.R. 480 (A.B.R., 1963); *United States v. Harrison,* 41 C.M.R. 595 (A.B.R. 1969); *United States v. Lindsey,* 41 C.M.R. 529 (A.B.R. 1969); *United States v. Rockenbach,* 43 C.M.R. 805 (A.C.M.R. 1971); *United States v. O'Neal,* 48 C.M.R. 89 (A.C.M.R. 1973). Appellate records in which the sex of the victim of a forcible sodomy charge is not specified: See *United States v. Farrell,* 24 C.M.R. 118 (1957); *United States v. Davis,* 41 C.M.R. 217 (1970); *United States v. Falls,* 44 C.M.R. 48 (1971) and 44 C.M.R. 748 (N.C.M.R. 1971).

35. In addition to cases cited below, see the case of an airman who accidentally suffocated his bunkmate in the course of forcibly sodomizing him, *United States v. Breeden,* 13 C.M.R. 805 (A.F.B.R. 1953); and in the case of the airman charged with a sodomitical assault on a sleeping soldier, *United States v. Butts,* 14 C.M.R. 596 (A.F.B.R. 1954). See also *United States v. Turner,* 18 C.M.R. 69 (1955); *United States v. Johnson,* 22 C.M.R. 289 (1957); *United States v. Goodman,* 33 C.M.R. 195 (1963); *United States v. Kindler,* 34 C.M.R. 174 (1964); *Silvero v. Chief of Naval Air Basic Training,* 428 F.2d 1009 (C. A. Fla. 1970).

36. *United States v. Holladay,* 36 C.M.R. 598 (A.B.R. 1966).

37. David S. Jonas, "Fraternization: Time for a Rational Defense of a Department of Defense Standard," *Military Law Review* 135 (1992): 37–129.

38. Wilton B. Persons Papers, Senior Officers Oral History Program, U.S. Army Military History Institute, 1985 interview: 460–64.

39. Paul H. Turney, "Relations Among the Ranks: Observations of and Comparisons Among the Service Policies and Fraternization Case Law, 1999," *Army Lawyer,* April 2000, 97–107.

40. *United States v. Cain,* 59 M.J. 285 (2004).

41. For similar cases, see *United States v. Free,* 14 C.M.R. 466 (N.B.R. 1953); *United States v. Lovejoy,* 42 C.M.R. 210 (1970); *United States v. Pitasi,* 44 C.M.R. 31 (1971).

42. *United States v. Free,* 14 C.M.R. 466 (1953).

43. 14 C.M.R. 468.

44. Ibid.

45. Ibid., 469–71.

46. Ibid.

47. For statistics, see http://siadapp.dior.whs.mil/personnel/MILITARY/rg0509f
.pdf (reporting number of female military personnel in September 2005);
www.womensmemorial.org/PDFs (reporting May 2006 statistics); see also
Government Office Accountability Report to Congressional Requesters:
*Military Personnel: Reporting Additional Servicemember Demographics Could
Enhance Congressional Oversight,* September 2005, 10–11, 38.

Bitter Fruit: Constitutional Gender Equality Comes to the Military

1. See amicus curiae brief, *United States v. Virginia*, 515 U.S. 518 (1996), of Lt.
Col. Rhonda Cornum et al. (nos. 94-1941, 94-2107).

2. Jean Bethke Elshtain, *Women and War* (New York: Basic Books, 1987), 3–13.

3. Linda Bird Francke, "Women in the Military: The Military Culture of
Harassment: The Dynamics of the Masculine Mystique," *America's Military
Today: The Challenge of Militarism*, ed. Tod Ensign (New York: New Press,
2004), 134–35.

4. Mark Danner, *Torture and Truth: America, Abu Ghraib, and the War on Terror*
(New York: New York Review of Books, 2004), 14.

5. Virginia Woolf, "On Being Ill," *Collected Essays,* vol. 4 (New York: Harcourt,
1967).

6. See Elaine Scarry, *The Body in Pain: The Making and Unmaking of the World*
(New York: Oxford University Press, 1985), 60.

7. Philippa Strum, *Women in the Barracks: The VMI Case and Equal Rights* (Lawrence:
University Press of Kansas, 2002), 2–35; Jeremy N. Jungreis, "Holding the Line at
VMI and the Citadel: The Preservation of a State's Right to Offer a Single-Gender
Military Education," *Florida State University Law Review* 23 (1996): 795.

8. Strum, *Women in the Barracks,* 40.

9. Jungreis, "Holding the Line at VMI and the Citadel," 801.

10. Strum, *Women in the Barracks,* 24, 36.

11. Ibid., 27.

12. *UnitedStates v. Virginia,* 766 F. Supp. 1407, 1425 (W.D. Va. 1991) (quoting VMI's study in 1996).

13. Strum, *Women in the Barracks,* 48–52.

14. Brief for Respondents, *United States v. Virginia,* 515 U.S. 518 (1996) (nos. 94-1941, 94-2107), at 12 (citation omitted).

15. *United States v. Virginia,* 515 U.S. 518 (1996).

16. Only Justice Scalia dissented. Chief Justice Rehnquist filed separate concurrence. Justice Thomas recused himself.

17. *United States v. Virginia,* 515 U.S. 518 (1996).

18. Strum, *Women in the Barracks,* 306–12.

19. *Bradwell v. Illinois,* 83 U.S. 130, 1414 (1873).

20. Strum, *Women in the Barracks,* 326.

21. Among numerous resources, see Human Rights Watch, *Firsthand Accounts of Torture of Iraqi Detainees by the U.S. Army's 82nd Airborne Division,* September 2005; David Rose, *Guantánamo: America's War on Human Rights* (London: Faber and Faber, 2005); U.S. Department of Justice Office of the Inspector General, *The September 11 Detainees: A Review of the Treatment of Aliens Held on Immigration Charges in Connection with the Investigation of the September 11 Attacks,* June 2003.

22. Mark Danner, "Abu Ghraib: The Hidden Story," *New York Review of Books,* October 7, 2004.

23. My argument for condemning Rumsfeld et al. contained in Frederick A. O. Schwarz Jr. and Aziz Huq, *Unchecked and Unbalanced: Presidential Power in a Time of Terror* (New York: New Press, forthcoming 2007), chap. 5.

24. Giorgio Agamben, *Homo Sacer: Sovereign Power and Bare Life* (Stanford, CA: Stanford University Press, 1998), 71–75.

25. Strum, *Women in the Barracks*, 50.

26. Jane Mayer, "The Memo," *New Yorker,* February 27, 2006.

27. *Break Them Down: The Systematic Use of Psychological Torture by U.S. Forces* (Physicians for Human Rights, 2005), 27, 32.

28. Executive Summary of Report of Albert T. Church (2005), 6–7; Independent Panel to Review Department of Defense Detention Operations (August 2004), 37.

29. Jane Mayer, "The Experiment," *New Yorker,* July 11 & 18, 2005, 60.

30. Kathleen N. Sullivan, "Constitutionalizing Women's Equality," *California Law Review* 90 (2002): 735, 752.

31. Sylvia Plath, "Cut," from *Ariel* (New York: Harper Perennial, 1999).

32. Meda Chesney-Lind, "Patriarchy, Crime, and Justice: Feminist Criminology in an Era of Backlash," *Feminist Criminology* 1 (2006): 6, 11–12.

33. Elshtain, *Women and War,* 169.

34. JoAnn Wypijewski, "Judgment Days: Lessons from the Abu Ghraib Courts-Martial," *Harper's,* February 2006, 39, 44.

35. Francke, "Women in the Military," 143.

36. Hannah Arendt, *Eichmann in Jerusalem: A Report on the Banality of Evil* (New York: Penguin Books, 1994), 287–88.

37. Quoted in *United States v. Virginia,* 515 U.S. 518, 602–03 (1996) (Scalia dissenting).

38. Quoting language of Hannah Arendt (*Eichmann in Jerusalem,* 288), who makes a slightly different point. While not certain Arendt would disagree, I am not invoking her authority for the substantive point.

39. *United States v. Virginia,* 515 U.S. 518, 542 (1996).

40. Wypijewski, "Judgement Days," 39, 41.

Photography/Pornography/Torture:
The Politics of Seeing Abu Ghraib

1. Katharine Viner, "The Sexual Sadism of Our Culture, in Peace and in War," *Guardian*, May 22, 2004.

2. Rush Limbaugh, www.rushlimbaugh.com.

3. Laura Kipnis, *Bound and Gagged: Pornography and the Politics of Fantasy in America* (Durham, NC: Duke University Press, 1999).

4. Cathy Hong, "How Could Women Do That?" *Salon*, May 7, 2004, http://archive.salon.com/mwt/feature/2004/05/07/abuse_gender/.

5. Maureen Dowd, "Torture Chicks Gone Wild," *New York Times*, January 30, 2005, www.nytimes.com/2005/01/30/opinion/.

6. Barbara Ehrenreich, "What Abu Ghraib Taught Me," *AlterNet*, May 20, 2004.

7. Susan Sontag, "Regarding the Torture of Others," *New York Times*, May 23, 2004, http://donswaim.com/nytimes.sontag.html.

8. Angela Carter, *The Sadeian Woman: And the Ideology of Pornography* (New York: Pantheon Books, 1978).

9. Linda Williams, *Hard Core: Power, Pleasure, and the "Frenzy of the Visible"* (Berkeley: University of California Press, 1990).

10. Janis Karpinski in conversation with Tara McKelvey.

11. Lynndie England in an interview with Brian Maass of Denver's CBS TV station KCNC. Found online at www.cbsnews.com/stories/2004/05/s2/iraq/main616921.shtml.

12. From trial of Lynndie England. LexisNexis Transcript Provider Service, online at www.lexisnexis.com/news/.

13. See note 10 above.

14. From trial of Lynndie England. LexisNexis Transcript Provider Service, www.lexisnexis.com/news/.

15. Ibid.

16. JoAnn Wypijewsi, "Judgment Days: Lessons from the Abu Ghraib Courts-Martial," *Harper's,* February 2006, 39–50.

17. Della Sentilles, "Beyond the Frame: The Torturers and the Tortured in Abu Ghraib" (unpublished thesis, Yale University, May 2005).

18. Kayla Williams, *Love My Rifle More Than You: Young and Female in the U.S. Army* (New York: W. W. Norton, 2005).

19. Ibid.

20. Ibid.

Gender Trouble at Abu Ghraib?

1. Scott Higham, Josh White, and Christian Davenport, "A Prison on the Brink," *Washington Post,* May 9, 2004. Additional Abu Ghraib photographs are reproduced in Mark Danner's 2004 book *Torture and Truth,* 217–24, and still more can be found at http://salon.com/news/.

2. Susan Brison, "Torture, or 'Good Old American Pornography,'" *Chronicle of Higher Education* 50 (June 4, 2004): 10.

3. Henry Giroux, "What Might Education Mean After Abu Ghraib?" *Comparative Studies of South Asia, Africa and the Middle East* 24, no. 1 (2004): 8.

4. Luke Harding, "The Other Prisoners," *Guardian,* May 20, 2004.

5. Cynthia Enloe. "Wielding Masculinity Inside Abu Ghraib: Making Feminist Sense of an American Military Scandal," *Asian Journal of Women's Studies* 10, no. 3 (2004): 91.

6. M. S. Embser-Herbert, "When Women Abuse Power, Too," *Washington Post,* May 16, 2004.

7. George W. Bush, "President Outlines Steps to Help Iraq Achieve Democracy and Freedom," May 24, 2005, www.whitehouse.gov/news/.

8. David Thibault, "Abu Ghraib Is a Feminist's Dream, Says Military Expert," May 10, 2004, www.cnsnews.com.

9. Peggy Noonan, "A Humiliation for America," *Opinion Journal,* May 6, 2004.

10. George Neumayr, "Thelma and Louise in Iraq," *American Spectator,* May 5, 2004, www.spectator.org.

11. It is perhaps no surprise that many other right-wing pundits, seeking to appropriate the Abu Ghraib images for partisan ends, did so by citing the alleged ubiquity of pornography, and especially gay porn, in American culture (see Frank Rich, "It Was the Porn that Made Them Do It," *The New York Times Magazine,* May 30, 2004). On this telling, England and her cohorts are marshaled in an effort to combat the excesses of a permissive culture whose primary causes, of course, include the rise of women's and gay liberation movements, both of which celebrate a promiscuous, if not depraved, conception of sexual freedom.

12. Barbara Ehrenreich, "Feminism's Assumptions Upended," *Los Angeles Times,* June 4, 2004.

13. Ibid.

14. Cathy Hong, "How Could Women Do That?" *Salon,* May 7, 2004, http://archive.salon.com/mwt/feature/2004/05/07/abuse_gender/.

15. As of March 2006, ten soldiers have been prosecuted and convicted in the Abu Ghraib affair. Their punishments, for offenses including dereliction of duty, maltreating prisoners, assault, battery, indecent acts, and conspiracy, range from demotion to ten years' imprisonment. Lynndie England, following a botched plea bargain, was dishonorably discharged and sentenced to three years in prison (Eric Schmitt, "Iraq Abuse Trial Is Again Limited to Lower Ranks," *New York Times,* March 23, 2006).

16. Karen J. Greenberg and Joshua L. Dratel, eds., *The Torture Papers: The Road to Abu Ghraib* (New York: Cambridge University Press, 2005), 909.

17. Ibid, 448–49.

18. Ibid, 1007.

19. "Abu Ghraib Was 'Animal House' at Night," www.cnn.com, August 25, 2005.

20. See Jasbir K. Puar, "Abu Ghraib: Arguing Against Exceptionalism," *Feminist Studies* 30, no. 2 (2004): 522–54.

21. With the exception of that involving fake menstrual blood, which is related in Erik Saar and Viveca Novak, *Inside the Wire* (New York: Penguin, 2005), 225–229, these incidents as well as others like them are related in the Taguba and Fay-Jones reports in Greenberg and Dratel, *The Torture Papers*, 416–17, 466–528, 1073–95.

22. For a more complete account of my reading of Butler on gender, see Timothy Kaufman-Osborn, *Creatures of Prometheus: Gender and the Politics of Technology* (Lanham, MD: Rowman & Littlefield, 1997), 120–36.

23. Judith Butler, *Gender Trouble* (New York: Routledge, 1990), 6.

24. Greenberg and Dratel, *The Torture Papers*, 989.

25. Department of the Army, *Field Manual 34-52: Intelligence Interogation*, September 28, 1992, www.fas.org/irp/doddir/army/.

26. In response to the abuses reported at Abu Ghraib and elsewhere, a proposed new field manual governing "detainee treatment," including interrogation procedures, was prepared and then posted on the Pentagon's website, only to be withdrawn shortly thereafter. It is not without significance that this manual includes the following statement: "[Office of the Secretary of Defense] is the sole release authority for photographs or videos of detainees" (Joint Chiefs of Staff, 2005, II–25).

27. On "softening up" prisoners, as well as the way in which such practices blur the line between these efforts and formal interrogations, consider the following passage contained in a letter written by Sgt. Ivan Frederick, the senior enlisted officer convicted in the Abu Ghraib scandal: "Military intelligence has encouraged and told us 'Great job.' They usually don't allow others to watch them interrogate, but since they like the way I run the prison, they've made an exception. We help getting them to talk with the way we handle them. We've had a very high rate with our style of getting them to break. They usually end up breaking within hours." (Quoted in Michelle Brown, "'Setting the Conditions' for Abu Ghraib: The Prison Nation Abroad," *American Quarterly* 57, no. 3 [2005]: 978).

28. Field Manual 34-52, v.

29. Mark Bowden, "The Dark Art of Interrogation," *Atlantic Monthly,* October 2005, 57–58.

30. The precise role of the CIA at Abu Ghraib remains unclear because, as the Schlesinger and Fay-Jones reports note, the agency "was allowed to conduct its interrogations separately," it operated "outside the established local rules and procedures," and its prisoners, "known locally as 'Ghost Detainees,' were not accounted for in the detention system" (in Greenberg and Dratel, *The Torture Papers,* 942, 1024).

31. Central Intelligence Agency, *Counterintelligence Interrogation,* 1963, www.gwu .edu (October 28, 2005). Also references Central Intelligence Agency, *Human Resource Exploitation Training Manual,* 1983, www.gwu.edu/-nsarchiv/.

32. The seventeen techniques in *Field Manual 34-52* are listed as follows: direct questioning; incentive; emotional love; emotional hate; fear-up (harsh); fear-up (mild); fear-down; pride and ego-up; pride and ego-down; futility; we know all; file and dossier; establish your identity; repetition; rapid fire; silent; and change of scene, secs. 3-14 through 3–20. Exactly how *34-52* functioned at Abu Ghraib is confused by the fact that its original version, produced in 1987, circulated throughout Iraq's detention facilities, even though it had been revised and superseded by the 1992 version. This later version deleted the 1987 version's very broad authorization to control "all aspects of interrogations," including "lighting, heating, and configuration of the interrogation room, as well as food, shelter, and clothing given to the source." (Department of the Army, *Field Manual 34-52: "Intelligence Interrogation," 1987, 3-2.)* That the earlier authorization to control all aspects of interrogations" received official endorsement is indicated by the fact that, on October 12, 2003, Lt. Gen. Sanchez issued a "new [sic] interrogation and counterresistance policy," which included the very language that had been deleted from the 1992 version (Douglas Jehl and Eric Schmitt, "Prison Interrogations in Iraq Seen as Yielding Little Data on Rebels," *The New York Times,* May 27, 2004).

33. *FieldManual 34-52, 1992.*

34. Greenberg and Dratel, *The Torture Papers*, 1004.

35. Scheherezade Faramarzi, "Former Iraqi Prisoner Says U.S. Jailers Humiliated Him," Associated Press Online, 2004, http://web.lexis-nexis.com.

36. Randall M. Schmidt, *Investigation into FBI Allegations of Detainee Abuse at Guantánamo Bay, Cuba Detention Facility (The Schmidt Report)*, June 9, 2005, http://balkin.blogspot.com. For a table that charts the "evolution of interrogation techniques" at Guantánamo, including the temporary approval of "sleep adjustment," light and auditory deprivation, removal of clothing, hooding, isolation for up to thirty days, the use of stress positions, and the manipulation of prisoners' phobias (e.g., through the use of dogs), see the Schlesinger report in Greenberg and Dratel, *The Torture Papers*, 966–67.

37. Schmidt, *Schmidt Report*, 7, 16, 19–20.

38. Kate Zernike, "Behind Failed Abu Ghraib Plea, A Tale of Breakups and Betrayal," *New York Times*, May 16, 2005.

39. Douglas Jehl, Eric Schmitt, and Kate Zernike, "U.S. Rules on Prisoners Seen as a Back and Forth of Mixed Messages to G.I.s," *New York Times*, June 22, 2004.

40. In much the same vein, the Fay-Jones report states that "the use of dogs to 'fear up' detainees was generally unquestioned and stems in part from the interrogation techniques and counterresistance policy distributed from CJTF [Combined Joint Task Force] 180, JTF [Joint Task Force] 170, and CJTF" (Greenberg and Dratel, *The Torture Papers*, 1084). See Kate Zernike and David Rohde, "Forced Nudity Is Seen as a Pervasive Pattern, Not Isolated Incidents," *New York Times*, June 8, 2004.

41. Kate Zernike, "Prison Guard Calls Abuse Routine and Sometimes Amusing," *New York Times*, May 16, 2004.

42. Enloe, "Wielding Masculinity Inside Abu Ghraib," 100. On the masculinization of the interrogators' culture, consider the following quotation

from Sgt. First Class Anthony Novacek, an instructor in the approved techniques of *Field Manual 34-52* at Fort Huachuca, Arizona. Teaching his new students that, even upon arrival, they already possess considerable intelligence-gathering skills, he offers the following example: "You're down at Jimbo's Beach Shack, approaching unknown females." Success, he continues, involves "assessing the target, speaking her language, learning her needs and appearing to be the only way she can satisfy them." (Quoted in Jess Bravin, "Interrogation School Tells Army Recruits How Grilling Works: 30 Techniques in 16 Weeks," *Wall Street Journal*, April 26, 2002.)

43. See, for example, Howard Schneider, "In Breaking Taboos, Photos Add Insult to Injury," *Washington Post*, May 7, 2004.

44. Enloe, "Wielding Masculinity Inside Abu Ghraib," 99.

45. Among other elements, a more complete explanation would require exploration of the masculinized culture of the American penal system. Several of the reservists at the center of the prisoner abuse scandal were assigned to Abu Ghraib precisely because they had experience working in American prisons. Within these prisons, abuse not uncommonly assumes forms very similar to that meted out at Abu Ghraib: "In Pennsylvania and some other states, inmates are routinely stripped in front of other inmates before being moved to a new prison or a new unit within their prison. In Arizona, male inmates at the Maricopa County jail in Phoenix are made to wear women's pink underwear as a form of humiliation." (Fox Butterfield, "Mistreatment of Prisoners Is Called Routine in U.S.," *New York Times*, May 8, 2004.)

46. Carol Burke, "Pernicious Cohesion," in *It's Our Military, Too! Women and the U.S. Military*, ed. Judith Hicks Stiehm (Philadelphia: Temple University Press, 1996), 214.

47. Ibid., 214–16.

48. Ibid., 205.

49. Susan Faludi, "The Naked Citadel," *New Yorker*, September 5, 1994, 70. That this misogynistic abuse often assumes a racist character as well is indicated

by the fact that new cadets at the Citadel were often warned by their older peers about "food contamination" from the germ-filled hands and the hair follicles of its all-black mess-hall staff.

50. R. Claire Snyder, *Citizen-Soldiers and Manly Warriors* (Lanham, MD: Rowman & Littlefield, 1999), 151.

51. For an account of the combination of homophobia and homoeroticism in the U.S. Navy's basic training, see Steven Zeeland, *Sailors and Sexuality* (New York: Haworth, 1995). Zeeland describes "Navy initiation rituals involving cross-dressing, spanking, simulated oral and anal sex, simulated ejaculation, nipple piercing, and anal penetration with objects or fingers, such as the famous 'crossing the line ceremony.'"

52. Snyder, *Citizen-Soldiers*, 151.

53. Kirk Johnson, "Guard Featured in Abuse Photos Says She Was Following Orders," *New York Times*, May 11, 2004.

54. David Cloud, "Psychologist Calls Private in Abu Ghraib Photographs 'Overly Compliant,'" *The New York Times*, September 24, 2005.

55. David Cloud, "Private Found Guilty in Abu Ghraib Abuse," *New York Times*, September 27, 2005.

56. Zillah Eisenstein, 2004. "Sexual Humiliation, Gender Confusion and the Horrors at Abu Ghraib," 2004, www.peacewomen.org.

57. Mark Danner, *Torture and Truth: America, Abu Ghraib and the War on Terror* (New York: New York Review of Books, 2004), 47.

Women's Role in Mob Violence: Lynchings and Abu Ghraib

1. Walter White, *Rope and Faggot: A Biography of Judge Lynch*, quoted in Dora Apel, *Imagery of Lynching: Black Men, White Women, and the Mob* (New Brunswick, NJ: Rutgers University Press, 2004), 88.

2. Naomi Klein, "'Never Before!' Our Amnesiac Torture Debate," *Nation*, December 26, 2005.

3. "Letter from Charles Lynch to William Hay, May 11, 1782," in *Lynching in America: A History in Documents*, ed. Christopher Waldrep (New York: NYU Press, 2006), 36.

4. Ibid.

5. See Dora Apel, "Torture Culture: Lynching Photographs and the Images of Abu Ghraib," *Art Journal*, Summer 2005, for more discussion on the connections between torture and the preservation of white masculinity in lynching and Abu Ghraib photos.

6. See Jean H. Baker, *Sisters: The Lives of America's Suffragists* (New York: Hill and Wang, 2005) for more information about how different women reconciled race and gender with social activism.

7. Robyn Wiegman, "The Anatomy of a Lynching," in *Lynching in America*, 21.

8. "Woman's Impatience Revealed as Cause of Porter's Death," *New York Negro World*, May 29, 1920, in *100 Years of Lynchings*, ed. Ralph Ginzburg (Baltimore, MD: Black Classic Press, 1988), 130.

9. Image reprinted in Apel, *Imagery of Lynching*, 89.

10. "Female GI in Abuse Photos Talks: Says She Was Just Following Orders," May 12, 2004, available at www.cbsnews.com/stories/2004/05/12/iraq/main616921.shtml.

11. Seymour Hersh, "Torture at Abu Ghraib," *New Yorker*, May 10, 2004.

12. Ibid.

13. Ibid.

14. All of the Abu Ghraib photographs discussed in this essay can be viewed at www.antiwar.com/news/.

15. "Boy Unsexes Negro Before Mob Lynches Him, Chicago *Defender*, October 13, 1917, in *100 Years of Lynchings*, 113.

16. James Allen, ed., *Without Sanctuary: Lynching Photography in America* (Santa Fe, NM: Twin Palms Publishers, 2005). See plates 95 and 96 for images.

17. Susan Sontag, "On Photography and Violence," *New Yorker*, December 9, 2002.

18. Ginzburg, *100 Years of Lynchings*, 270.

Pawn, Scapegoat, or Collaborator?
U.S. Military Women and Detainee Abuse in Iraq

1. Kirsten Scharnberg, "Stresses of Battle Hit Female GIs Hard," *Chicago Tribune*, March 20, 2005.

2. Amnesty International, *Casualties of War: Women's Bodies, Women's Lives* (London, 2004).

3. National Council for Research on Women, *Missing—Information about U.S. Military Abuse of Women* (New York, July 21, 2004), www.ncrw.org/misinfo/.

4. Suzanne Goldenberg, "Woman Soldier Claims Sex Harassment in Iraq," *Guardian*, June 20, 2006.

5. Amnesty International, *U.S.A.—Guantánamo and Beyond: The Continuing Pursuit of Unchecked Executive Power* (London, 2005); Human Rights Watch, *"No Blood, No Foul": Soldiers' Accounts of Detainee Abuse in Iraq*, July 2006, 18.3.

6. Human Rights Watch, *Getting Away with Torture? Command Responsibility for the U.S. Abuse of Detainees*, April 2005, 17.1; Human Rights Watch, *"No Blood, No Foul,"* 1–3.

7. Human Rights Watch, *"No Blood, No Foul,"* 52.

8. Ibid., 1.

9. Josh White, "Abu Ghraib Tactics Were First Used at Guantánamo," *Washington Post*, July 14, 2005; Tim Golden, "Army Faltered in Investigating Detainee Abuse," *New York Times*, May 22, 2005; Emily Bazelon, "From Bagram to Abu Ghraib," *Mother Jones*, March/April 2005.

10. Suzanne Goldenberg, "We Did It for Fun, Claimed Iraq Jail Accused," *Guardian*, August 4, 2004.

11. Ibid.

12. Human Rights Watch, *"No Blood, No Foul,"* 24–25.

13. Susan Taylor Martin, "Report Steers Clear of Interrogators' Boss," *St. Petersburg Times,* May 8, 2004.

14. Human Rights First, *Where Are They Now? End Torture Now Campaign*, www.humanrightsfirst.org.

15. Douglas Jehl, "Army Details Scale of Abuse of Prisoners in an Afghan Jail," *New York Times*, March 12, 2005.

16. "Fort Huachuca Officer Criticized in Army Probe," staff report, Knight Ridder Newspapers, *Arizona Daily Star*, March 26, 2005; "Carolyn Wood," www.Answers.com/topic/carolyn-wood.

17. "Demotion for Abu Ghraib Commander," BBC News, May 6, 2005.

18. Ibid.

19. Amnesty International, U.S.A. *Guantánamo and Beyond*, 13.

20. Human Rights Watch, *"No Blood, No Foul,"* 3.

21. White, "Abu Ghraib Tactics Were First Used at Guantánamo."

22. Human Rights First, *Where Are They Now?*

23. "Dishonorable Service," editorial, *New York Times,* August 3, 2006.

24. Deborah Pearlstein, "Abusive Promotions," *American Prospect,* October 20, 2004.

25. Kayla Williams, *Love My Rifle More Than You: Young and Female in the U.S. Army* (New York: W. W. Norton, 2005), 246–250.

The Military Made Me Do It:
Double Standards and Psychic Injuries at Abu Ghraib

1. Rush Limbaugh, *Rush Limbaugh Show,* May 3, 2004.

2. Ann Coulter, *Hannity & Colmes,* FOX News Channel, May 5, 2004.

3. Peggy Noonan, "A Humiliation for America," *OpinionJournal,* May 6, 2004.

4. Linda Chavez, "Sexual Tension in the Military," *Catholic Exchange,* May 6, 2004; and on www.townhall.com.

5. George Neumayr, "Thelma and Louise in Iraq," *American Spectator,* May 5, 2004.

6. Sahih Bukhari 4:54, no. 464, narrated by Imran bin Husain.

About the Contributors

Francine D'Amico is associate professor of political science and director of undergraduate studies in international relations at the Maxwell School of Citizenship and Public Affairs at Syracuse University. She is coeditor with Dr. Laurie Weinstein of *Gender Camouflage: Women and the U.S. Military* (New York University Press, 1999).

Angela Y. Davis is known for her ongoing work to combat all forms of oppression in the United States and abroad. Over the years she has been active as a student, teacher, writer, scholar, and activist/organizer. Davis is the author of many books, including *Are Prisons Obsolete?*, *Angela Davis: An Autobiography*, and her forthcoming *Prisons and History* (Columbia University Press).

Ada Calhoun, a senior editor at *Nerve,* has been a frequent contributor to the *New York Times Book Review* and a contributing editor at *New York* magazine.

Elizabeth Maddock Dillon has taught at Yale since 1997. She is the author of *The Gender of Freedom: Fictions of Liberalism and the Literary Public Sphere* (Stanford University Press, 2004). She received her PhD in comparative literature from University of California at Berkeley in 1995. Before coming to Yale, she held a Mellon Postdoctoral Fellowship in the department of comparative literature at Cornell University.

Eve Ensler is a playwright/performer/activist and the award-winning author of *The Vagina Monologues* (Villard, 2002). She is founder and artistic director of V-Day, a global movement to end violence against women and girls (www .vday.org). Ensler's other plays include *Conviction, Lemonade, The Depot, Floating Rhoda and the Glue Man,* and *Extraordinary Measures.*

Ilene Feinman, PhD, is associate professor of democratic participation at California State University–Monterey Bay. She received her PhD in 1997 through the history of consciousness program at University of California, Santa Cruz. Her book, *Citizenship Rites: Feminist Soldiers and Feminist Antimilitarists* (New York University Press, 2000), was noted in the *Chronicle of Higher Education* as a groundbreaking work on women, the U.S. military, and militarism. Her current research employs her usual method of participant observation and focuses on the gendered and racialized constructions of militarism and peace activism. Dr. Feinman is a longtime peace activist and organizer. Dr. Feinman thanks the Institute for Public Accuracy, Air America, and several anonymous readers on earlier drafts of this essay for helping her to present and hone the arguments set forth in this piece.

Barbara Finlay is a professor of sociology and former director of women's studies at Texas A&M University in College Station, Texas. She has published numerous articles and books on women and gender issues, most recently *George W. Bush and the War on Women* (Zed Books, 2006).

Laura Frost is a professor of English at Yale, where she teaches twentieth-century literature, gender studies, and the history of sexuality. She has published articles on visual culture and on modern and contemporary authors, including James Joyce, D. H. Lawrence, Virginia Woolf, Sylvia Plath, Erica Jong, and Kathryn Harrison. Her first book is *Sex Drives: Fantasies of Fascism in Literary Modernism* (Cornell University Press, 2001). She is at work on a book on modernism and pleasure, and a project on narrative and 9/11.

Karen J. Greenberg is the executive director of the Center on Law and Security at New York University School of Law. She is the editor of the *NYU Review of Law and Security,* coeditor of *The Torture Papers: The Road to Abu Ghraib,* and editor of the books *Al Qaeda Now* and *The Torture Debate* *in America* (Cambridge University Press). She is a frequent writer and commentator on issues related to national security, terrorism, and torture.

Elizabeth L. Hillman is a professor of law at Rutgers School of Law-Camden, where she teaches courses on military law, the Constitution, and legal history. A veteran of seven years on active duty in the U.S. Air Force, she taught history at the United States Air Force Academy before earning her JD and PhD in history at Yale. Her book, *Defending America: Military Culture and the Cold War Court-Martial,* was published by Princeton University Press in 2005.

Aziz Huq directs the Liberty and National Security Project at the Brennan Center for Justice at New York University. He is coauthor of *Unchecked and Unbalanced: Presidential Power in a Time of Terror* (New Press, 2007), and is a 2006 Carnegie Scholars Fellow.

Kristine A. Huskey teaches in the International Human Rights Law Clinic at American University, Washington College of Law. She spent eight years practicing international litigation at Shearman & Sterling, LLP, and was an adjunct professor on human rights and humanitarian law at the American University School of Public Affairs. She has also been a resident guest lecturer on international litigation and human rights and humanitarian law at Victoria University of Wellington (New Zealand) School of Law. Huskey graduated Phi Beta Kappa and magna cum laude from Columbia University and received her JD from the University of Texas School of Law.

Timothy Kaufman-Osborn is interim dean of the faculty at Whitman College as well as the Baker Ferguson Professor of Politics and Leadership. He is the author of three books as well as over twenty scholarly articles on topics including capital punishment, the discipline of political science, feminist theory, and American pragmatism. From 2001–2003, he served as president of the Western Political Science Association, and he is currently a member of the executive council of the American Political Science Association as well as president of the American Civil Liberties Union of Washington. Kaufman-Osborn is the recipient of numerous awards for his scholarship and teaching, including the Western Political Science Association's Pi Sigma Alpha and Betty Nesvold Women and Politics Awards; the Robert Fluno Award for Distinguished Teaching in the Social Sciences; and the Whitman College Town-Gown Award.

Janis Karpinski is the former commanding general of Abu Ghraib. She is the author of *One Woman's Army: The Commanding General of Abu Ghraib Tells Her Story* (Miramax Books, 2005).

Riva Khoshaba, a Yale Law School graduate, has interviewed refugees and torture survivors in the Balkans and worked on a class-action lawsuit on behalf of Iraqi civilians who were detained at Abu Ghraib. She is an attorney in Washington, D.C.

Lucinda Marshall is a feminist artist, writer, and activist. She is the founder of the Feminist Peace Network (www.feministpeacenetwork.org). Her work has been published in numerous publications in the U.S. and internationally, including *CounterPunch, AlterNet, Dissident Voice, Off Our Backs,* the *Progressive, Countercurrents, Z Magazine,* and *Common Dreams.*

Steven H. Miles, MD, a professor of medicine at the Center for Bioethics at the University of Minnesota, is the author of *Oath Betrayed: Torture, Medical Complicity, and the War on Terror* (Random House, 2006). Dr. Miles has written extensively on geriatric medicine including nursing home care, the care of persons with Alzheimer's disease, the use of restraints, and end-of-life care. He has served as a consultant to the FDA and to numerous professional associations on restraint policy for nursing homes and hospitals.

Jumana Musa is a human rights attorney and activist. She is currently the advocacy director for domestic human rights and international justice for Amnesty International USA. Formerly, she worked as a police attorney for the National Network to End Domestic Violence and handled international relations and immigration issues as a fellow in the office of Representative Jesse L. Jackson Jr. Musa holds a BA in international relations from Brown University and a JD from Georgetown University Law Center.

Lila Rajiva is a journalist and writer based in Baltimore. She has written for *Dissident Voice, CounterPunch, Antiwar, AlterNet, Common Dreams, MoneyWeek,* the *Indian Express, India-West, Himal Southasian,* and the *Baltimore Chronicle.* She is the author of *The Language of Empire: Abu Ghraib and the American Media* (Monthly Review, 2005), the first book analyzing the media coverage of the Abu Ghraib scandal. She has an advanced degree in politics from Johns Hopkins University and has taught courses on the media at the University of Maryland, Baltimore County.

Erin Solaro has been a radical feminist, army reserve officer, defense analyst, historian, and journalist. She has appeared on public and network television and talk radio, and published more than twenty articles on military affairs, including two series from Iraq and Afghanistan, in the *Seattle Post-Intelligencer,* the *Baltimore Sun,* the *Christian Science Monitor,* the U.S. Naval Institute's *Proceedings,* and the *Marine Corps Gazette.* She is the author of *Women in the Line of Fire: What You Should Know About Women in the Military* (Seal Press, 2006).

Katharine Viner is features editor of the *Guardian,* London. For eight years she edited the *Guardian Weekend* magazine and was twice named Newspaper

Magazine Editor of the Year. She is coeditor, with Alan Rickman, of the play *My Name Is Rachel Corrie*, which won Best New Play in the 2006 Theatregoers' Choice Awards and was shortlisted for an Olivier and a South Bank Award. She has also been a judge for the Orange Prize for Fiction.

LaNitra Walker is a doctoral candidate in art history with a certificate in African American studies at Duke University. She is currently writing her dissertation on South African artist Irma Stern. Walker's research focuses on African and African American art, and she has presented her work at the College Art Association and the African Studies Association annual meetings. She has also written for the *Journal of Asian and African Studies* and is a frequent contributor to the *American Prospect* online magazine.

Acknowledgments

Special thanks to my editor, Brooke Warner, at Seal Press for coming up with the idea for the anthology and for asking me to work on it—and for her patience and forbearance during the process.

To Eric Lupfer of William Morris for helping me through the logistics of working on a book.

To Karen Greenberg of the Center on Law and Security at New York University School of Law for providing institutional (and personal) support.

To Mark Danner for recommending me for the project.

To all the contributors, of course, for their great essays.

To Ron Rosenbaum for his support, advice, and enthusiasm for my work.

To Jameel Jaffer and others at the ACLU, for the government documents they've obtained through the Freedom of Information Act that make books like this one possible.

To Michael Tomasky, Sarah Blustain, and Erin Pressley of the *American Prospect*, Philip Turner of Carroll & Graf, Betsy Reed of the *Nation*, and Julia Savacool of *Marie Claire* magazine.

To Ren Weschler for his thoughtful comments about the subject.

To Elizabeth Spellmire for her help with the project.

To my parents, John McKelvey and Lee Purcell; my brothers, Kerry and Sean McKelvey; Ada Calhoun and Neal Medlyn; Judy Warner and Max Berley; Peter Schjeldahl and Brooke Alderson; Anna Riegel and Anton Wellstein; Tasha Lance and Ken Rogoff; Belinda Luscombe and Jeremy Edmiston; Rita Rodriguez; Errol Morris; Mark Rosenthal; Murray Waas; Jeff Dubner; Alan Wade; Jessica Stern; Carol Memmott; Bob Burns; Emma Rigney; Josh Siegel; Daniel Heyman; Matthew Berger; Jonathan Marks; Asra Nomani; Joel Achenbach; Negar Azimi; Jim Bamford; Chris Spolar; Jan Goodwin; Donovan Webster; and Robert Kostrzewa.

Most of all to my children, Lidia Jean, Julia, and Xander, for their love, affection, and sense of humor—all of which makes me optimistic about the future despite the dark subjects that I somehow keep writing about.

About the Editor

Tara McKelvey is a senior editor at *The American Prospect* and the author of *Monstering: Inside America's Policy of Secret Interrogations and Torture in the Terror War* (Carroll & Graf). She is also a 2006-2007 research fellow at New York University School of Law's Center on Law and Security and a contributing editor at *Marie Claire*. She lives with her three children in Washington, D.C.

Credits

Selected Titles from Seal Press

For more than thirty years, Seal Press has published groundbreaking books. By women. For women. Visit our website at www.sealpress.com.

Pissed Off: On Women and Anger by Spike Gillespie. $14.95, 1-58005-162-6. An amped-up and personal self-help book that encourages women to go ahead and use that middle finger without being closed off to the notion of forgiveness.

Voices of Resistance: Muslim Women on War, Faith, and Sexuality edited by Sarah Husain. $16.95, 1-58005-181-2. A collection of essays and poetry on war, faith, and sexuality, this book reveals the anger, pride, and pain of Muslim women.

Women in Overdrive: Find Balance and Overcome Burnout at Any Age by Nora Isaacs. $14.95, 1-58005-161-8. For women who take on more than they can handle, this book highlights how women of different age sets are affected by overdrive and what they can do to avoid burnout.

Women in the Line of Fire: What You Should Know About Women in the Military by Erin Solaro. $15.95, 1-58005-174-X. A wake-up call on the damage and repercussions of government neglect, rightist fervor, and feminist ambivalence about women in the military.

Nobody Passes: Rejecting the Rules of Gender and Conformity by Mattilda a.k.a. Matt Bernstein Sycamore. $15.95, 1-58005-184-7. A timely and thought-provoking collection of essays that confronts and challenges the notion of belonging by examining the perilous intersections of identity, categorization, and community.

Testosterone Files: My Hormonal and Social Transformation from Female to Male by Max Wolf Valerio. $15.95, 1-58005-173-1. A gripping transsexual memoir that focuses on testosterone's role in the author's emotional, perceptual, and physical transformation.